Christine Mathis-Rimes

CRUEL
SANCTUARY

A young woman's battle to escape from
a fanatical religious sect

Christine Mathis-Rimes

CRUEL
SANCTUARY

A young woman's battle to escape from
a fanatical religious sect

Cruel Sanctuary: 978-1-86151-998-6

First published in Great Britain in 2018

Copyright ©2018

Cover Design and artwork - Ray Lipscombe

Christine Mathis has asserted her right under the Copyright Designs and Patents Act 1988 to be identified as the author of this work.

A CIP catalogue record for this book is available from the British Library.

CONTENTS

The family before joining the Bruderhof, 1942

The family after joining the Bruderhof, 1944

FOREWORD

When I was a very young child, Christine lived in the last house at the end of my street and she and her husband Jörg were close family friends. They had a shared history with my father and Nana, which I always felt unified our families. It is a history of 'The Community' (as the Bruderhof was always referred to), and I was privy to many conversations about their life there, both good and bad.

To my innocent young girl's ears, the 'Good' related to farm life, wildlife, ponies, walks in the countryside and solid friendships. 'Bad' aspects always included talk about the Community's Break Up; of families being separated and disbanded, leaving a gaping wound of hurt and an overwhelming sense of moral injustice. I didn't understand this talk for a long time, and I couldn't relate it to my own everyday 'normal' life.

Christine was quite simply the warmest person I knew, besides my own mother. Her house at the end of the street was like an extension of my own home, where my sister, brothers and I were always welcomed and loved. It was a lovely haven which always smelt of home cooking and Earl Grey tea. When I think of Christine, my mind always goes back to these early memories of bright red poppies, raspberry bushes, pet rabbits, singing, recorder lessons, bare feet and sunny days. Always sunny days! Despite the struggles of her life, and perhaps because of them, Christine had a love of life and a sense of fun that was simply contagious, and wonderful to me in my early years.

Christine has a gift for storytelling. She once held a weekly 'story club' at her home, for the children of our street, and I remember the excitement I felt before each one. Christine would draw her young listeners in with her sparkly voice, her glistening eyes and her joyous, cascading laugh, of which there are many echoes in her book.

An important role model to me throughout my life, Christine has remained a close friend and trusted confidante; distance has not been a barrier to our closeness. She has told a truly remarkable story in 'Cruel Sanctuary', a true-to-herself story, which will resonate with so many others who have suffered as a direct result of cult living. Christine's truth however has taken some finding. The influential people and religious institutions of her life have been carefully 'unpicked' and re-woven in a way which seems to enable her to make sense of who she is and who she can be. Her unwavering faith in the potential goodness of human nature, despite encountering so much of its badness, reflect a spirit, a soul, which has largely been healed, and found a level of peace: the 'life-light' which Christine writes about as being within all people is so strikingly prevalent in herself, and will, I'm sure, continue to glow brightly and steadfastly into her future.

Rebecca Holz Rogers

ACKNOWLEDGEMENTS

I would like to thank with all my heart Jörg, my husband, who has helped me along the way and walked my path with me, supporting and encouraging me with his constancy and love. To my three children, Giovanna, Marcella and Jonathan, who have been my inspiration, joy, and encouragers, my love and thanks. To Jon's dear partner Fiona, thanks from my heart. Without her I simply would never have managed; you have never failed me. To John, who so kindly listened to me and read my manuscript, giving me advice and encouragement, with such honesty and warmth, my thanks. To my wonderful friend Rebecca, thank you so much for your loving words, your kindness and our happy connection.

My thanks to Chris Newton for the excellent work in editing my manuscript without losing the essence of it. And to Ray for his lovely cover design, my sincere thanks.

My parents after arriving at the Bruderhof, 1943 or 1944

PROLOGUE

How beautiful is creation. As I walk through this Gloucestershire village I am proud to be able to call it 'my' village at last. My life has taken me from village to farm, from town to city, from continent to continent, leaving me rootless and almost cultureless. Now I am back where I was when I first drew breath, and after more than five years, I can at last say 'my village, my area, my county'. I can feel I belong, with joy and pride.

I pass by a perfect, scraggly hawthorn tree, not a bush in a hedge as one frequently sees but a tree – bare now, as this is January. This wonderful tree is full of what seems like hundreds of chirping sparrows. They twitter and cheep, quite undisturbed by passing people and dogs, knowing their perfect safety within those matted, gnarled branches.

Walking to the village centre, my heart is leaping

with the cheeky, sprightly river Churn as, split in two and running on either side of the path, it giggles its way down to the old mill house, where in times gone by it helped run that mill well and faithfully. Its rippling, laughing voices join together as one again later on, at the edge of the village.

Today has been so precious and healing to my soul. Walking under a crystal blue sky along our merry Churn, I watch a blue tit flit jerkily from branch to branch of a huge bare willow tree. Across the river I see a greenfinch, seemingly more peaceful by nature than the tit, just enjoying his wonderful habitat. The trees that line the merry river are so grand and majestic. The river is like a child, impossible to rein in in its effervescent joy; each tree is like a solid, loving father, ever watchful, peaceful and guiding. They stand bare against the blue of the sky, patiently waiting for the season of fruitfulness. The branches wait quietly for the time when they will put forth buds to turn into leaf and blossom. I feel my heart is in harmony with Creation and God; my heart walks in step with its being as I feel so close to the source. So lovely it is to walk with the Divine Being in my aloneness – no, I am not lonely right now, just alone with my God, within me, part of its Creation. Oh lovely, lovely peace.

As I turn right over the little humped wooden bridge taking me back amongst the houses, I stop for a moment or two, many thoughts going through my mind. I am thinking of my beautiful children when they were small, and the joy we had playing pooh sticks, which reminded me of Pooh Bear and Piglet, Eeyore and Tigger. They brought a contented, lazy peace to our family in days gone by, a happy cuddliness, as they had done during my own childhood, when my father introduced these characters to me and my brothers and sisters, very often with a twinkle in his eye.

I leave the little bridge and follow the path between the small houses, houses built especially for folks who need a bit of care from the state. That seems an unfortunate term, because 'the state' translates into real people with caring minds and hearts, I hope, even if they are trying to just earn a living. My mind starts to think of the needs and pains of people living here, which in turn makes me think of my own life, a life with much pain behind me, but a life rich in a thousand and one victories in life-light and love. A life in which I am discovering wholeness and healing. And now my real story begins.

CHAPTER 1

The innocent years

Overhill Road, the Silver Birches in Stratton, Cirencester, on a beautiful September day in 1938, was where my life started. I was told that my mother had a difficult time during my birth and that I was wrapped up and laid on the mantelpiece and left there for a while just after my birth and before I drew my first breath. Apparently she needed much care, and the baby at that moment was the secondary concern. However, after a while the doctor got me going and helped me to start breathing, and fortunately I've been breathing ever since. My parents were young, 21 and 20 years old, and now they had me and my older brother Nigel (three and a half) to care for.

My father Robert was a miller's son and was at the time in partnership with my grandfather. The mill was quite close, over some allotments and down a couple of small roads, so Daddy could be at work in a very short time. However he did own a car, an MG, I believe. Legend has it that Grandfather Maurice was the first man in the village to own a car and that he had a 'heavy foot on the accelerator'.

Our house was a semi-detached, still being built when my parents returned from their honeymoon. Soon after they returned it had been finished and they happily moved from my grandparents' house into their own. They planted two silver birches in the front garden and No. 24 became known as 'Silver Birches' or 'The Birches'.

Memories of those days are sketchy, but vivid. Nigel and I would be taken to the mill and we would play around there. My memories are of horses, pigs – yes, pigs! Grain everywhere, sacks, lorries, and men loading them with huge, heavy sacks, almost obliterating the men holding them. It always looked to me as though the sacks had legs, and each sack would then jump onto the lorry, when a man would appear from behind it.

In those days Daddy seemed to be full of fun. My memory is of a constantly happy, beaming face. He would pick Nigel up, put him in a full grain hopper, and as the grain ran into the sacks on the floor below and Nigel began to vanish from my sight, Daddy would snatch him out, both of them laughing. Then it was my turn. As I started to sink with the grain it never occurred to me that my father might fail to grab me in time and let me go down the chute to the floor below and into a waiting sack. I just knew for sure that this game was perfectly safe and that I would be hauled back out just in the nick of time. How different were my days to become! But for now, they were secure, understandable and happy. I was after all less than four years old at this blissful time, a brief interlude which somehow seemed eternal.

The River Churn ran the mill. It seemed to come in deep and run out across the fields shallow. My mother would take us for walks along its edge and through the fields. She called each flower we passed by name. Each blossom was so perfectly and wonderfully made, and soon I could name them all. Each mighty tree had a name, and those majestic ones I knew by name too. To a little child even hawthorns and willows had strength and character, but oaks were powerful and regal. In those days we picked flowers and blossoms and took them home to decorate our home with – we seemed never to be without a vase of flowers in the centre of

3

our dining room table.

The river was my friend. It flowed deeply and quietly to the mill house, but once past it, it rippled, giggled and rattled over pebbles as it went on its way. One day it took on a darkness in its deeper and quiet side. I gathered from adult conversation that a little girl, not too much older than I was at the time, had drowned in it. I looked deeply into the river one day and felt it was hiding a dark, sad secret. I became afraid of its power to do a thing like that.

Later I was to hear of an earlier tragedy concerning my own family. My grandparents had been taking a family walk one Sunday with several of their 12 children, including my father. Some of the little ones ran ahead and five-year-old Janet and three-year-old Colin slipped into the river. My father, who was about six, managed to catch hold of Colin's legs and pull him out, but when he tried to get Janet, she was out of reach. She drowned, and my father, so young, saw it happen. He didn't talk of it much, but when he did he would look above me, past me, not meeting my eyes with his. I would look into his face and he passed me; I could feel pain that was still there in him. I tried to make him talk more by asking questions, with the faint nebulous feeling that if he could talk about it he might be less distant, less sad. If, I thought, he could throw up, he would feel better. I had seen my baby sister throw up and she had gone from grisly to laughing. She had been named Janet after my little drowned auntie, who never lived to be an aunt.

But most of the time, my mother and father laughed a lot and seemed full of living. There were times when they piled us three children onto their tandem and the next thing I knew, we'd be whistling through the air with trees racing by us in the opposite direction. I can feel the wind in my hair now. It was quite exhilarating. My parents did the work – we three, Nigel, Janet and I, just sat watching the world go by. And what a wonderful world it was; made especially for us!

There was a baby basket seat in front of my father, then behind him on the crossbar Nigel or I sat, in a little seat attached to it. Then came my mother, and behind her was the last child's seat. If you sat right at the back, you could see our parent's legs pumping up and down in unison. It made me feel so safe; at such times I knew there was nothing they could not do. In them was total security.

I remember a day when I must have displeased Daddy. We had a long rough wooden table, with two benches either side. The benches were upholstered along the seat part and covered with a blue material, dull to look at but wonderfully soft to sit or run on. The table's end and one side were up against a wall, and so was the bench I was walking along. Daddy's face was like thunder, and he strode up to grab me. I squealed and ran the length of the bench into the corner. He strode down on the other side of the table to lean over and grab me. I squealed again and ran back the other way, not quite sure whether this was a game or if I had reason to fear him. The soft upholstered bench felt so good to my bare feet, but my heart was in my mouth as I ran up and down it, trying to keep my eye on Daddy at the same time, as he looked rather dangerous by now. He had a long arm, but not long enough to grab me it seemed.

At last Daddy stood still, looking at me, and suddenly the thunderclouds parted and light beamed from his face and the laughter followed. How strange adults could be! But now I was safe from whatever had come between adult and child. I breathed a sigh of relief.

We had swapped houses with Grandpa and Grandma at some point during this time. I guess it was just before Janet was born. We went to live at the Mill, and our grandparents went to live at The Silver Birches, Overhill Road. The Mill had been so much part of my life that the move is not something which stands out in my memory. However, it did relieve me of the two old ladies at Overhill Road. They had watched me looking through our front window one day and I guess I had had my thumb in my mouth. As I looked out and across the road, there they were at their window, mimicking me, each with a thumb in her mouth and waving her fingers back and forth. At that moment, they changed in my imagination from humans to black witches – I felt frightened, yet sad at how grown-ups could behave. Perhaps it was the first of life's encounters with something close to mockery. Or were they having fun? Either way, it felt bad to me. With the move to the Mill no one overlooked us.

It was around that time that Daddy introduced Nigel and me to AA Milne's Winnie the Pooh stories. The cold dark winter evenings were wonderful as I lived through each story with my father's deep brown voice behind them. I am sure there were other stories too, and story time seemed to lead to Christmas time. Christmas pops up in my memory as a brightly-lit tree, my grandparents and other people filling the house and milling around, with grown-up talk that floated way above my head. There was a dolls' house, and although my parents had made it and filled it with little people, beds, chairs, cupboards and so forth, for some reason it was Father Christmas who had brought it to me from them. How I loved that dolls' house!

There was good food too, eaten round the freshly-scrubbed wooden table, mostly by the grown-ups and Nigel. I wasn't so interested in the food, and Janet was still too little to choose. She only got what was put into her mouth by some over-excited grown-up. No doubt we all landed in church during the Christmas days too, as my parents and grandparents were all very sincere Christians and Methodists.

I remember the word 'Ashcroft' would pop up every so often, like pop-up tarts, during adult discourses. Later I found out that the name referred to the church on Ashcroft Road that my family attended. During those times, if I was taken to church, it certainly didn't impress me. However, my parents' faith and understanding of Christ's love certainly did reach me in a sort of gentle, firm, quiet way. Their faith was safe and real. More than the words (which I can't remember), it was like dew falling on the grass and watering the heart.

* * *

Soon came the time when the everlasting uprooting was to begin. I would guess that it was my father's sincerity about life and his faith which was at the bottom of it. It began to turn into idealism, and the result started to shake my life to the core. It seems that having an ideal is one thing, but being idealistic is another (maybe idealistic people have made their ideal into a religion).

My parents left the Rimes Mill and Grandfather and Grandmother Rimes and went to live in Herefordshire, in a house they shared with three other families in an effort at community living – a sharing and caring type of thing. Of this time I have 'flash-bulb' memories. I remember that no longer could I call the bedroom Janet and I shared ours, as we shared it with two other babies; Susan and Jenny. Nigel seemed to have a corner to himself, but when we played there was always this little toddler at our elbows, ready to pull to bits or knock down anything we had created or built. When I walked into the kitchen to see Mummy, I would find another mother at the kitchen sink, bathing her toddler in it rather than the potatoes or beetroots or carrots. I would wander into some big hallway and find Jenny's mother on her hands and knees washing the red tiled floor. When at last I located my own Mummy, she would be picking raspberries along the long rows of raspberry canes, and it was almost like looking for a needle in a haystack. She appeared slightly changed from the mother I had known – still her, but not quite as carefree.

One day Nigel and I were building in the sandpit. It was right next to the end of a stone building, and along the side of this building were clumps of nettles. As we played, for what seemed like the hundredth time, 'Tuppenny' appeared (his real name was Geoffrey), the very toddler who was bathed in the kitchen sink. As he was about to crash into Nigel's castle, Nigel, without looking up, gave him a shove. The next thing we knew was that a loud scream came from one of the clumps of nettles. As if summoned by a bell, three mothers appeared, my mother amongst them, and of course, Tuppenny's mother. She snatched up her precious babe and ran for the kitchen. My mother came towards her offspring, and the third mother vanished into thin air.

'Who pushed Geoffrey into the nettles?' my mother asked. No answer, as neither of us felt we had – not deliberately into the nettles.

She asked again. No answer.

'Was it you, Nigel?'

'Nope', he replied.

'All right then, both go and sit on your beds until you can tell me who did it.'

As I walked through the kitchen to find the stairs,

who should be occupying the kitchen sink, still whining, but little Tuppenny, with his mother standing there, splashing him with water and crooning. Wouldn't any mother be the same?

Ah well, life was starting to turn unfair. This was the first 'unfairness' I remember, my introduction into the fact that life isn't fair.

I sat on my bed, bored and alone, for what seemed a very long time. When the endlessness became unbearable, I decided to go and tell Mummy that I had pushed Tuppenny into the nettles – perhaps that was all she was waiting to hear. Seconds later I found her and told her what I thought she was waiting to hear. She turned to me from her work of folding washing and said, 'All right, don't do it again.'

As I went outside again, I could hear my mother calling Nigel to tell him he could return to his play now. This was another first in my experience of life. It was the first time I had taken on someone's guilt, although it would not be the last. It had been an easy one though.

* * *

This place we now lived in was called 'Adams Cot'. I have a very little memory of our very short time there.

Whether it was during this time I may never know, but some friends of my parents had been on at them for some time about wishing they had children of their own and how they would like to 'borrow' one of us. I remember suddenly being taken by a very gushing woman into her home, and having to spend what seemed like ages and ages in the care of her and her husband. It could have been years, but my mother later told me when questioned that it was more like a long weekend. It was an awful experience, and to this day, I do not quite understand my feelings over it.

I do not remember what happened. What I do remember is that I was terrified of Mrs Bird, who was to be avoided at all costs. Mr Bird paled into the shadows by comparison. I was desperately lonely, and the whole time I felt like a used object rather than a little human being who did in fact count and have feelings. I was there to oblige Mrs Bird, to be used for her fancies, and it left me feeling like a thing, a thing with fear and shame, a thing to be picked up and petted when wanted, then to be discarded when no longer needed. But as I said, I don't remember anything – not even going back home.

Life did return to 'normal'. My father in particular seemed always to be very happy, but I began to realise that he was a man on a mission, a man of conscience, a man who thought life out; his deep thinking was leading him to an ideal. Mummy had always been carefree and full of fun and probably didn't weigh life as heavily as Daddy. She was very happy with the Jesus she knew (I do not recall my parents using his name much, or speaking religiously) and rather preferred not to question him on anything. She loved God's creation; she loved her children and her husband. She also loved the fact that my parents had owned a house and a garden and had the wherewithal to put three square meals on the table. She enjoyed washing and ironing, her lipstick, her hairdresser and pretty clothes. Both my parents loved dancing and playing the piano, and singing too. Not that Daddy could play (well, not very well) but he could sing. He had the most wonderful, velvet, dark brown bass voice, and loved listening to Paul Robeson. Mummy could play and sing most beautifully. She was a bright soprano star in those days, but later, as life took a turn for the heavy, she became an alto. The heavy bit started when my father began talking to my mother about community living. That is, *real* community living. Adams Cot had been a failure in his mind, and he wanted to move on.

CHAPTER 2

A conspiracy of adults

About six miles from the Mill, near Ashton Keynes, my father had discovered a little village, an international community of Christians called the Bruderhof. He had met its members through delivering grain to their farm. I can imagine his delight when he found out that they were all pacifists. A few years earlier he had been called up to military service and refused to go. During his tribunal he had said that on the grounds of his Christian faith, he could not go to war. Apparently his sincerity got him off without even having to do alternative service – maybe the Mill provided the excuse? However he was free to live as was, and he began to worry about why he should have freedom while thousands were putting their lives on the line to 'save' their country. He even had a brother who had been shot down over Africa and become a prisoner of war.

As my father listened more and more to these Bruderhof people, an ideal began to take shape and grow. Now, some years on, he felt that if he could live with them it would put his faith to positive action rather than the inaction he felt from not playing his part for his country. He could become an example to the world of what he believed was Christ's way, a way which would reflect the Kingdom of God. This was their ideal.

I imagine that it took quite some time to persuade my mother. She told me of the times when she and my father would walk up and down the raspberry canes picking the fruit and he would be trying to persuade her to agree with his thoughts and convictions. She said she simply could not understand why anyone would want to give up the life they had to follow such a lifestyle. It was all extremely alien to her. Her father had fought in the First World War and although, or maybe because, it had caused the family great hardship, my mother's people were very patriotic. The Rimes family, my father's people, were 'away with the fairies' perhaps; free thinkers. They couldn't just accept and live, they were always in need of digging deeper. But gradually she became persuaded.

Later she told me that my father had said, 'Would you like your son to be killed, or for him to kill? That's what war is about.' That made her understand what my father was saying, and maybe it was more evocative and poignant for my mother as Nigel was her blood child and not my father's. She said she just took a look at Nigel's very young face, this new creation, and felt she would do anything to save him.

How persuasive our speech, and how fickle the mind! How unwittingly do we cross the boundaries and manipulate each other's minds, thus enabling us to twist our own hearts; our own being becomes bruised for a while. But so history is made. It is the mind that seems to make history, not your being, not the heart.

* * *

One day, a lorry rolled up in the yard of Adams Cot and out slid two red-bearded giants. I felt awed rather than afraid. I stood at a safe distance and observed. They had clearly arrived from another world. Their beards were long and flowing and rather uncared for. They had clothes that looked as if they should have been worn by fairytale people, like Snow White's dwarves. Their trousers ended in tight little girly bands, just below the knee, and they had collarless black jackets with bright shirts underneath. They were giants with a purpose, wreathed in smiles of the victory kind. They were like fishermen who had landed a big one, and they were happy with their catch, which seemed to make them very merry.

One of them endeavoured to make contact with me, but I backed off, feeling very unsure of what they were. They became more human when I realised that they could speak – and in a language that I understood. I slowly warmed to them, but it was not long before I noticed that they were loading the lorry up with the mattress from my bed. My sister Janet's followed. It was outrageous!

Then I noticed that several of my parents' possessions were also being hauled up onto the lorry. The lorry took on a sinister hue, and so did the creatures loading it. Their happy faces turned possessive and grey-green, and behind the smiles burned an ominous purpose. I began to feel shaky. My doll's cot was thrown onto this infamous lorry, followed by my precious dolls' house. Everything was becoming quite suspect.

In fact it was the overture to an insecure new world and a very different life to follow. I was four years and eight months old and my warm, secure, love-filled, taken-for-granted world was starting to show cracks and threatening to fall apart.

At one stage in the game that was playing out before me, I noticed that my parents were not at all indignant about what these two giants were doing. They exchanged words in a friendly way and seemed to be part of this, making it seem more like a conspiracy of adults. So these men were doing their looting with my parents' permission. In fact my father in particular was actually enjoying it!

Next thing I knew we were rushing and bumping along in the lorry towards goodness knows where. I was in the cab along with Adam, our little black dog, Nigel and the driver. Adam sat at my feet and looked up frequently, holding me with his beautiful velvet brown eyes and telling me that although he was small, he would take care of me. Nigel seemed angry in his silence. I had no idea how my parents with Janet managed it, but some long while later we all found each other again on a farm out in the hills of Shropshire – not that I knew that's where it was at the time. But my family was all intact, all together again.

From then on it was like taking every step in the dark, with no light to shed on it. So it was sink or swim, stand or fall, bend or don't bend. I was on the first day of the first course which was going to hone very finely my inborn gift for survival, which is rebellion, not conforming, following my own spirit, my being.

I discovered later that my parents had intended to join the Cotswold Bruderhof community, but they had missed the boat and been taken to one at Wheathill Farm in Shropshire instead. During all the procrastination while my parents had been making up their minds to join, the Cotswold community had packed up and moved to Paraguay in South America. So when my father finally got round to travelling the six miles to Ashton Keynes to announce his intention of joining them, he found they had left. His search had then revealed that three British members of the sect, as I suppose it must be called, had gone up to Shropshire and bought a very run-down farm, classed as a Grade C farm, to live on, as so many British people had shown interest in their way of living and wanted to join them. The Home Office had said that all members of the Cotswold community would have to leave the country, or they would have to intern the German members, because the war was still on. There had apparently been stories flying around amongst the neighbouring farms and villages that the Bruderhof in Ashton Keynes were ploughing their fields in the shape of the Swastika, and the feelings of discomfort were growing because they thought these people were Nazis. In fact this international community had been chucked out of Germany by Hitler's SS because they would not conform to his regime. By the time my parents joined the Bruderhof, several of the British members who had gone out to Paraguay had returned, to 'support' and I might add, to 'train' those in this new beginning in England.

So here we found ourselves in the hills of Shropshire, in a run-down farm which would provide plenty of 'working together' for all of us, and reduced to two very small rooms in a cottage that I believe must have been built by the original Adam. It was tiny and had neither toilet nor kitchen nor hall, nor space for toys of the smallest kind, nor entrance hall, even of the most minuscule sort. No paint, no light, no nothing!

The back room, which was very dark indeed, was fitted with a bunk bed and a cot, thoughtfully and no doubt lovingly prepared for Nigel, Janet and me. In one corner was a screen, the kind used sometimes in doctors' offices, behind which stood a white enamel bucket. I vaguely wondered why it stood there all hidden, but it was the only thing in the house that was in pristine condition. I quickly learned that it was supposed to be a toilet. The front room, or the first one you walked into straight from the yard, was absolutely filled with a bed which at a pinch could fit two people in. Maybe this was for my mother and father? It had never occurred to me before that they actually shared a bed, but they would certainly be safer sharing a bed in this unfriendly and oddly dangerous-looking place.

Right at the bottom of this double bed and pushed right up against it was a table. The bed would prove essential for sitting on at the table, as there was not room enough for five chairs around it. I have no memory of actually settling in, as it is next to impossible to 'settle' in such a bleak place. Everything that meant life, light, love and security was ripped away. Our psyches were not prepared for this 'settling'. I registered that I was now a nomad, although I did not know the word of course, so 'settling' was not in my imagination. Instinct told me that now I was to prepare to be unsettled for life, or as long as it took. It was a very unpleasant feeling and I felt extremely insecure.

I remember many smiling faces around and about. The women wore odd pieces of cloth, uniformly black with white dots, tied around their heads and tied in a little tight knot under their chins. Again the fairy-tale images came to mind and I wondered if they were witches. Were they to be trusted? What might lurk behind those sweet smiles? Could I accept the apple that was offered? Were they not in fact like the witch in Snow White? But they seemed quite friendly, given the chance. The men were all dressed identically to our original giants. Everybody laughed and looked jolly. They would pass by with a friendly smile, but the smile was not a connecting one; it seemed more like an overlooking, dreamy, distant smile; almost condescending. Something that was more 'worthy' than loving.

As I remember back to the little girl that was me, it is mostly emotion that comes whooshing over me rather than memories of events, activities and so forth. I felt no joy, love, warmth, excitement. My childish heart was full of apprehension, fear and anxiety. It was difficult to eat and sleeping was cold and fitful, and I just went into freeze mode.

My father seemed oblivious to the traumatic life they had dumped us into. My mother however was not oblivious; she was suffering, just as I was, from great unhappiness, she later told me. At one point she had run away, weeping in anguish over her lost life. She told me that she had run off across the farm and on finding a haystack she had slid to the ground, hiding behind it. A Sister named Barbara had found her, and was able, with her kindness and conviction over the life they were leading, to bring Mummy back to accepting that she and my father were doing 'the right thing'. My mother said to me, 'From that point, once I found acceptance, I found happiness'. Well, she may have found a form of happiness, but as I see it she suffered for the rest of her life through 'accepting' a life which was never truly for her.

I do remember certain events that served to bring me out of my freeze and awakened interest in life again, if not without the insecurity, and I became a cautious and sometimes reluctant child, always looking and waiting to see what was around the next corner.

One morning as we sat at breakfast in our pocket-hanky sized cottage, Nigel and I sitting on our parents' bed end, Janet on Mummy's lap, Daddy on a chair next to her and squashed against the wall, a Shire horse poked its head through the open window, between our parents' heads, and with one wide open-mouthed crunch, it ate the flowers from the vase in the centre of the table, the very last thing left to us that spoke of our life at home. The flowers on the table had been the fine and beautiful thread that held so strong, the promise of safety, the last vestige of connection between Mummy and me. Nothing else in the tiny, cold cottage belonged to us. In fact what WAS there inside? Nothing – nothing at all save the bare essentials of existence. All our toys had vanished in the move. Later we were to understand that now everything belonged to everybody – no one owned anything.

One day Nigel and I climbed up a barn wall and looking over it we saw, amongst other things, our toys, waiting to be doled out to other children for birthdays or Christmas. That hurt – it cut deep. I couldn't even cry; I felt betrayed. Nigel, by now almost nine years old, was angry and not afraid to express it.

Nigel investigated and found that all the Shire horses the Brothers owned lived in the stone barn attached to our abode. This was, we were told, the last farm in England to keep up farming with only Shire horses rather than tractors. This ideal was soon to be shattered however, as the Brothers found that it was vitally important to put food on the table and they needed to keep up with the rest of the farming world. The slow but beautiful creatures, elegant and sleek, some a little fiery, all with such integrity, were gradually replaced by tractors.

Another early memory; I was standing at the gate to the kindergarten, my mother close beside me. She was talking to a very smiley witch-woman. This woman seemed genuine enough, and her smile quite real. Then my ears caught 'just leave her and walk away, she'll be all right'. My hand, having already been surreptitiously slipped into my mother's hand, tightened. But as if on command, my mother's hand was coldly pulled from mine and she started to walk up the hill and away, not even looking back. For the first time in my life I opened my mouth and howled like a wounded animal. I was as much frightened by my own useless cry as by the loss of my mother. My father, Nigel and Janet had already vanished. *Parents beware, lest your Ideal overrides and suffocates your Love!* My parents were already losing themselves in preference for the Tribe, the Christian Brotherhood. The first wee taste of George Orwell's *Animal Farm* was upon me.

No doubt I was collected that evening at 5.30 by my mother and taken 'home'. It was part of the daily schedule to be taken to children's departments at 8 in the morning and collected again at 5.30, but nothing had been explained to me, (or maybe I had not been able to comprehend the explanation for such an abnormal kind of living,) so on the first day I thought I had been abandoned. Now I realise that Nigel was in the community school, Janet in the baby house, I in the kindergarten and my parents working in various community departments all day. At 6 pm my father came home – or was supposed to – and at 7 my parents left us in the care of a designated person – a different person each night – to go to a communal supper for adults and then a meeting afterwards, coming home between 10 pm and midnight when we already slept. Community families rose in the mornings at 7 am and so we children spent two and a half hours in 24 with our mothers and fathers. In our case my father was always busy on the farm and in the office and worked longer hours so that we saw even less of him.

We children ate dinner and supper in the children's departments – only breakfast was eaten at home. Breakfast consisted of porridge collected from the communal kitchen and half cold by the time it arrived at our mean cottage. Sometimes we had a piece of bread and Marmite or jam as well. I could hardly swallow my breakfast because the anxiety would set in as I anticipated the daily kindergarten ordeal.

As time went by I think I became resigned to this strange life, and perhaps started to feel safer in the rhythm of the daily routine. My kindergarten experience was short lived, as I was graduated into pre-school the September I turned five, just three months after our arrival. By now I began to feel safe and even happy with my little playmates, but I avoided adults like the plague.

Around this time it was deemed safe for me to go home on my own without being 'collected'. Our home doors were never locked; in fact nothing save the Servant's (minister's) office and the Steward's office were locked. Perhaps this office contained some cash – which of course belonged to everyone, since the adults believed they 'had all things in common'! This is a verse found in the Bible pertaining to the first Christians, but in my adult view, it was taken out of context or misunderstood or both. The problem is that when enthusiasm becomes idealism, which then becomes a religion and this religion takes over, it becomes a lethal cocktail which crushes the spirit and truth in the individual.

My Bruderhof experience helped me to appreciate the difference between 'religion' and 'spirituality'. Spirit is connected to God / Universe / Source – unconditional love. In fact Spirit IS God / Universe / Source, unconditional love. Unconditional love is born of Spirit, and Spirit grows and blossoms into unconditional love. How beautiful is the circle of life! Love given and received without condition is so delightful, glorious, peaceful, joyous; simply Love-ly! It is like living in Spirit, only with your body still attached—Heavenly! Blissful!

Religion is totally devoid of Spirit, being man-made, moralistic, rules without heart, controlling, dogmatic; in fact conditional 'love' (I hate to use the word love in this context) seems to be the dictator of anything with religion as its root. Let's be honest can we ever understand what real love is if there is always a condition put on it? 'IF you are good, you may have an apple! IF you say sorry, we will admit you back into our circle. IF you repent you will go to heaven when you die [die? Do we ever die?] IF you are nice, we will give you a gift.' On our farm community, the Bruderhof, this was called 'clear love,' and people who lost their hearts to it were highly revered.

I only talk of these things now so that in case I mention 'religion' or 'spirit' again you will understand where I am coming from.

As time moved on and I became more accustomed to life in this unique community farm, I started to notice the trees, the birds, the flowers, blossoms, small animals such as rabbits and hedgehogs, ladybirds, butterflies, greenfinches, swallows, primroses, and even discovered my dear friends the birch trees, like those I had known outside the front door of my real home, before the life I had been so connected to had been uprooted. One day I came across a little fast-flowing babbling stream and my heart just sang with delight. Sure, it was not the River Churn, but still it was flowing water, sparkling and laughing over pebbles and stones. I began to feel the flow of life-love in my veins again. My freeze started to melt and I felt in tune with the Universe again. Oh blessed and healing Creation! Even now my heart swells with peace, joy and love at the memory.

* * *

My pre-school year seemed to be spent growing used to this new and absurd life that my parents had fallen for. I was very happy with life amongst my child friends and loved the peace and harmony of the beauty of creation all around me. The very soil of a newly-ploughed field gave me such enormous joy and security and love. What bliss to climb a gate and gaze across a field of tender spring wheat coming up through the warming, rich soil! Unlike our farm's rabbit catcher, I fell utterly in love with all the thousands of rabbits that inhabit a C farm, which at this point it still was. I was beginning to sort the approachable adults from the unapproachable, the ones I still needed to be invisible to. By now I realised that all the adults were in fact genuine humans, rather than blundering giants and dark-witches.

Until we were elevated to 'schoolchildren', we were required to take a rather lengthy nap in the middle of the day. This made me feel extremely self-conscious and slightly anxious at first. Lying in silence and not being allowed to say a word to anyone, like sausage rolls on a very hard wooden floor – well, one felt exposed, very naked, and strangely vulnerable.

Once I found a voice amongst the children, I misled them in a few ways. There was an apple tree with small, very deeply-coloured red apples at the bottom of the pre-school field. I encouraged David to go with me to this tree. We filled our pockets to bulging under my encouragement (David was a very good boy as far as the adults were concerned and needed a little guidance from me!) just before having to lie down on those infernal half-inch-thick mattresses on the floor that served as beds. Lying next to David, I whispered to him to pull the blanket over his head and enjoy the apples. If we were fully covered we couldn't be discovered. Quickly covering my own head, I began to crunch, at the same time shoving the rest of my precious booty under the very flimsy bit of rag that served as my pillow. These apples were, and still are, the best tasting I have ever had.

It felt funny and sneaky to be with my head on the hidden, forbidden, bumpy apples. I also found, for the first time in my life, how good it felt to win a small battle with an enemy, in this case the adults.

Suddenly the blanket was whipped back from my undercover operation, which made me jump. As my head jerked, the daylight revealing an upset, red-faced adult hovering above. All the apples slithered out from beneath my flimsy pillow, rolling dismally over toward David on the one side and whoever it was on the other. David was caught too, after confessing, which cost him much. I felt vaguely sorry for him. My happy bubble of revenge was burst. But why was I seeking revenge, why were adults my enemy? At the age of five I had no way of asking, let alone of finding answers. All I knew was that I was in for it.

The lady hovering above our heads trying to look severe was Madge. I saw as we stood up on her very UN-commanding command that she stood not an awful lot higher than we did. In fact she was so tiny that I felt the immediate urge to protect and defend her. I could sense in my childish way that her spirit felt tiny too. She seemed to feel so out of place in the position of disciplinary adult. Yet this was her role and Big Brother expected it of her. I believe that at this point she was fairly new to 'the life'.

After a very gentle-voiced telling off, she told us 'put out your hands'. She explained in some meek way

31

that she had to 'smack' us. I had never been 'smacked' in my life, so I watched with bated breath as her hand started descending on to mine. I see it to this day, all in slow motion. I was revolted, feeling how weak it was that an adult should hit a child, the united Brotherhood's way of disciplining children, obviously alien to Madge. This was indeed a different world.

As her hand made contact, all she could manage were soft, slow strokes across the back of my hand, about three of them. Then I realised why I needed to protect Madge, my teacher (all adults were addressed by their first names – this was the 'brotherly' way to do things) Adults in this commune also had feelings, sad and happy, and some of them needed protecting from the others. In this case I was the protector – of course, only in my heart.

In fact Madge was the dearest, gentlest little lady that anyone could encounter and later, on the day she married our Headmaster, her countenance bore an expression of pure bliss. (Her husband was the exact opposite – an outspoken, loud man who quite smoothly and easily would hit a student on the head with a loud crack, using any book to hand but without malice and seemingly not much gifted in empathy!)

CHAPTER 3

Life in the Commune

My parents, at least my father, seemed quite happy most of the time. Life was filled with school, music, harvest festivals, Christmases, Easters, haymaking, planting potatoes, harvesting strawberries, riding horses, and all manner of farm and garden occupations. Unusually for a Christian church, we children got to celebrate the summer solstice and winter equinox. I think a few innocent adults sneaked these festivities in for a while, until it was found that they were 'not in the right spirit' in celebrating them and these wonderful occasions came to an abrupt end. I heard the word 'Druids'; they had celebrated the summer solstice, and they were pagans, a part of the

Antichrist, therefore we must distance ourselves from such wrong. But while these occasions lasted, my childlike heart was filled with bliss. I have a very dear friend who seems to find a way to celebrate these times with others, and to this day when he tells me about it, my heart sings with a kind of unexplained happiness.

What else did we children do? We dug underground houses, made wigwams and climbed trees of every kind and all sizes. The older boys, my brother being one of them, built a wonderful tree house and any of us who could climb high enough would collect all the conkers from beneath the horse chestnut tree and carry them up to the house, golden treasures of untold value. We dug a swimming pool in a stream on one of the fields and christened it the 'mud puddle' as it left us all with brown beards after a swim, but we still kept swimming, six strokes across and eight strokes from end to end.

There was so much to do to occupy young minds and hearts. Lots of the harvesting was done by us children. In fact it would get so tiresome during the blackberry harvest for instance that I devised a quicker method which would, I hoped, hoodwink the adults. We were severely ordered to pick a certain minimum number of punnets a day. This became too much for me, so I would go and strip the elderberry branches into my punnet and then carefully pick a layer of blackberries to lie on top, putting it beside all the other filled punnets while a teacher marked one more up to me. This gave me time to rabbit hunt or dig at molehills, in case I might find a mole, before starting on my next punnet. I never was found out, so there was no need for guilt as my heart was happy and what the grown-ups didn't know I was all right with. This attitude was to stand me in good stead in years to come.

During my years at school we did quite a lot of drama, putting on plays for Christmas and weddings etc. I was very lucky because I loved singing and drama and could lose myself in another world. I was picked for interesting parts much of the time. I was required to sing my part quite often, which was much easier than speaking it, and I could totally absorb myself into this with great comfort and would feel very protected and safe. It was almost heavenly to be able to live on a different level, somewhere where no one could touch me, and yet I was performing in front of many adults who normally had great power over me; when I was performing, they had none. I guess when playing a part in a drama you are bringing some kind of message to others and they are listening. For a voiceless one within a sect this can be very powerful.

We were severely brainwashed and one of the teachings was to tell us 'you are nothing'. You only become of any import when you are crushed underfoot like the grape with many others to make wine; then you are a kind of holy wine and no longer an individual. The other story hammered into us was that like a grain of wheat, you are nothing alone. Only when you are ground down with many other grains are you worthy of being made into a loaf of bread that can help the starving, so as to 'save' others. You as an individual are nothing at all. In fact they sing a song which says 'I want to be nothing, yes nothing'. It is sung with very grave faces, and becomes a total insult to creation that we are part of. I guess that the author may have been worried about 'egotism' but it sure has taken on a very sinister face in this Commune.

So with the prison bars building slowly but surely around me, I was free for short periods to live by acting through my singing in these dramas. It was as if I was lifted up on angel wings – so very beautiful. Up there you could breathe lovely, fresh, sparkling air.

Later as a teenager I was asked, as were we all, what I wanted to 'train' in. I said I would like to go into music and singing. This was immediately cut down with scorn and I was told 'That is no help to us or anyone else. You must choose something that will be helpful, and sacrifice your own wish for the greater good'. One could never do anything just for sheer joy, only if it would 'help' mankind and especially the kind of man living on the Bruderhof. 'Sacrifice', a word bandied about in the commune, and a word which was constantly bringing me another step nearer to being a complete nothing.

'Sacrifice' was a big concept to accept, but swallow it I did, and nothing came of a career in singing, nor of playing my beloved violin to a professional standard. It was later in life that I was helped by a very dear and 'in tune' soul to mend and heal my life and find myself, my truth. At this stage in childhood I was on the way to losing myself. But I digress...

Looking back, this community in the Shropshire hills was mostly made up of very young grown-ups, many still in their twenties when they had joined. As human beings, we have a tendency toward striving for an ideal when dissatisfied with life in general, especially when young. Before long this can turn to idealism. It is my experience that when you become idealistic, you feel the need to strive constantly for perfection. Since we will always make mistakes, this can be a very unwise and harmful course to take. When religion is added to this idealism, it becomes quite toxic.

All who joined the Bruderhof at its beginning in Shropshire did so during and just after WWII; my parents joined later. They were all pacifists. Therein lies a huge debate that I am not here to solve, but suffice to say that these were young people who were genuinely looking for answers to what to them were huge world and life issues. It was war versus peace – and how could they reconcile killing others in war with what they had learned from the Bible, 'thou shalt not kill'? Having found what they thought was the answer, and feeling well satisfied, now perhaps the arrogance set in. It was partly this cloud of arrogance that seemed to suffocate and dull my little life.

It was made very clear to Nigel and me that we were not on the same level, 'not as pure' as the children who had been born into the community. When another little girl, Linda, came with her parents shortly after our arrival, although well greeted and with joy at the expansion of the 'church community', I understood from remarks by teachers and various adults overheard that she was also on this less acceptable level. She and we were tainted by 'the world spirit'. This, in the loaded language of a sect/cult, means a negative spirit. There were other children who came from 'outside' who also never quite made the grade in the sense that you were always a little beneath those 'born on the Bruderhof'. If you put this together with the religious idealism of becoming 'nothing', you gradually accept that you *are* nothing. The word 'outside' was used constantly to describe the difference between us on the 'inside' and the rest of the world. We children heard the word so much that we frequently used it. We had a language all of its own on the Bruderhof.

One day I was invited to another family for Sunday morning breakfast because one of their children had a birthday. There were many visiting guests in those days and each family would host them. A guest woman was present on this particular morning. The Bruderhof folks all wore a sort of old-fashioned peasant clothing and the women wore a head covering of black with white polka dots. It was considered 'chaste' and 'pure' to cover your body to the utmost, at least where the women were concerned. The oldest child of this family, around nine years of age asked their guest, 'Do you live outside?' Her reply was a very curt, 'No, I do not, I live in a house!' Having taken a long look at the clothes she wore, the child's next question was, 'What are you wearing underneath?' I knew why he asked, as by now I could understand the mindset of Bruderhof children, but I was highly embarrassed as I also knew the real world. This child was trying to grasp whether she had a 'normal' bulky dress underneath her very tight pencil skirt. She was horrified at the child's questions and made a very smart exit as soon as the meal was over. The parents just smiled sweetly at their son's ignorance and said not a word. In their minds it seemed sweet that at age nine he already understood that we were different from 'the world'. He was being a little ambassador for the Bruderhof in letting her know that she could dress in a less worldly way.

During our sojourn in the Shropshire Bruderhof community, we moved from house to shed to barn many times within a few years as our family grew and grew. It was the belief that 'God gives life and God takes life' that helped my parents to have so many children, I believe. By the time my parents were 45 they had 12 living children, with two more miscarried. My mother shared with me the fact that a miscarriage brought great grief. The Bruderhof attitude was to be silent about such things, and certainly a parent didn't share such experiences with a child. Empathy was there between mother and mother, but woe upon you if you 'gave in' to too much sadness, to too much emotion of any kind for that matter. Also to stop copulation because you wanted no more children was seen as a sin. In fact the Bruderhof was heavily tainted by belief in male supremacy.

At the age of approximately seven I was still totally innocent of any of the true facts of human physical life and how a baby came into being. I had noticed that almost every family had a baby during the year my brother Andrew was born. All families had a new baby by November that year, all bar one couple who had no children at all. The adults, including my parents, said that babies came from God and that the angels brought them from Heaven. It was God who decided who could have a baby at any given time.

One cold winter night, having given the Jeffries (the couple with no children) a lot of thought, I decided that I should do something about it. Audrey, the wife, was my teacher at this point in time and I felt that she deserved a baby as I knew that everyone wanted a baby! To me a baby human was the most wonderful part of all of creation. Why was this God so unfair? We had heaps of children in our family – they had none! I sincerely told God that this couple needed to have the joy of a baby and what was he/she waiting for? Thomas and Audrey had been waiting a lifetime. It was a very long time since they had got married – probably at least a year!

By now we were living in the old farmhouse, a three-storey building in the old style with very thick walls. We lived up under the roof. The window sills were deep and covered in red tiles. I perched up on our bedroom sill and looked up into the heavens, watching stars and expecting an angel to come flying past with a baby in its arms to deliver to the Jeffries. I got colder and colder, but still I had to see this sight and know that God had made right his position with the couple. I felt there had been a promise and I would wait. But it was midwinter and we had no heating. Gradually the cold won out and I crept sadly back to bed to get warm.

The next thing I knew, Daddy was waking us and announcing happily that Thomas and Audrey had had a baby daughter in the night. I was at once absolutely delighted, yet I felt so cheated. I went in to Mummy and told her my story of the night, wondering how I had missed the angel when I had been watching so carefully. I can't recall her answer, but she gave me a hug, something that occurred seldom. In fact after our Bruderhof entry, hugs were something my parents seemed to leave out of our lives except on rare occasions out of sight of others.

Some time after this incident, my mother took me into her confidence and told me the truth about how girls and boys developed and how babies came into being, where they were stored in safety and security until they were nine months old and ready to be born.

She suggested that I keep it to myself and not share with my friends as they probably didn't know, and it was their parents' privilege to tell them! Most parents never did, and I sensed that my mother's safety depended on my silence, so I kept it. To demonstrate this innocence, when I was nineteen a girl of twenty-one asked me why Jane was knitting a baby jacket. I said that I expected it was for her baby. 'But she hasn't got a baby!' she said. As the conversation progressed I realised that this young woman still lived with the fairyland concept of childbirth. She hadn't therefore noticed that Jane was not just pregnant but close to the time of her baby's birth. This almost took my breath away, but as she pushed for knowledge I was left with the task of explaining the facts of life to a young woman my senior.

Opposing emotions followed me throughout those times, and later I was to find this stark contrast and confusion in emotion following me throughout my Bruderhof years. I had to accept love and fear, joy and anxiety, deep sadness, anger with a tight lid placed on it, and the confusion of being shown concern one minute and total indifference the next by the same people, as if I counted for nothing. It was so confusing. One minute something was 'right' and of God, and a short time later the same attitude or behaviour was 'wrong' and came from a 'wrong spirit'. It was wrong to be too happy, happiness had to be controlled. If a bunch of children were heard to giggle or laugh, there was an immediate appearance by an adult to reinstate control. It was wrong to be angry – in fact that was an arch sin. It was wrong to be sad, and wrong indeed to be fearful.

There was a gradual loss of parental love. I say 'gradual' because for a child a month is a long time and a year a very long time, and my parents began to let go of us children more and more, until we belonged to the community rather than to them. In adult terms this happened over a very short period. I know they loved us and on the rare occasions when we were alone with them, with no onlookers or eavesdroppers, they became their true selves once again, and seemed real. However they were mostly loyal firstly to the Brotherhood.

I could rely on, and felt great love from, the Universe. But my insecurity seemed to grow out of all proportion. Belonging to no one (for that's how I felt), is it any wonder I felt hugely insecure? Where did I get the unconditional love that each creature deserves and thrives on? From creation itself! I would wander off over the fields of our large farm and feel full to the brim with love. Love for and from the Universe, the

Source, and the one who I knew in my heart embodied unconditional love, Christ Jesus. This was someone I knew. This was the Being who loved me, and I him. He used to walk the Earth, and now his Spirit was with me as before.

Strangely I had heard no stories about Jesus except in a vague way from adults talking high above my head. I knew the Spirit's love before I could reason, and I knew that Christ embodied this love. Where adults in this religious life seemed not to know such love as a group (although I am sure that sometimes they did) I was still connected, even though I was often so pained amongst others – the adults. Often during my journey on Earth, Christians in particular have asked me 'when and how were you converted?' I never was converted. This is difficult to tell people you love, as if they are 'Christians' it makes most of them feel very ill at ease, and indeed I have found that they will start trying to 'convert' me or patronise me, even feeling sorry for me rather desperately, in case I should spend eternity in Hell. What many can't accept is that God/Universe/Source has no need of a Bible to tell you about love, helpful though some may find it. Christ is more than able to be in you without you ever reading a book. Indeed, before the complication of the Book, we are all in Christ and Christ in us. Yes, we may walk off our path and need to come back to it to find joy, but we are still part of the whole God and it part of us. We are the Whole and the Whole is the One. Who is the great I Am? Maybe we all are. And the I Am is us?

I felt deeply sad much of the time, yet very deeply happy out in nature, with my child friends, and on the rare occasions when we were just with our parents. I often felt lost, alone, abandoned, guilty that I was not perfect in all I was required to be. I didn't belong. Great fear set in at times. I felt fear for my parents, needing to keep them safe, especially after seven o'clock in the evening when we had been put to bed and they were in this very unsafe place, the Adult Supper, and Meeting to follow.

As time went on I was to realise that in this Christian community, if anyone put a foot wrong, disagreed with the Servants of the Word (Ministers) or anyone in charge, they were deemed to be 'in a wrong spirit' and could get all kinds of punishment in varying degrees. This was called 'Church discipline'. You might not be allowed to talk to anyone for days, even weeks. This was called the 'small exclusion' – being shunned. No one made eye contact with you in these circumstances. The more serious form of Church discipline was the 'great exclusion', which meant being sent to live alone without one's other family members, sometimes right out of the community and into 'the evil world', until such time as it was deemed possible to re-unite with the unlucky wayward one, if he or she was deemed repentant and asked forgiveness.

Another Church discipline for adults was a ban on attending 'Brotherhood' (members') meetings for a certain amount of time, which again depended on how remorseful a person was or wasn't. As I grew older I noticed that on the whole, those who asked forgiveness in tears were lovey-doveyed back into 'unity' more quickly. Even as a child I could see that often these tears came out of fear. Parents who had been parted from their children stood to be sent straight back out if they were not seen to be repentant in the most devastating way. Fear will act on any mother or father if they love enough and are desperate enough to be with their children. So I have seen tears stream in desperate fear.

One night when I was perhaps 11 years old, my father stayed at home instead of going to the meeting. Even though it was the most wonderful thing to happen, having him home, my heart began to pound with anxiety. I knew something was very wrong. I was afraid to ask, yet felt compelled to. 'Daddy, why aren't you going to the meeting?'

He told me with such a shame in his voice that he could hardly speak, 'I have some things that I need to think about and repent of'. He then went on to explain that the Brothers felt he hadn't helped Mummy enough and had spent too much time on the farm and in the office. I sat there wondering why only a short time ago Daddy had been told he needed to work long hours for the sake of the Church. When I was sent by my mother to ask if Daddy was coming home, one 'Brother' had said, 'But Christine, you know your father is working for the Church – he can't come yet!' Very often, to this day, Community members say things that sound fickle and contradictive. Unpredictability from those who hold the power seat is the name of the game, and emotionally it makes for a very anxious, torn, shredded, confused heart.

My father was absent from meetings for some time. I didn't know what was worse, having him home in shame for being 'in the wrong spirit', or not having him home because he was 'in the right spirit'.

I remember night after night, before I could sleep, putting my entire family into safety. I would lie with my head on one end of the pillow, push my fist under the other end and hunch it up so that I had formed a nice cosy cave for all my family to spend the hours of darkness, thus keeping them safe. I would lie there and visualise my mother, then my father, as I helped them into the safety of my snug warm pillow cave. Then I would visualise each brother and sister in turn and put them in. When they were all safe I'd pull the blanket right up over my head and the pillow and know that for this night at least they were safe. It was a great responsibility for a child to keep her entire family safe – I guess it should have been the parents' job really.

Security became a deeper issue for me. I was a very sensitive child and sensed things before I could reason about them. Almost from the beginning of our Wheathill Bruderhof days Nigel was used and treated differently from myself and the other children; not by my parents, I hasten to add, but by all other adults who interacted with us. Slowly this began to filter down to the other children, as children will respond almost unknowingly to an 'atmosphere'. It is hard to find words to cover this, but it was very obvious to me. Nigel was a lesser being in the eyes, minds and hearts of the adults, or at least of the adults who interacted most with us children. Some very dear adults were kind to Nigel, but generally these grown-ups were the ones who were 'living in the wrong spirit' themselves. Nigel was so looked down upon. I began to hurt on his behalf but couldn't put word or even reason to this unhappy knowing.

One day we schoolchildren were gathered together and asked to sit under a tree with our teacher to listen to what she had to say. The subject was Nigel. To my horror she said what a naughty boy he was, and that he brought the wrong atmosphere into 'the life'. (This meant the 'holy' life of the Bruderhof as she perceived it.) I was still quite young and knew of nothing that Nigel had done to hurt anyone.

This woman proceeded to ask us all what we thought should be done about this bad boy. Of course Nigel was right there, but he could say nothing. I was sick inside and very upset, but equally could say nothing. Thankfully all the children were silent and there was an awkward moment for this teacher; then she hastily turned the conversation to something else and we dispersed. I remember nothing else of this incident. From now on I would need to protect my brother very carefully to keep him secure and safe. It was a huge burden for me, as I had taken his strength and protection for granted and now the tables were turned.

Everything was done 'in unity' on the Bruderhof. That is to say the members spent long hours mulling over what should be done, and said, over practical matters, such as where to spend what kind of money on this and that, and equally what to do with this child or that adult over any misconduct that was concerned worthy of 'united' discussion. A member might feel it was 'wrong' that the children were nicking apples from the communal trees, or that they had been found to be playing 'impure games'. This would be brought to the Brotherhood (circle of membership), or in some cases the teachers' circle, and a 'united' front would be reached. Then the parents would come home and mete out the unanimously agreed punishment to their children.

I believe that mostly this so called 'unity' was really conformity – conformity to those in positions of power. Although it was preached that 'we all sit on the same bench', in fact if a person who had no power questioned one who had, they were often deemed to be 'in the wrong spirit', and Church discipline would be meted out. A father could be excluded and separated from his wife and children if he refused to thrash his child on the decision of a 'united' brotherhood. Thus the life of brotherhood was strongly fear-based. Even to this day the Bruderhof operates in the same way. I understand that recently, after a decision to identify with the poor of the world and start eating very little, one father protested as his children were crying with hunger, and this ended in separation from his family. (This is hearsay, but I can well believe it as it comes from someone who was present.) In this case he would either need to repent, saying how wrong he was and how sorry he is, or suffer, maybe for life, this horrendous separation. Strangely, divorce is not tolerated, as it is a 'sin' as far as this church community is concerned, but forced separation (by fear) is all right!

We all have choice over most things in our lives, but in this situation the choice would be very difficult. Either you must find a way to live with insincerity, go back and pretend to beg forgiveness so as to live with your family and accept your children's suffering, or decide that you can't do this and find peace living alone, with no contact with children and wife and still the worry for your children's well-being clinging to your heart. Very difficult, especially when the wife is so brainwashed that she has sided with the Brotherhood against her husband. This, in my view, is also out of fear.

There *is* such a thing as unity with other humans, and it is profoundly beautiful. It is the spirit and heart that bring about this blessed state, not the mind. No decisions made solely with the mind can bring about such precious unity. Mind doesn't do it, but heart does. Love brings this gift – the love that is unconditional. Since being sent away from the Bruderhof at the age of 23 to fend for myself because I was 'not in the right spirit', I have been blessed so deeply in this area of unity in spirit with others, and I have found that very often human minds have quite different beliefs and we come to very different conclusions in our understanding of life – yet there is this most wonderful and precious gift between us, unity in spirit. The fruit of this always seems to be peace, love, joy and happiness, an experience quite divine. Or could it be that peace, love, joy and happiness bring unity? I guess it can be either way, as life is a circle (or a triangle), not a line.

With time I was to find out why Nigel was treated so badly, and the eventual abuse he suffered. In the meantime, I needed to defend him.

Wheathill Bruderhof comprised three farms in the Clee Hills of Shropshire. At first we all lived on Lower Bromdon Farm. When Upper Bromdon Farm was added to the property our school was moved up there for a while. Life was good, when we were alone without adults, but with the adults I always felt a little anxious, not knowing what would be around the next corner.

Near to our school was a cherry orchard where we used to play during recess times. The fruit was a treat at harvest time and the trees were great to climb. We did the kinds of things country children do. We played with conkers, dug holes in the ground, threw balls about and made up our own games.

One day at recess time I wandered out into the grassy orchard on my own and went over to join my playmates already at play. Some of them had erected a kind of tent with an old grey blanket. I strolled over and lifted the flap to see three little girls with one of the little boys. They were playing what they called 'milking the cows'. This consisted of the boy on all fours having his penis stroked by the girls in turn—all with rather grave faces – although I detected that the boy was quite enjoying it. I was invited to join in, but felt quite averse to this game, so I just walked away, as even at age six or seven I felt a little uncomfortable. I sensed too that it would be more than frowned upon by the adults.

It seemed not long after this that a third farm was purchased, and the school was moved to Cleeton Court, some two and a half miles from the other two farms as the road ran. It was closer as the bird flies and sometimes we managed the birds' direct way, except that as we couldn't fly we had to go over the fields, walking along and into ditches, breaking through hedges and climbing gates and fences, dodging cow-pats and watching that the bull was not in our path.

All the children, of all ages, walked to school. In winter it was hard going as the snow was often quite thick and would last for several months. If there was a wind the snow would drift and fill in the narrow country lane. The men would have to get the spades out and start digging to allow children, horses and carts and tractors, plus one or two cars to pass along, so as to reach their various destinations. During spring, summer and autumn it was sheer delight to walk to school most of the time. We had no adult supervision and just went off alone until we could catch up with a friend or two; most of us had several siblings with us anyway, some in tow and some doing the towing. So we were seldom alone.

One day when I was nine years old I found myself walking alone and didn't much mind. I heard the clop of a horse coming up from behind and turned to see that a horse-drawn cart was gaining on me, driven by the 'brother' who brought the milk down to school each day. As he came alongside, I jumped up onto the cart for a ride. I believed all the adults were people who knew everything, were always right and could be trusted. I did trust them; at least my mind did, but not always my heart. We were always taught to obey the adults. There seemed no distinction between our parents and any other adult.

I stood just behind the driver's seat enjoying the realisation that I would arrive at school on time after all, when the most disconcerting thing happened. This man put his arm around me, still holding on to the reins with the other, and slowly his hand found its way inside my clothing and between my legs. His fumbling filled me with dread. Immediately the wonderful mechanism that we call fight, flight or freeze kicked in, and I used the first two. I hit hard at the man with my elbow, almost at the same time jumping off the wagon. I can't remember what happened after this, but somehow I did get to school. This had been a 'brother', someone we were supposed to trust as much as our parents! I think I understood how Chicken Licken in our storybook felt when she thought the sky had fallen. For a split second on that wagon I had felt crushed and threatened with being overpowered. My trust had been dashed.

When I got home that evening I told my mother. She was visibly horrified and said in a low, trying-to-contain-anger voice, that she would have to speak to someone about this. She told me not to worry, she would deal. Having dumped it on my mother, I let it go. I now know that several of the small girls had experience of this man that had gone much further than mine. I believe none of us had been older than 10 and some had been very tiny indeed.

What followed my revelation to my mother was far more traumatic than the actual deed this man had taken on me had been. Suddenly it felt like all hell had been let loose on us children. A black atmosphere descended upon the whole community. If I had been an artist I could have made a painting depicting what black hellishness is like when humans all wield the sword of ego power and fear is upon the land.

If this suffocating black cloud was not enough, my father came home one day and had a 'serious talk' with me. I remember nothing of what was said except that he tried to convey to me that the 'Brotherhood' found that we children had been in an 'evil spirit' and had played in an 'impure way' and therefore it had been decided that he should give me a thrashing, at which, although I was nearly ten, he grabbed me, threw me over his knee, lifted my skirt and gave me the prescribed thrashing. He had never in his life hit or smacked, let alone thrashed, any of us before. Later I was to hear from other 'Exits' (people who had left the Brotherhood) that many children had received the same treatment. It had been conveyed to us that we children must have been 'in an evil spirit' to induce the milk wagon 'Brother' to sexually assault us. Or at least that was the impression it left me with.

Even after all these years, as I relate this story I feel the hurt, anger, shame, injustice, indeed loathing of such an act rise up in me. Oh dear God, how I hated religion!

Although my father was protected from this knowledge, he was the one who introduced me to sexual abuse through this act of his, decided upon by Christians in their 'clear love'. This was far worse than the abuse by the 'wagon' brother. It is quite impossible for me to find words to describe why this felt like sexual abuse, especially as I was absolutely innocent still of sex or sexual feelings. Yet it aroused in me an enormous and fierce awakening of anger and shame surrounding sex, a thing I didn't know existed, and still would have no knowledge of for years to come.

That aside, I was confused as to why all this fear-anger from the adults towards the children was loaded onto me. What had I done wrong? At the time I forgave my father unquestioningly, as I knew he wasn't himself. His real self had split off from his true personality, in the effort to follow what his thinking said was 'clear love', and to be in 'unity' with the Brothers. Later, when I was in my early twenties, I was left with emptiness, a shame of self, even self-loathing, and this experience with my father was only one small root of a growing tree.

It was around this time that my brother Nigel simply vanished. I was now in a state of paralysis. I was beginning to not think, not know, not feel; even breathing had to be done quietly. In fact, emotionally I felt that if I could stop breathing I would be all right.

I had come home one day to find a couple named Peter and Olive in our home. They announced that they would be caring for us. They were trying to be all niceness, but they had not told us why they were there. Mummy and Daddy failed to come home, and we spent the hour before bed with Peter and Olive, with no explanations.

The sequence of events is a bit blurred. At one point it seemed that I was alone, with no idea where my brothers and sisters had gone. I was later to hear that they had all been farmed out to various people because my parents were among a host of those who had been found guilty of 'wrong', and therefore been 'put into exclusion'. Peter and Olive didn't seem to last the evening, as they too vanished.

Next thing I knew I was taken to live in a badly-converted granary with a single woman named Ivy to care for me. At one point there were two younger girls in this place with me, one around eight years old and one six. At night I remember Ivy would tell us in a very sharp voice to be quiet if we moved in bed. This admonition would wake us, as although we may have been moving, we were still asleep. It seemed not long before I found myself alone with Ivy – the other two children had vanished as well. I was not allowed to go to school – later I found there was no school in process – and I was informed by my carer that I could not talk to anyone, especially any of the children. I was at 'home' all day cleaning and generally lolling about. I oscillated between anxiety and a state of paralysis, as if I was frozen. This state was easier to cope with and I guess I could have stayed in it, but my longing, love and heartache for my family would bring me out of it into anxiety.

CHAPTER 4

Rebellion and exclusion

What seemed like an eternity of living in this fearsome isolation may have in fact been only a short time, although it could have stretched beyond what any child can comprehend in time. Meanwhile spring was well into its promise of new life and this kept me company and my heart in tune with life. Otherwise I might just have curled up and died.

One day I was informed that I should go up to the Plateau, a field on high ground which adjoined the houses of the small village that was the Bruderhof. I was not told why. I wandered up the path that took me steeply up to the top. My feet seemed to be obedient while my mind was frozen, yet my heart was cocooned in itself with my wonderful Universe, my God, my love, my Source.

As I walked up the last three steps that led me through the hedge gap and onto the Plateau, I looked across the field – and saw children. My friends were sitting dotted around the edge of the field, none of them close enough to be able to talk to each other. The sight of them knocked me out of my isolated world for a split second, but then in another split second I was back into it again. Before I could wonder what to do, the daughter of the Minister, a girl of about 16, strode over to me in her long voluminous peasant dress and told me to sit down under the hedge on a blanket, which she provided. She then handed me a piece of paper and a pencil and told me, 'Write down what you have done wrong'. She was clearly acting on instruction from her father and mother.

This acted as the slap I needed to bring me out of my freeze and into reality, the reality of what religious ego and power can do to life and lives, bringing chaos to mind, soul and spirit, killing the heart whilst leaving the body alive and kicking. Now my spirit, mind and body became one again, and I rebelled. I didn't kick, scream or shout. I mentally put my foot down and said to myself silently: 'NO! I won't be bent or crushed or broken under anyone's power. Not any more. I won't write a word!'

It was bliss; my rebellion had brought me back in touch with myself. Calm and beauty drenched and washed my soul as peace filled me to the brim, and I sat listening to the birdsong and watched as the first bumble bee struggled up from the ground and with a long, loud, lazy buzz started out on its nectar-seeking journey. Blossoms were wild with joy in the hedges and gardens, while shy flowers, golden celandines, delicate primroses and white wood anemones blowing gently in the slight breeze, peeped out from between the roots of the trees that grew wide and tall around the hedge under which I sat. The sun was shining, and no one could touch me. I was in a bubble of light and security.

How long I sat there I will never know. I saw every child and adult from a distance. No human voice was heard. At one point the same girl – to me an adult – brought me something to eat. I don't remember eating it. I just sat in my peaceful state.

All of a sudden my unwritten paper was being collected, but nothing was said about its empty whiteness. The next thing I remember I was back in my granary room. Who knows how I got there? Maybe on the wings of a dove? In spite of everything, I still felt protected.

I still did not know where any of the members of my family were. I didn't think forward or back. That would have been too painful. Nigel had not been on the Plateau; I would have known him, even at a distance. He would have come to take care of me. The flash of hope of seeing him was quickly tucked back into my heart so as not to spoil the beauty of the Universe with my deep pain. I was later to find out that he had been put into 'the Great Exclusion', at the age of just 12. He stayed there for half a year. Nigel's exclusion pad was a small, beat-up old gypsy caravan which had no water, no heating and no toilet. All it had was a bed, two high-backed chairs and I believe a small table. Every day a Brother would go and dump a plate of food on the steps of the caravan, and like a frightened dog, Nigel would come out and pick it up to carry in and eat after the man had disappeared.

There came a day when I was informed that we were to celebrate Easter. If I had known the word 'hypocrites', trying to deceive the Spirit with false goodness, this would have summed up my feeling of indignation, even allowing a hidden anger to rage within. Being angry was a great sin, so only I could know that I was angry.

On the Wheathill Bruderhof we always celebrated Easter, and it was usually a beautiful occasion. Most of our parents were young adults, and quite spontaneous, genuinely into their faith and joyous during such ceremonies. We would all get up before dawn on Easter morning and go to a field on the farm where an enormous fire had been built, as yet unlit. We would stand around this in a huge circle, babies in their parents' arms, along with a few 'old' people, 40 years old, maybe even a few who were 50. When all were gathered, someone would put a torch to the fire and it would go up in one huge mass of flame, making the logs stand out black against the red, orange and yellow fire-glow, sparks flying upward to meet the fast fading stars of the night. It was quite awe inspiring. Mostly it was so well timed that as the fire finally spent itself and became a heap of glowing ash the sun rose in all its glory, throwing light and new life-giving energy over all Creation. As the sun's first glow appeared over the horizon, someone would burst into song and all joined in with a mighty sound. The song would be one of the Easter Resurrection and new life, of which we knew many and all by heart; we never needed books to sing out there under the sky. Many songs were sung, and as we became quiet between each song we would hear the thousands of happy songbirds in their wonderful dawn chorus in field, hedge and copse.

On these occasions I would feel safe and profoundly happy; my heart would fly to join the angels. I was truly amongst the angelic realm, living in the moment with love, joy and peace. The love was Source love, unconditional and all-encompassing. I would look up into Daddy's face, then across to Mummy, and recognise there that they too, for the moment, were secure in peace and sublimely happy.

As we climbed the incline that led us back to the centre of our village community, there was no shouting, but a quiet, joyous anticipation of more to come – a kind of expectancy. Once parents had taken time to pop home, change babies and take the youngest to the baby and toddler house, we would gather in the dining room to eat a wonderful farmhouse breakfast meal – home-made brown bread, thick home-made butter, hard-boiled coloured Easter eggs, marmalade or strawberry jam and coffee; the only time we ever had coffee. During the meal, I seem to remember that the Easter story was read out loud. The choir would sing and sometimes the children's choir or soloists, or children would perform a small play to suit the occasion. Anyone who had a gift for playing piano would give us the joy of some beautiful music.

And yet anger and indignation rose within me at being told that we were to celebrate Easter. How can a child celebrate anything with any joy with their whole world upside down? All that was real life had been taken away with no explanation, just gone, lost, never to be found or experienced again. With my new-found sense of rebellion and independence I was *not* going to celebrate Easter with this bunch of confusing, confused grown-ups; grown-ups who would seemingly thrive on making pain for children, and other grown-ups too for that matter. Weren't my parents in pain? Were my parents alone, somewhere on the Earth? I had thought and wondered about Mummy and Daddy and something deep inside was assuring me that they hadn't died, but that they were being disciplined in the infamous way that Christianity feels is necessary for cleansing the soul, a warped kind of Christianity that says that you must repent and you can't do so unless you have been punished in some way. It was very confusing, as I deeply loved Christ, Jesus, as I knew him, the Christ whom I knew my parents loved too. Somewhere, in some life, I had met Christ personally and knew that he was unconditional love —not that I knew the word 'unconditional', but I knew it meant. It was the very essence of life. Without it there was no life. There could be breathing without unconditional love, but breathing alone is not life. Love makes life. Love IS life. Breathing is what we do for our physical continuance on Earth; love we are eternally. Breathing is a line, it starts, it stops. Love is a circle, it never ends.

So how could we celebrate Easter without love in action? The circle seemed to have been viciously torn apart.

I was informed that I should go to the dining room on Easter morning. Thankfully there had been no fire and outdoor welcome of the light. I wouldn't have been able to do that in the 'dis-grace' I felt myself in.

I remember arriving at the hall and being gently nudged through a crowd into a seat on a bench which ran along one of the very long tables that I recognised so well. I dutifully sat in my place next to an adult whom I knew very well, by the name of Peggy. There was a joyless song to start and a long silence (the silence was used at every meal so that people could give thanks in their own minds and hearts) which seemed never ending.

Next thing I knew, Peggy was nudging me in the ribs and telling me, in a kindly voice, to eat. I could not eat. What's more, even if I could have I wouldn't have. Little did I know it then, but I guess I was on a protest, a sit-in.

After a while, Peggy bent her head toward my ear and whispered, 'don't be so silly, eat your breakfast'. I didn't move. I just sat. This meal was to be a celebration, but what had I to celebrate?

The dining room was large, and as I sneaked a look around I could see other children through a kind of haze. There was not a child I didn't know on the Bruderhof, all of them, old and young, my mates, yet I didn't recognise one in that Hall. I couldn't see any of my brothers and sisters there either. I will never know if they were or not.

I have no memory of what happened after breakfast, so let's jump forward. I was now being told to go up to the Plateau, and there I could hunt for my Easter nest!

Every year at Easter the 'Easter Hares' hid nests of goodies for us children and we would have fun in field and wood, up trees, underground, hunting for our prize. This year was apparently to be no different. I wandered up to the high-up field and as I stepped through the gap in the hedge again, I was amazed to hear children's voices, their raucous sound wafting across to me in a very inviting way. Looking to my right and across the field near the hedge at right angles to where I stood, I saw a group of children chanting triumphantly together. I walked slowly across to them and as I got near I saw one of my sisters with a great long stick beating at the hedge. Along with all the others, she was shouting in rhythm and hitting an Easter nest to smithereens, whilst chanting 'Donald Parris' Easter nest!' Donald was the one they must surely be punishing for the state we all found ourselves in, as he was the man who was in charge, the 'Servant of the Word', the expression used for 'Minister' on the Bruderhof.

My heart swelled with pride to see my sister so boldly hitting at the heart of the matter. As I walked up close I noticed that two of the Minister's children, were standing in the little crowd and my heart just broke for them. I wanted to stop my sister but was torn between pride in her and anguish for my two friends. Never have I been so close to pain and happy victory both tugging at my heart with equal force.

After this followed a period of what seemed a long isolation again, a time of being in 'Exclusion' with Ivy still my guardian. In a strange kind of upside-down way my child heart felt sorry for Ivy. Maybe it was the lack of conviction that any child can feel in an adult when the adult hasn't their heart in the matter. It felt such a long time, though, it could have been a mere day, I don't know. I have little memory of this time.

I do have a vivid memory of one day when I was told by a grown-up that I could go home. I can't remember the person – just the voice. I stood in the middle of the room on the bare unpolished floor boards and felt frozen to those boards. It was as if heavy magnets were holding me down. I tried to think but could not remember where my home was. Where was the apartment that I had last known as home? Where were my parents, where my brothers and sisters? I did not know, but I made a step into the outdoors and stood in a sort of state of suspension, in limbo.

My next memory is very vivid. I was standing outside the door of the third-floor apartment of the old farmhouse. I opened the door very cautiously and there were both my parents, standing side by side in the middle of the room with my younger siblings milling around in an air of unruly happiness. Andrew, in true Andrew style, was beaming, his whole face radiating the bliss of being back with his parents and siblings. Heather was standing quietly by Mummy, perhaps more cautious and maybe not quite trusting her safety, yet the shy happiness was there on her face. Janet, the one who had shown her feelings up on the Plateau that Easter day, appeared more robust and trusting, ever the vivacious one, more in control of her feelings. Then to my delight I saw my baby brother Michael there too.

Both parents looked at me with a solemn contained joy, tinged with guilt, and holding their arms out they said my name and I walked towards them as in a dream. They hugged me, almost as if they were not supposed to but couldn't resist. I couldn't cry or laugh. My inside was almost disbelieving. I couldn't entirely trust this moment of reunion. It was wonderful to be back with my family, but a frozen, bewildered child can't become understanding and accepting from one second to the next as if the nightmare had never happened.

Also, we were still not complete; my younger siblings were there, but Nigel wasn't. And he was my protector, the fun one, the one with a mind of his own which he could share with me. And there had been no explanations. The fear was still hanging in the air, so I didn't dare ask where Nigel was, in dread that they might say he had gone forever.

My parents were kind of apologetic in manner, and seemed changed. There were things being withheld from me, but what? They seemed uncertain. Dare I trust my parents completely? I loved them so deeply, but no longer could I show this to them, nor indeed to myself, because I needed to leave a reserve. I needed to reserve the possibility that they might vanish again. If you don't love too deeply, the love, when broken, won't hurt so much. It seemed at that moment that although my parents looked the same, I would need to get used to different characters as parents.

It might have helped me to know security again if my mother and father had been able to hug me, kiss me, be more demonstrative, but for some reason they could not. They had slowly succumbed to the Bruderhof attitude to 'emotionalism'; showing emotion was seen as from the dark domain. Being 'sentimental' was a sin. Accordingly there was little touch and contact.

The human child is a very precious part of creation, and in spite of crippling trauma, they can adapt very immediately to real love when it comes from the parents' truth, from the parents' true heart. After a while, in the end, it was my parents' love that came through, surpassing and surmounting my broken spirit in the days to follow, and I was able to begin to find myself again.

Somehow during this confusing time, Nigel was suddenly reunited with us and we were a complete family again. I have no memory of how this happened. I was never given any explanations at the time; it just was so good to know he was safe and back with us. Only later did I hear Nigel's story.

After this reunion my parents did convey to me, as well as they could, that the Brothers and Sisters had made a big mistake and done wrong to us children.

Their little chat with me did help to disperse some confusion within me. I felt lighter.

Then came the day when my parents told me that I was invited to a Brotherhood meeting. I was terrified. The Brotherhood meeting was a gathering of all adult members that took place every evening after we had gone to bed. It was this Brotherhood that had caused so much pain. It was they who had put me into a state of such fear that it was at times difficult even to breathe. What could they want with me? What terrible thing had I done to deserve this?

I heard my voice as if it came from somewhere else saying, 'I'm not going!' I was so fearful and angry that I had the strength to defy my parents and stand up for myself at that moment. With expressing my real feeling came a small return of self-respect and a warm kind of energy, with the ice around me starting to drip, and I cried silently. This was the first time in all the weeks of isolated horror that I had been able to cry.

My parents realised that I was terror-struck and explained that all children were invited to the meeting because the grown-ups wanted to say sorry to us children. So although it made me feel sick, that night I joined the throng. With every step into the hall my fear grew until I walked like a robot with something else making me move. I sat next to my parents and froze again, both with cold and fear. Some man's voice started up and gave a vague kind of apology to the children, simply saying 'We did wrong and we want you to know that we are sorry. We also want to tell you that it is now forgiven and put behind and should never be spoken of again'. There was still no explanation of why we had been treated 'wrongly'.

After this short message we were told we could now go home to bed. We were not to speak of it again, so I was unable to talk to my parents about all that had happened. They offered no more either.

Later when I was a young adult, and no longer part of the Bruderhof, I asked my mother what had happened during the time I have just described. Even then it took courage for her, but she told me in some detail what had gone on. I believe the first part of the problem had been that Brother Rodney, the milk cart man, had sexually abused most of the young girls. We children had been given a thrashing because we were 'in an impure spirit' since this had happened to us. In the minds of the adults, the children seemed as much at fault as the paedophile. Amongst the Brotherhood some had protested about the treatment of the children, my parents amongst them. This had sent these parents into 'Church discipline', exclusion, as they were showing themselves to be in an 'evil spirit' by questioning the 'Servant of the Word' (the Minister), and the rest who stood with him. I am sure there were other disagreements and issues that surfaced in the Brotherhood meeting, but as far as I was concerned this was the key to what had happened to my life. The man who had abused us was put into 'Church discipline', exclusion, and later returned to the Brotherhood to be reunited and 'forgiven'. He was later sent to the communities in Paraguay and I am led to believe he re-offended there; so much for the discipline. He needed help, but not of their kind. This man had committed a crime, but the Bruderhof never let the law in. They do appear to be above the law.

The Bruderhof in Shropshire comprised three farms. During this crazy, confused time the parents who had been expelled had been split up, all the women on one farm and the men on another. Eventually they had managed to get messages out to each other and to three of the Brothers who had been journeying in Europe. Plans were made and the exiles gathered together one evening just after the Brotherhood meeting had started. The building where the meeting was taking place was a Nissen hut, the communal dining room. It had an entrance at both ends of the building. My parents told me that they had one half of the excluded ones at one end, while at the other end of the hall an equal number of people were standing at the ready. At the pre-arranged time they all marched into the hall, to the shock of those good souls sitting there, and in their own way, took over. The Minister in charge apparently started to get physical, but this didn't work out for him.

During the time of upheaval this Minister had been physically abusive to several adults and children, my aunt being one of them. Later, after much suffering through being excluded, having been taken from my two little cousins, her children (and my uncle, who was a member, but allowed this treatment of his wife after at first protesting his disagreement), after being made to live in a cottage on her own, she finally broke and left the community for good. I missed her terribly and it felt as if part of my heart had been torn out.

The adults managed to get things together and life started to go forward in a more peaceful way. There was naturally a trail of traumatised people, especially the children. None of us were offered any counselling help, or explanations. The religious creed always was to 'forgive', and since everything and everyone was forgiven in a tribal act of the head, rather than an individual act of the heart, the trauma got swept under the carpet and left emotions polarized inside. And as we restricted the light, we could never really savour the truth over this whole experience. The word 'forgive' also meant to forget. I know that most of us never really forgave until years later. What you haven't grasped and held you cannot let go of. Forgiveness involves letting go, to free up your own soul. What we were being asked to do in 'forgiving' was for the sake of the perpetrator, to forgive them so that they could feel good. The religious Bruderhof rituals also said that it would be a sin to ever talk again of what had happened, so things were even more locked up in my being, and my soul remained trampled.

Later in life Nigel himself, as well as my parents, told me what had happened to him. He had been sent to live on his own in a gypsy caravan, five fields away from the collection of housing that made up the Bruderhof community. This caravan was well known to us as we had often played in it. It was approximately ten foot by five, unheated, no water, no toilet, an absolutely bare caravan, though beautifully decorated on the outside and horse drawn when needed. Nigel had been set up with a bed, a very small table and two chairs. Six little wooden steps led up to the door in the rear of this humble abode and on these steps was left, every day, a tray of food. The Brother who delivered the tray neither spoke nor looked in to see how he was. Once in a while the headmaster of the school would be sent to talk to him; mostly that turned into an interrogation. He also received a longer interrogation from the Minister once in a while. Half the time he couldn't understand what they were asking him as they used words that meant nothing to him. The Bruderhof members have a fixation with purity versus sex (as Nigel was born 'out of wedlock' he was automatically tainted with, in their eyes, 'original sin' which left him less 'pure' than others). Anything sexual, masturbation, wet dreams, imagining performing any act of sex, seeing someone half naked, dressing in any way that could show the form of your body, was a sin. Nigel began to realise that the adults were asking him whether he had committed such a sin. However this only came to him slowly and fleetingly. In trying to understand what they wanted him to answer he was desperately trying to see clearly, but he had to do so through their very deep dark fog. He remembers some words, even though they meant nothing to him. During the interrogations the word 'penetrate' was used and, 'have you penetrated'? By now Nigel was so frustrated and angry, having no idea what this man was talking about, that he answered 'yes' as he thought this might get him some peace from the constant interrogation. He felt that was what they were looking for.

Of course, it had the opposite effect. Following this he received a beating from the Minister that left him bleeding from his mouth, nose and ears. For this thrashing Nigel had been taken to the office of the man, Donald Parris, and whilst the beating was taking place my father walked in and seeing Nigel in this state shouted, 'Donald, LET HIM GO!' I don't know what followed. Nigel tells me that prior to this he had run away. The beating may have had to do with this too. He had taken a bike, leaving after dark, and cycled through the most awful weather for what seemed hours. He stopped in one town, I understand Birmingham, and went to the police to tell them what was happening to him. However a very friendly policeman, after giving him a meal and getting all the information from him, got in touch with my father to go and pick his son up, which he did the following morning. In all Nigel was alone in exclusion for six months.

Nigel made many wonderful discoveries about nature. Plants, trees, animals, birds, and the sky at night lifted his spirits greatly as he loved it all and was in awe of this beautiful creation, our wonderful planet. He also loved reading, and at night, after midnight, when all the grown-ups had gone to bed bar the night watchman, he would sneak over the fields back to the houses, dodging the man on night watch, and take books from the library. To do this he really needed a torch, so he sneaked into our family apartment one night and looked in his room to see if his torch was still there. It was! Nigel described to me the awful agony of his need to listen to the music of his brothers and sisters breathing, to peep and make sure that Mum and Dad were all right, but fear of being caught by the night watchman, of causing trouble for our parents in front of the 'Brotherhood' should they be hauled up to give account, thus giving them more pain and shame, made him leave as silently as he had arrived. He took his torch for comfort as well as practical use, along with his sheath knife, which was still in a box under his bed. That was because he thought he might have to defend himself against Donald if he attacked him again.

As I have said, the adults had an obsession with 'purity'. The children born whilst their parents were members of the Brotherhood were the top of the range. The ones born 'outside' came next, and if you had the misfortune to be born out of wedlock before your parents were members, you were on the bottom rung of the ladder. In fact you were bound to bring your mother's 'sin' with you and you remained tainted with 'impurity'. Nigel was on this bottom rung. Of course neither he nor I understood their reasoning at the time. Slowly we were to find out, as life on the Bruderhof unfolded.

Nigel tells me that he had times of great peace as he learned to live alone, even with no human contact, no one to talk to, and without the security of parents to confide in and trust. He found solace and support in nature. Creation became very real for him. Nature was very close to his heart, and this was the way he survived this time. However I was, in the most deeply shattering way, bereaved. I still had no idea what had happened to my brother. During this time I found myself without my best friend as well, because she too had been put into solitary confinement. It felt as if the world had crumbled.

Nigel tells me that he also had times of terrible fear. Here, in his own words, is some of what he wrote to me about his time of solitary confinement in the gipsy caravan. This he wrote years later when he was an adult with his own wife and children, and living far from his childhood experiences.

It must have been near the end of March when the winds began to blow. Each day they got stronger and the clouds scudded across the sky. At night the moon, now almost full, seemed to be travelling at an incredible speed, forging ahead through an overcast sky that thickened by the hour. And then there was no moon and it began to rain. It came sheeting down and as the night advanced the rain gave way to howling wind. It grew in intensity, and suddenly everything seemed to explode. The door burst open with a loud roar, the stove flared up and went out and even the storm lantern was extinguished. Simultaneously there was a brilliant flash of lightning and an incredible crash of thunder and the wind began to howl and whine. The caravan swayed and creaked as the door kept banging back and forth. I huddled in my corner in sheer terror and I could feel a scream deep down inside me trying to surge up like vomit. But it couldn't come up. Down below the caravan something began to thump on the floor as it tossed around like a small boat in a turbulent sea. And suddenly I knew that the Devil was there and he had finally come to get me. Groping in the darkness, I found my sheath knife and clutching it before me, I waited for the beast to come and get me. Still the hurricane grew in intensity. The caravan was rocking on its springs like a wild animal trying to break loose, and the Devil was down below pounding on the floor like a madman.

The wind was shrieking. Lightning flashed almost continuously as thunder roared, creating weird forms before me and the thunder seemed to give the beat to the violent thumping under the floor.

Suddenly something seemed to snap inside me and I was filled with fury. I leaped to my feet, casting aside the blankets. If the time had come to die I would go down fighting. I ran through the caravan door and leaped out into the darkness, forgetting the six steps down to the ground. I fell flat on my face in the mud and still clutching my knife turned to face the Devil before he could jump me.

And then the scream came out with all the pent-up fury. 'Come and get me, you stinking bastard!'

That scream must have scared the living shit out of the horned one, because with the next flash of lightning I could see that there was nobody under the caravan. I spun round, trying to determine the direction of his attack on me. He was hiding from me. 'You dastardly coward. Come and face me like a man!' I screamed. He must be hiding behind the straw stack. I began running round the straw stack trying to catch Old Nick. There were moments when I could have sworn that I had seen him dodging round the next corner, but he always escaped my fury.

And then I was climbing up the straw stack. If I could get to the very top and dig in between the bales, I would be able to see him when he tried to climb up to get me.

For how long the storm went on I do not know. Without doubt I had gone out of my mind for a time, and then I began to feel the friendly warmth of the straw. Slowly the wind abated, the clouds began to break up and the bright light of the full moon shone down on me. Suddenly I was filled with a wonderful, warm glow and a feeling of deep peace came flooding into my being. I heard a voice of indescribable beauty inside my head saying, 'Calm down my son. You need never fear anything again. You have fought your battle against the evil one and discovered that he does not exist except in your imagination. From now on you are protected and nothing can ever harm you again.' And just as suddenly as it had come the great warmth and the beautiful voice had gone. The moon vanished behind clouds again and the wind came back. But the fury of it had gone, and now it was only a strong wind. I snuggled down in the straw stack and went to sleep in perfect peace and tranquillity.

In the morning the wind was still almost gale force, but I climbed down from my fortress to get something to eat. I looked under the caravan and saw that the metal brake shoe on its chain had broken loose from its housing and was dangling down and swaying in the wind. That was what had made the thumping sound. My imagination had done the rest.

But how do you explain that incredible voice inside my head at the time of the lull in the tempest?

Over fifty years have gone by since that fearsome night and I have been in many situations that were much worse, but I can truthfully declare that I have never again experienced the naked terror that filled me that night, as a 12-year-old boy, alone in a gipsy caravan during a violent storm.

CHAPTER 5

Paraguay

I have little recollection in any detail of the time that followed these tempestuous experiences. There are happenings that stand out in my memory in an isolated kind of way. I remember one day a sadness that settled down upon all the grown-ups. But it wasn't frightening – the atmosphere was of endings, sad endings that shouldn't be. A kind of childlike helplessness was upon them. There was a couple who had four children, three boys and the youngest a very blonde little girl, a lovely-looking toddler. Their father, Sydney, was being spoken of in hushed whispers. It came to my ears that he had died. Next thing I remember we were all gathered at the bottom of the drive and welcoming the mother of the family back from hospital, where I think she must have been with her husband. All the women were dressed in long black or blue dresses. My next memory is of us children being allowed, indeed asked, to go out without any adults accompanying to pick wild flowers. It must have been around June, because I remember the glorious heavenly sight and the scent of wild roses and honeysuckle, of walking through long uncut grass, of white daisies, buzzing bees, warm sunshine and above all the love and security that Creation covers me with. It was a beautiful day and I felt strong again.

My next memory is of visiting a room with my father. Beneath the window on the table was a long, large box and all the flowers we had gathered decorated the whole room, table and all. I had also visited Sydney with my father when Sydney had lain in bed quite ill in this same room, or so it felt. He and Daddy had chatted and laughed together, and I felt happy to see them this way. It could be that my mind is mixing up the two occasions, but Sydney was one of the few adults I had had no fear of, and who treated me as a whole person. So my heart was split between happiness to be able to know him with love, and sadness that it appeared that I would never see him again – and I never did.

This then was death? Death was the ending of life – for ever? I felt so sad for his children. But inside I comforted myself, because I knew that death wasn't really the end. I thought of the lovely shiny conkers. They were as precious as gold, but kept too long they would wither, mould and lose their glory. I planted one once in a pot and its shell rotted, but out of its kernel grew a most beautiful strong little horse chestnut tree. My mother and I planted it out near the wooded area and no doubt it still lives to this day, dropping its beautiful conkers for other children to gather, and holding them in their hands, feeling the awesome beauty of life close to their hearts.

* * *

One lovely memory is of the Christmas I received a gift which was unparalleled by any other in my experience. Christmas was always special. There were very few presents, but it was a time of celebration, great food, sweets and chocolates (otherwise unknown), and lots of family time. There was much singing, dramas acted by children or adults, choral and solo singers and everywhere was beautifully decorated with fir branches, stars, icicles, hearts in red, with gold and silver and candles on every Christmas tree. To this day

I love a Christmas tree shining with real burning candles.

This Christmas I was amazed when a very big present appeared with my name on it. Normally presents were very humble, such as a hand-made wooden box, a beautifully-carved lid and inside a Mars bar. As I unwrapped my present from its brown paper I saw that it was a violin! My joy was so great that I hardly dared open the lid completely in case it evaporated and turned out to be a trick of my mind. My parents both watched me with such shiny expectant faces that I opened it and just gently fondled it, loving every moment as my whole family shared my joy. I remember its smell to this day! As time passed and I learned to play my violin I grew to love it almost as if it were alive.

We shared a deeper and deeper friendship and it evoked a kind of love that I have no words for. Music is beauty to the soul that you can wrap your heart around. My violin, such a joyous instrument and so well loved! Out of a violin one can draw lots of various notes and sounds, some very deep, some high and purely pitched, emphasising various tones and vibrations, all of which seem to touch some part of the physical body as well as the soul. Even as I played the four open strings alone, my soul and body vibrated in unison.

There was a day when my parents told us at breakfast time of a decision that had been made in a Brotherhood meeting the night before. This was mid-1952. We were not often involved with Brotherhood matters, but this time it concerned us. We were to be sent overseas, to Primavera, Paraguay, to live in one of three Bruderhof communities out in South America. It had happened before to others, and we were used to hearing about families travelling back and forth between continents, but this time it was our family.

I felt split in half. Part of me was excited, as I knew it entailed a four-week journey over land and sea, but the other half felt very apprehensive. It would mean saying goodbye, for what might be forever, to my school friends, not to mention the fields, woods, trees, flowers and blossoms, streams and hills that I knew so well and loved so much.

The preparation for our journey turned out to be quite happy, as folks seemed to be extra nice to us, and we received new clothes and shoes, which was very pleasing, even if they were of the peculiar design of the Bruderhof 'peasant fashion'. I was thirteen years old by now and looking back, with the experiences of my own children, I realise that it is very difficult to move house, school, county and country at that age. However, all I could do was follow.

My parents did stick up for Nigel and won his plea to stay in England. He was almost 17 years old and wanted to go into the RAF and learn to fly when he was 18. He certainly did not want to stay one minute longer in this community than he had to. My parents made arrangements with one of our many uncles for him to live with our Uncle Edgar's family until such time as he would be able to learn to become a pilot. Uncle Edgar, our father's brother, owned a farm down in Devon.

Each year that we had lived on the Bruderhof community we had had a visit from our paternal grandparents and one aunt from our mother's side of the family. Later I learned from my grandfather that this happened because each year he gave money to the Bruderhof, which was meant to be a loan, although he knew that he would never see the money back, and never did. He held no grudge, saying 'never lend anything if you really need it back'. So thanks to my grandparents' big heartedness, we were privileged to see some of our many relatives. I loved my grandparents and aunt very much and hardest of all was the knowledge that I may never see them again.

Our departure date dawned just as winter set in. We left Wheathill Bruderhof on a wet, cold day, headed for Southampton where our ship, the

Alcantara, was docked. There had been a farewell 'love meal' prior to us leaving. It was so tough leaving Nigel in England, although it was slightly easier knowing where he was this time and also knowing that he had chosen and been granted his choice. He clearly looked forward with happiness to the prospect of becoming a pilot – and being rid of the Bruderhof folks! This knowledge eased me slightly. I can't actually remember saying goodbye to him and I believe, as I did many times in my life, that I had blocked the pain of it, almost not accepting that I might never see him again –it was simply too much. We did know that we might never see our loved ones again, but it was impossible to embrace that fact, so it was easier to block it out.

The sight of the ship which was to be our home for three weeks took my breath away. It seemed enormous and so very regal. It seemed to gleam white as it sat in dock, all its portholes watching us like kindly eyes of welcome.

My parents certainly had their hands full with eight of their own children to watch and care for and one other, a nineteen-year-old girl from Germany called Necki. The Bruderhof had been a very international venture from the start. Necki had come with her mother and brother from Germany to join the Bruderhof and as has always happened, the Brotherhood deemed it necessary to part Necki from her mother as their relationship as mother and daughter could become too emotional for the good of the church – or so it was explained to me by a wise old 'sister'.

So there we were waiting to board the *Alcantara*, watching my father dash about with luggage as he separated what needed to go with us into the cabins from what would go into the hold. Soon we were walking up and onto the ship. Never in my life had I imagined the beauty, might and strength that seemed to emanate from this man-created wonder. It was awesome.

The next thing I remember was a small host of Spanish *mozos* (stewards) helping us to find our cabins. They were happy people, beaming as if they hadn't a care in the world. Of course they must have had cares, but they were so carefree compared to the adults in the community. They could be very spontaneous and happy at times, but most of the time there seemed an undercurrent of care, watchfulness and seriousness, much darker than the sunny faces of these Spanish waiters.

We were given three cabins, each with two bunk beds in it, thus making room for four people to sleep. I shared a cabin with my sisters Janet and Heather, while my parents had the baby and toddler of the family Hazel and Marion in with them and my brothers Andrew, Michael and Martin were in the third cabin. Strangely I do not remember where Necki slept – it could have been with us, but from here on I remember not an awful lot of her. I do remember that much of my father's concentration went into looking after Necki's whereabouts as all the various and happy mosos were very interested in her, which seemed to make my father a little nervous. At nineteen she seemed to me to be an adult and should be able to take care of herself, I thought.

The journey from England to Buenos Aires, Argentina, was beautiful in every way. To start with all the ship's crew as well as the other passengers seemed so happy to know us; the food was unimaginable, so delicious and included fruits, meats and vegetables that we had never tasted before and didn't know they grew on this Earth. Everyone seemed to know only happiness. It was like Heaven – there was an energy, an atmosphere of freedom. My heart seemed to fly like a bird on the wing soaring up and up, tasting a delightful freedom that began to help me know myself. My soul tasted joy, love, light and peace. Even my mother, after she had recovered from her sea sickness, was my carefree, happy mother again. This remained with me for the full four weeks we were to spend on our journey.

As our ship ploughed through the Bay of Biscay, as predicted by the sailors we were thrown about, pitching and tossing, which made Mummy and Martin very sick. We seemed to be passing through a storm at one point. I went across the decks, enjoying the wind and rain and having to hold on to posts and rails to keep myself upright. My father caught up with me and pulled me under a sort of awning, and we stayed there chatting. It was so good to talk with Daddy and just enjoy his company without him being called away to greater and more important life issues.

The rain stopped, but the wind still raged. I noticed quite a few people around the railings of the deck were holding necklaces, slowly twisting them in their fingers and apparently trying to count the beads. They were also mumbling, which seemed a little dubious to me. I asked my father what these people were doing and he told me they were afraid of the storm and were praying for it to cease. I was surprised that they were afraid at first, but then I realised for the first time that the elements could be powerful and overwhelm mere humans. I stood quietly beside my father taking this in. I decided that he must not be afraid as he seemed content to chat rather than pray, although he had never prayed in this moaning manner, which was a new experience for me anyway.

The rest of the family were in their cabins by now and as it was already dusk we both decided to go down too. To get to our cabins we had to go downstairs; they went first straight ahead then turned at right angles to the left. As I put my foot on the first step the ship pitched and I flew down to the first landing, hitting it with force. As I landed the ship tossed and I continued falling until I got to the very bottom. The next day I was black and blue from my hip to my ankle. Over the time of our journey it went from blue to green and then yellow, then vanished. Even this accident did not take the happiness and joy from me; I was so blissfully happy that this seemed to wipe out any pain.

It wasn't long as we headed south around the globe before we left the grey, heavy early December skies of the north behind. I had done enough geography at school and looked at enough maps to know and follow exactly where we were. This made the trip even more exciting. Our first port of call was Vigo, Spain; then followed Lisbon, Portugal. Standing high above on the top deck, we would watch the loading and unloading by huge cranes of various cargos.

The next place we set sail for were the Canary Islands, docking at Las Palmas. Here we were to stay for some while, so my father decided we should spend the day on land enjoying this beautiful island. We couldn't disembark for a while as there was much unloading going on, using up a large part of the quayside with dangerous unloading equipment.

The odours and perfumes of a new land greeted us, and it was very lovely and quite intoxicating. We older children hung over the railings of the ship with a bird's eye view, watching and smelling the exciting new scents wafting on the gentle air. After a while we disembarked and rented two pony carts to take us round the island. It was great fun. The ponies were fast and seemed as happy as the people. The sun was blazing and it felt as if we were in a bubble of protection in this wonderful light. The market we stopped off at was a treasure trove for any child. The only problem was that we had no money; or rather we children took it for granted that we had none, so we asked for nothing, as none was ever seen whilst living on the Bruderhof. My delight was enormous when my father produced some cash and with a broad smile gave us some each to spend. I bought a very lovely square silk scarf, not for myself but to wrap around my violin inside its box. I have it to this day – it reminds me of my father and my violin, both of whom I am now missing.

We set sail again for the South American continent, specifically Brazil. Soon the Canary Islands were lost to our view and I found what it felt like to be on a ship sailing along with no land in sight for days on end. So far the ship had seemed like a gigantic, powerful and very safe vessel, but now it seemed to shrink, becoming smaller and weaker like a helpless, small unknowing baby, very vulnerable in the midst of a world of nothing but water and sea creatures. Although our ship was powering along it seemed to slip, slide and drift along, getting nowhere. Yet the screw at the back of the ship was still working powerfully with a fearful commotion, leaving in its wake a deep ditch filling constantly with white spray.

The sea was beautiful, deep, calm and mighty, its colour an amazing blue, almost lapis lazuli, patched with greens here and there. This ocean was home to many sea creatures, some of which swam in shoals and shone with a light that was delicate yet clear and bright—a kind of iridescent light and almost square in shape. There were flying fish too. These also came in shoals and seemed such happy creatures, afraid of nothing. It would not have surprised me to hear them sing, in soprano voices with harmonies!

I can't remember if it was during this phase of our journey, but at some point there were schools of dolphins following us, also rising and dipping alongside our Alcantara home. The greatest beauty was the night sky. With no cities and towns to throw up light, the moon, the stars and constellations were as clear and bright and wonderful as anyone can imagine. It felt safer at night than in the day because of this amazing canopy of our Universe, its bright lights shining from a velvet black sky holding us safe in its care and loveliness. I could imagine I could see land during the night, even though as the sun rose it was clear that there was still none in view.

During this part of the journey there was great excitement generated by the crew for us passengers, and especially for the children. There were other families on board but none as large as ours, which was perhaps why crew members would come to us to relate what was going on, also bringing us sweetmeats, cakes and the like left over in First Class. The crew also seemed to enjoy our family, which was something to relish while it lasted. Back home on the Bruderhof I had never felt truly appreciated, never special, let alone genuinely loved or adored by any other adults other than my parents on rare and precious occasions. The Brotherhood members were afraid that praise and love could encourage the great sin of pride. One must 'fight against pride' at all costs.

One morning as we all sat up on the highest deck, Hazel in her playpen and the rest of us playing cards, drawing or writing, with the two youngest just running about, two beaming mozos approached us, saying that we were about to cross the equator and would our parents allow them to take us into the First Class part of the ship, where some kind of maritime celebration would be going on.

We all traipsed along through the forbidden doors into First Class and up to the deck that housed the swimming pool. Our two delightful Spanish *mozos companieros* left us by the pool and vanished, only to reappear with a huge plate of the most excellent cookies, cakes, pies and biscuits, goodies that I hadn't even imagined existed. There was much laughter and noise around us among the First Class passengers, but even though their language was English I didn't really understand what it was all about. We were now crossing the Equator, and all of a sudden some unsuspecting passengers were picked up and thrown into the pool, one after another, some screaming with laughter yet trying to run away. It was of course wonderfully hot weather and none were the worse for wear, in fact they seemed happy to have been picked on. I was worried that I could be chosen for this flying dip treatment, but thankfully we were guided back out of First Class by our mosos very soon after this.

It wasn't long after that that I noticed what I thought could be land to our right. If it was land it was very far off, and not even my father could tell for sure. Next morning when we woke we could indeed see land, and I felt much excited, realising that I was getting my first glimpse of Brazil.

We sailed closer and closer to land and into our first port of call, Recife. It all felt so exciting, looking down onto the quayside watching the dock workers. Many of these people were really black. I had never seen a brown person in my life, let alone a black one. I thought they were just beautiful, and it was amazing how Creation had so artistically woven all these different colours into the human being. From our perch up on the Deck I could see below us only the very white smiling teeth and the whites of some men's eyes, so dark was their skin.

Soon we were disembarking and enjoying everything and everybody close up. I was thrilled at the sights, the sounds and the scents of this wonderful land.

As we journeyed down the coast we stopped at several towns and cities. Rio de Janeiro lies just about on the Tropic of Capricorn, south of the Equator. We had learned about such matters in geography lessons in our Bruderhof school, but I had long forgotten it. One day as I walked over the deck I saws that I had no shadow. Looking up to the sun I realised that it was directly overhead and remembered that December the 21st, our winter solstice in the west, was the summer solstice in the tropics and that at this time the sun was right overhead at midday. Sure enough we were just about on that date.

It was right at this time that we sailed into Rio de Janeiro, a sight to behold. As the sun rose, shining delicately upon the harbour of Rio, how utterly, breathtakingly magnificent the sight appeared.

Having docked, we spent the day on Copacabana Beach. It was all utterly glorious. At this time, as a newly sprouted teen, I knew nothing of the pain and terrible need that clung to those beautiful mountainsides around Rio, or the painfully poor and hungry human beings living in thousands of shanty huts. I only saw and knew the wonder and beauty of Creation. I was simply awestruck.

We sailed on. From the port of Santos my parents took us on an all-day trip through mountainous regions and alongside a great river, as far I think as Sao Paulo, or it may have been Curitiba, I don't really remember, except that it was inland from Santos. I was so delighted at the beauty of this amazing land. The ship was docked for over 12 hours, giving us a nice chunk of time.

During this four-week journey Daddy had switched back to the father I had known before my Bruderhof days, which was sheer delight. Despite his responsibilities he seemed to have a constant beaming smile. My mother was just as happy and so much freer again, spending much time with my baby sister and the younger children. Back on the Bruderhof the baby would be parted from her at six weeks of age for the biggest part of the day, as with all mothers, but now she was with her round the clock, which seemed to suit her well.

After docking for very short periods along the Brazilian coast we found ourselves arriving in Montevideo, Uruguay. There had been a Bruderhof established a few years before just outside Montevideo, and the next thing I remember is being happily carted off to spend a few hours with Bruderhof folks in 'our' Bruderhof home at 'El Arado'. It was a small community and rather happy-go-lucky compared to the more established communities. There was a very free kind of excitement at meeting us and lots of iced orange and lemon juice with home-made biscuits was handed out. There were also piles of oranges, tangerines and other fruits unknown to us, all free for the taking. The English members there were particularly interested in anything my parents could tell them about the UK. They had been away from their home country for about twelve years and international communication was not good at the time. Sometimes you had to wait for weeks for a letter to arrive. There was radio contact too, but nothing like we had known it in the West.

I sat there silently taking it all in and as time went on, I began to feel anxious. My anxiety grew until just as it was at a pitch that began to feel unbearable, my father got up, saying that we better get back to the ship sooner rather than later. In spite of the happy atmosphere amongst the folks we had just left, I was immensely relieved to be back on board ship. There was a delightful freedom in being away from the Bruderhof and the religious atmosphere that seemed to suffocate me, the religion that said this is right and that is wrong, and if you crossed the line and got anything wrong, the dreadful guilt one suffered, even if it had been an innocent mistake.

Back on the Alcantara, all the free delight and secure love came racing back into my soul and I was safe with my family again. I missed Nigel, but it was a different kind of missing as I knew he was safe with our uncle and aunt and looking forward to becoming a pilot. I felt proud of his determination.

My happiness was to be short lived, as it was not very far from Montevideo to Buenos Aires, Argentina. That Christmas Eve I found myself having to leave the ship that had given me a safe home life for three weeks, and in tears I recall standing on the quayside with my mother and brothers and sisters while Necki helped my father to count up all the luggage that belonged to us and saw that it was transported to the right place to be reloaded onto a river boat. Still waters run deep; my tears ran deep and silent. Necki worked hard with my father while I tried to help my mother by making sure my young siblings stayed together while we waited there in the hot sun on the quayside.

The next thing I remember is walking into a huge old building called a hotel, somewhere in the great concrete city of Buenos Aires, and being guided by someone up the bare wooden stairs and along a corridor to a two-room apartment. I had no notion of the normal world and didn't know what a hotel was, and certainly not that you had to pay to stay there. We somehow managed to get all eleven of us into the two rooms with enough space to put Christmas decorations out on the smallish wooden table that graced the corner of one room. I was later to learn that this was probably the scruffiest, dingiest hotel in the whole of Buenos Aires.

My mother set about unpacking various things and organising us children to get cleaned up before traipsing off down those wide wooden stairs and into a dining hall. After the meal we all went back upstairs and our parents told us to go into one of the rooms with Necki while they went next door to set up a surprise. After a while Necki vanished, but she returned very quickly, saying we could all go with her into the next room. We went in to find a candlelit grotto of love and beauty, all decorated by my parents to welcome in and celebrate Christmas Eve and Christmas Day. From somewhere, as if by magic, a huge fir branch 'Christmas Tree' had appeared, and it stood in the corner all decorated with stars, hearts, tinsel and brown cookies hung on with scarlet ribbon. There were also small gifts for each one to be opened on Christmas day. The table seemed to be almost collapsing with bowls of exotic fruits, biscuits and sweets.

Daddy read us a story about a 'Little Christmas Tree' which was one that all could understand, bar the baby and toddler of the family. Christmas party games followed, as this was one of my mother's specialities; they always brought forth her wonderful giggles which

I loved her so much for, and which had been sadly lacking over the past years. Then we sang and sang all the many Christmas songs we knew, and when we had had enough of singing we enjoyed what had been tempting us all evening – the food on the table.

Our first Christmas passed over in the tropical midsummer heat and left a confusion of emotions – great happiness, freedom to love and be loved, apprehension, and a foreboding, a sense of loss, with an open-ended newness that was incomprehensible and unfathomable. During our stay of almost a week in Buenos Aires we met up with a Belgian / Argentinean family whom my parents knew to be friends of the Bruderhof communities. Stan and Hela invited us to their apartment up on the 15ᵗʰ floor of a high-rise building. I had never ever heard of nor seen such buildings, and it was scary to find ourselves high up in the sky over looking this vast city. This couple had two tiny children and I felt worried for their safety living in such a precarious place. We enjoyed their company very much as they were very happy and entertaining to spend time with.

At one point my father took me out into the city alone. This was very special for me. My violin had become unglued down one side due to the heat of the cabin wall against which it had stood. We seemed to walk for miles until at last my father stopped at a small shabby-looking shop, telling hopefully that there was a man inside who was a violin maker and might mend my instrument. Sure enough there was, and he did. He was a small, grey-haired jolly man and very happy to oblige us. It was a lovely day for two reasons: my beautiful mellow, resonant instrument was fixed and well, and I was spending the first day alone with my father in almost ten years. He was actually my carer, MY Daddy, instead of a nebulous group of people whom I didn't really belong to. A grand man with a velvet deep-brown voice and an ever-ready twinkle in his eye, he was himself again. This sounds like the description of a man in his fifties or more, but he was just 35 years old and had found joy and fun again. Should he ever have exchanged his heart's feeling for his brain's thinking? Should he have exchanged his moral, religious thinking for his happy-joyous-loving heart? Whatever the answer, for the moment I was sublimely happy and very safe.

Some days later we found ourselves on the most beautiful river boat you can imagine. It was painted white, and so was everything on board. It was spacious, and glided up the river like a huge swan under an azure blue sky with a white hot sun blazing down by day and under a black star-spangled canopy by night. Boarding in La Plata, the river's mouth, we were quickly on the River Parana.

This part of our journey was uneventful and serene. At one point the Parana flows into the river Paraguay which was the one we were to follow, but first we had to disembark and board a smaller ship, I believe at Corrientes. What a kerfuffle. It seemed to take such an age with many shouting, hollering people pushing and shoving luggage and shouting for children to get out of the way, for those continuing the journey to board. How my parents managed I'll never know, but they did.

Soon after we started on this lap of our trip, we found ourselves stuck in the blazing hot sun, on a sandbank. No sooner were we freed up than we got stuck on the next sandbank. There were so many tug boats pushing and shoving, so many voices shouting and hollering, and it seemed we would never get free of the sand to sail further. Eventually, hours later, the sailors got us going again and a huge cheer went up.

We arrived in Asuncion, the capital of Paraguay, in early January. There was a Bruderhof House community there, and they had sent a contingent down to the harbour to pick us up and take us 'home'. We were greeted very warmly, but before I could take breath it seemed I was being put right on how I should behave, how I should make my bed, how wrong it was of my two sisters and me who shared the same bedroom to be talking and laughing during the siesta. One Bruderhof 'Sister' no older than 20 was particularly heavy on us, and every word she spoke was very severe, moralistic and indeed quite grim; nothing we did was right for her. I remember nothing to be excited about.

One day soon after this I found myself, along with the rest of the family, walking over a plank and onto the *Aurora B*, a little boat that resembled a tub. We had one more night's journey to complete up the river to the port of Rosario before the last leg of our journey by lorry over land, to our destination of Primavera, and the community we were to spend an unknown length of time with. I walked over this plank and looked back at my mother and saw anxiety written all over her face. To walk this narrow plank over deep water with no railings whatsoever, with an eleven-month-old baby in her arms, was too much. She was a small woman and suddenly she looked very fragile and no longer sure of anything.

I went back and helped some of my younger sisters and brothers, my heart in my mouth, and one by one, over into this awful, dirty, little tug boat while my father and some strange 'Brothers' helped my mother with the baby and the luggage. My older siblings managed for themselves.

Goodbyes were said amongst the grown-ups and we were led into the scruffiest, most dilapidated dining room you could imagine. The tables, all attached to the ceiling, were slid down poles to chair level and we were invited to sit at one long table. We hadn't long to wait before some sort of gruel was placed in front of each of us with a spoon to eat with. The gruel was in fact very tasty and filling, which was lucky as there was nothing more to eat.

After all the passengers had eaten, the tables were shoved back up to the ceiling and we were invited to lie on the floor on blankets for the night. We slept in one long row, in the middle of the dining canteen, my father at one end and my mother at the other. People had shown too much interest in our family for my parents' ease, and I wondered if they were worried that one of the little ones could be kidnapped. They needn't have worried as neither they nor most of their children could sleep much, so there was always someone awake and keeping watch over the little ones.

The one and only toilet for the passengers was a wooden structure surrounding a hole in the floor which I believed at that time just let everything through to bless the fish in the river. By now I am sure that even Paraguay has introduced health and safety. Maybe in those days it was reckoned that because the river is very wide at that point it could take some amount of human waste. I stand in awe of my parents' amazing ability to adjust with such a large family, given that they had been brought up in respectable homes with flush toilets; it is something I feel very proud of them for. During the 12 hours spent on the *Aurora B* my parents must have clocked up endless trips to the hole in the floor with one child or another.

Next day we arrived in Puerto Rosario, where we were faced with the same problems in disembarking. Narrow boards were carelessly slung together and we bounced our way along them off the boat, only to be met by a steep mud bank which we had to somehow negotiate. I remember feeling so sorry for my mother and wanting to protect her from all this complicated living that seemed to have hit us. No one had prepared her for this strange, precarious landing into her new life. She had simply obeyed the Brotherhood decision to send us to Paraguay, and felt she would go forward 'in trust' and not question.

After a while we found ourselves sitting on the back of an ex-army lorry, perched up on top of some of our luggage. The rest of our cargo was put on wagons, each pulled by two horses. We had brought many trunks, cases and containers and baggage of all kinds; however most of the luggage was not ours personally, but for the three Bruderhof communities in Primavera, Paraguay.

After what seemed like hours the lorry pulled to a halt in a village, one of the three Bruderhof communities. We were quickly surrounded by a multitude of men, women and children of all ages. My parents climbed down from the lorry to say hello to everyone, but when they came to help us children down a man wearing the scruffiest, bushiest beard stopped them and said quite seriously that we could not get close to any of the children as we were to spend three weeks in quarantine before joining them in the communal life. This man was named Hans and turned out to be the man in charge, 'The Servant of the Word', a Swiss member with an awful lot to say but with quite a twinkle in his eye.

After my parents had finished the rounds of hand-shaking we continued a short way through a village named Isla Margarita to one of the school houses where we were to live for the next three weeks. It was the beginning of January and so the summer Christmas holidays were on. I remember little of that first night except that it was alive with the non-stop chirping and piping, rasping and croaking of a myriad frogs, toads, cicadas, crickets and more.

It was a strange sensation and with wondering thoughts, I lay those following first nights in total darkness. The sensation of lying in suffocation, in humid heat, on a wooden bed and mattress filled with the most aromatic cedarwood shavings, and the confusing feelings and thoughts that I had landed in the back of beyond, was more than I could take in. I felt like flotsam on a vast ocean – no boundaries, nothing to hold on to, yet no doubt to be bound by Bruderhof rules and regulations. But I did have my parents and siblings, who were possibly feeling much as I was.

Over the following weeks I am unable to tell what happened in what order. It's all a bit of a hotchpotch, but certain things stand out. I remember being in quarantine in the School Wood in one large school hut with two classrooms where we as a family resided. The toilet was a large outhouse, a sort of hut built over a cavern. There was a well about a hundred yards from our 'home' from which we could draw water. Breakfast, as in England, we collected from the communal kitchen. It consisted of *yerba mate*, a herbal tea, and one slice of brown bread with sugar cane syrup to spread on it, or alternatively, pig fat. The other meals were taken in a communal dining room. Everything eaten was home grown. The three Bruderhofs, collectively named Primavera, had been built up from nothing to some amazingly fine villages, but everything was home-made. All houses were after the native style with stamped clay floors, thatched roofs and wattle and daub walls. There was no glass in the windows but there were shutters in the newer houses, with boards to slide one on top of another over the window apertures in the less advanced buildings. All the houses were what we would call bungalows. Isla Margarita, the community where our family had landed, was the largest. The Bruderhof communities were made up of many nationalities and with its founder having started in Germany and quite a few Swiss and Austrians also being members, the language generally spoken was German.

My father celebrated his birthday very soon after our arrival and on that morning, for breakfast, someone brought a huge, very flat cake for us to celebrate with. Although I had been taught German at school in England I really understood very little of what was being jabbered all around me. Josef, the man who had brought the cake, chatted away in German and none of us had a clue what he was saying except that we understood his very happy face and body language which were welcoming us very sincerely.

The children in Primavera were less friendly. As we were not allowed to integrate with them for the first three weeks we went around as a family investigating our new surroundings, and it could have been quite fun. However, we were greeted wherever we went on those first days by chants and taunts from children of 'nak nak Eulen' (a name they gave to a type of owl) and other such chants. This was because they wanted to let us know that they thought we looked like owls, as we have a tendency to rather large eyes in our family. But with the taunts came rotten oranges and lemons hurled at us too, one hitting me on the side of the head. Not having long started out on my teen life, this all had a profound influence on me. I had never thought about my looks, as this was not something ever discussed by the adults in the English Community, and the children had not really encountered bullying before. Suddenly I felt I must be horrendously ugly and was immensely ashamed. However, I was now the eldest of the family, and one day I got angry in English at one or two lads and a girl who were bullying one of my younger sisters. I felt enraged, and very protective of her. The three kids turned tail and vanished as my fury broke. I was quite shocked at myself (yet at peace too), being normally somewhat shy. That was the end of the taunts. However, I felt unnerved and fragile for quite some time.

Being in a new land, with a different language, amongst adults and children I didn't know, made me very insecure, even quite suspicious; I couldn't trust! My parents had already started to attend Brotherhood meetings in the evenings, which meant that the inevitable 'evening watch' would keep an eye on us. One evening a young woman named Nadine came as our 'watch'. How great was my delight when she spoke in lovely, perfect English with a British accent! It made me feel safe, and unlocked my tongue and my emotions, and I found we spoke and shared with ease and understanding. This, during our first three weeks in this new and weird situation, was my mainstay and joy. She became a good friend to my mother too, and remained someone I trusted.

Again it was the wonders and beauty of nature and creation that were there to comfort me. My words will never be sufficient to describe the exquisite beauty and infinite wonder of all that surrounded us. The exotic and perfumed blossoms on shrub and tree so wonderfully crafted; brilliant red flowers in the shape of rose hips at the edge of virgin forest twining themselves up taller vegetation with the sun on them, yet hiding in deep shade during the hottest time of day, such perfection. The open Camp lands with bright, glowing yellow flowers and secret fruits that no other land knew, all of this filled my heart to bursting. The monkeys in the very tall orange trees that grew wild along our path through the forest on our way to the swimming pool were fascinating, if a little awe-inspiring. Humming birds eagerly fed on nectar from the lovely big bright blossoms just outside our dwelling, so delicate and beautiful. The night sky was so familiar yet so different, because if you looked carefully the moon was upside down; for us children, instead of the man in the moon there was rabbit. You could see the Southern Cross and many other new constellations, and all so powerfully bright since there were absolutely no towns and cities to throw up light to distract from the heavens. It was wonderful.

CHAPTER 6

Adventures in the jungle

After our three weeks' quarantine we were moved to a house nearer the centre of the village. With summer holidays over, school could start up again. The quarantine had been a necessity in that situation. The people who had built up Primavera from absolutely nothing had lost many of their little ones to dysentery and other illnesses when they had first gone out to Paraguay. They also had had no hospital in the vicinity except for one very basic medical centre quite a distance away. Later several adults had died from various illnesses that we would not be too worried about with our fine medical services here in the UK; others had died from tragic accidents. Three British doctors just out of medical school had joined the Bruderhof, also a couple pharmacists and nurses, but it had taken some years to build up a hospital and now it didn't just serve us Community people but all the neighbours for miles around. They couldn't afford to have us bring any contagious diseases along. They had lost so many lives in the decade since first arriving in Paraguay. One wonders that they had been willing to sacrifice so much for a religious ideal.

Paraguay at the time still had no penicillin, and anaesthetics were hard to come by. It was all, I imagine, quite nightmarish for the adults at times. In fact I have great admiration for the way they all managed and what they achieved, even if mentally, emotionally and physically there was quite a lot of abuse meted out by adults, especially those in charge of various areas of 'the life'.

Although the Isla Margarita School was the largest of the three Community schools, there were only about 18 children in my class. Our class teacher, Marie, was German and therefore all classes she conducted were in German. It was very hard going for me at the start as I understood next to nothing she was saying. This is, however the fastest way to learn a language, and it was not too long before I started to learn. One subject that this teacher taught was Astronomy. We would gather in the class after communal supper and then go stargazing with her and learn all the names and positions of the planets and constellations, as seen from the southern hemisphere at various times of year. It was very powerful, peace-giving and wonderful, filling me with awe. Marie also taught Geography and History. Geography was self-evident as I could see the world atlas and follow it, but history was an absolute nightmare as long as my German was so sketchy. This bothered me greatly at first.

Our Spanish language teacher was also German and his name was Fritz. He soon gave up on me and told me to go home for the duration of his class as I was way behind the rest of the class with Spanish language and grammar – very complicated – and all that went with it. Our Chemistry teacher was English and that was great fun for me. I enjoyed the lessons and could understand what he was talking about in every detail, and even ask him to explain what I had not grasped.

The English teacher, Kathleen, was Scottish, a gentle, very intelligent woman who never got angry, shouted or put anyone down with snide comments when they didn't understand or manage something. If students were disruptive, and some were, she would just stop lecturing and stand there in silence until students noticed and shut up of their own accord. Many adults in Primavera were extremely sarcastic and cutting, even vindictive, and of course the children followed suit. I was not used to this; it felt like a very harsh, cold way of behaving, and I found myself quite hurt and confused over it on a daily basis. Kathleen was just the opposite and was balm to my heart. Of course it also helped that in those days I excelled in English, be it spelling, dictation, and grammar, literature, reading out loud – I loved it all. Now I have lost much, but at school it was more than OK.

A Swiss lady, Julia, was our arts and crafts teacher. She was a sweet little woman, but very pernickety, and she seemed never content with my work. I remember undoing a baby sweater that we each had to knit, so that it took me almost all year, or so it felt, of undoing and redoing it wrongly again! She was peacefully merciless in this lesson she was trying to give me, yet never gave up on me – I wished she would! I do remember that the end of year came and my baby sweater was unrecognisable. She took it with no words and an impassive face. However she didn't suffer from sarcasm.

Our art teacher was an eccentric American. I loved her because she admired all our work and was very genuine in her admiration. Her name was Ruth.

CHRISTINE MATHIS

Under her tuition I became a fine artist and was well pleased with myself as I had never been able to draw and had always hated art lessons. Now suddenly I was an artist! Sadly she only lasted for one year as teacher and I went back to being a non-artist.

In Paraguay, because of its close proximity to the equator, there is neither twilight or dawn as we know it in the west. The sun seemed to rise quite abruptly and wonderfully in all its glory and equally abruptly vanish too, around seven o'clock in the evening. The rising and setting were gloriously, dazzlingly beautiful. The joy they gave me every day I have no words for; it filled me with love, peace and happiness.

Because it was so very hot by midday, we would get up very early for school, in summer at five and in winter at five-thirty, and have breakfast at home, which was never more than one slice of bread and a cup of yerba mate. We would attend lessons, with a small break for a second breakfast of a drink of well water and a handful of peanuts. We'd go to lunch at twelve o'clock, then home for a siesta at twelve-thirty, and back to school at three and home again at five-thirty. During siesta time we would lie on the bed and if we remembered, under a mosquito net, peeling sugar cane sticks and cutting it into chunks, chewing and letting the wonderful fresh liquid roll down our throats as we lay there sweltering. When every drop of the delicious syrup had been swallowed, we would spit the pith out onto the earth floor beside the bed. After we had chewed our fill we would fall asleep until about ten to three, jump up, swallow a cup of yerba mate or eat a huge grapefruit and perhaps a handful of peanuts and dash back to school, arriving just in time.

All the bullying had stopped with our integration into school. Although I had my struggles again, being within this community group, and the way the adults behaved and what they expected me to be, I fell back into the pattern of happy ease with my child contemporaries, who mostly became good friends, but on the other hand there was mounting fear of the adults. They seemed to be of the opinion that you were either good or bad, right or wrong, in an 'evil spirit' or a 'good spirit'. There seemed to be no in between. I began to feel suffocated much of the time, especially when in any communal activity such as meal times, celebration times like weddings, or even school group activities. I felt trapped and I clearly remember wondering for the first time whether there would ever be an escape for me. I don't think I knew what I needed to escape from or what I would escape to.

Time and again Mother Earth came to my rescue, and the wonderful loving parts of the Universe that I could see and delight in gave me such warm security. We all walked barefoot most of the time. Often the sandy road was so hot that I would run from shade patch to shade patch so as not to burn my feet. I loved being barefoot; it made me feel one with the earth. There were no cars, and horse-drawn wagons were the main source of transport with an occasional lucky lift on a lorry. The *paraiso* trees that lined the part of the dirt road past our family house were often laden with green and yellow parakeets, cracking away at the seeds of the trees and making quite a din. One day my sister Janet found an abandoned nest with chicks in it. She brought them in and we fed the baby birds by chewing peanuts and letting the babies eat from our mouths and between our lips. They grew strong and matured and flew out, back into the trees, but they came each day to visit us until we moved to another house.

The flowers and tree blossoms were breathtakingly beautiful and the scents and perfumes, especially at night were, some delicate and others almost overpoweringly exotic and heady. The wildlife was fascinating and so different from what we had been used to in England. I remember one night being woken by a sort of quiet rushing sound as if from fairy folk – a loud yet silent sound. In the misty dawn light I saw a broad ribbon of travelling ants making their way across the bedroom I shared with my sisters Janet, Marion and Heather. They had come, quite undisturbed, up the outside wall, in through the window, up over Janet's mosquito net, along the floor, up over my net, then over Marion's. As they reached Heather's net and were moving purposefully up and over it to exit through the window on her side of the house, she must have somehow disturbed them, because they began to scatter in confusion and frustration and we saw hundreds and thousands of what now seemed huge creatures running in every direction. My parents were woken and with great speed my father filled little tin cans of water with kerosene, then stood the legs of my baby sisters' cots in the cans to prevent the ants crawling all over them should they run into the next room where they had been sleeping. It worked, and not a single ant got at the cots. The boys' room was further away from all the scattering ants, and as we watched from a distance they seemed to follow some invisible gridlines back into their column. They started filing out through the low window they had been headed for in the first place.

Another amazing experience was on the first Sunday when our family ventured out to go swimming. We had to walk through virgin forest to get to the swimming pool on the other side. As we walked along a well-trodden trail we heard noises coming from high up in the canopy. Looking up we saw two enormous monkeys high in the branches of wild orange trees. They were feasting and as we stopped to watch them, they started to make loud sort of grunting noises. I became a little anxious as I didn't feel protection from my father; after all he surely knew nothing about monkeys. These two enormous fellows started getting excited and within seconds they were hurling oranges at us. In reality I expect they only aimed one or two. It was fascinating, but scary, and time to get going fast.

The next thing I remember was arriving at our destination feeling so very hot, summer's humid heat wrapping us up in its blanket. I couldn't wait to get into the water. It turned out to be wonderfully cool, as it was in the shade of the trees. My older siblings and I could just about swim, but the younger half of the family had no idea. I have often wondered how my parents kept us all safe and floating as there were no such things as life belts, arm bands and the like. There seemed also to be no shallow end.

We were still in the early days of our Paraguayan experience and I was in our living room when out of the corner of my eye I saw movement just outside the window. I looked around and saw the head of an old man with snow-white hair and a beard. It was a little scary, but not scary enough to prevent me from going closer to the window to investigate. I had reached the window sill just as this man passed within inches of me. He said in a very deep, gruff voice 'Hallo, wie gehts?' (Hello, how are you?) Now I knew he was German but not his name. I didn't need to ask, as he informed me very briskly as he passed 'Ich heisse Otto' (I am called Otto).

So this was the little man some of the children had told me about. He was a lot smaller than me. The Paraguayans named him the 'Forest Spirit'. He would walk very fast to keep up with others, but when he wanted to be alone he had the habit of enjoying his own company and going for walks in the forest – hence Forest Spirit. Being so short, broad and white gave him quite some presence.

Otto would help the hospital by gathering fruit for its kitchen. The fruit trees close to the hospital were generally reserved for the sick and needy, but often, under cover of darkness, the children would nick the fruit from orange and tangerine, from guayaba, banana and peach trees, all from the lower branches. One day Otto went with Castorina, a young Paraguayan girl doing nurse training in our hospital, to gather tangerines for the meals in the hospital and found that all the lower branches, those within reach, were bare, the fruit having been taken by the children. That day he was a sight for sore eyes, all dressed in the home-made trousers from the Isla Margarita sewing room, saggy, baggy and washed-out blue. These excuses for trousers were hung upon him by some very sturdy home-made cowhide braces.

Otto got himself a ladder to climb for the tangerines on the higher branches. Tangerine trees are very bushy, with dark green shiny leaves and sharp thorns. Among them two types of snakes love to hide, up on top of the trees where they catch birds. These *nasanina* snakes are six to seven feet long and quite thin. One kind will attack if provoked, while the other escapes with the speed of summer lightning.

Otto put the ladder against the tree and boldly ascended the heights with confidence, but then all of a sudden he came tumbling back down, the ladder on top of him. As he scrambled out from under the ladder he was performing a wild and furious rain dance. Castorina, being a native, knew exactly what had happened. A tree snake had managed to slide down Otto's baggy trousers and was lashing around trying to escape. Otto, being a puritanical Brother, tried freeing the creature without losing his trousers. This was difficult, as all the men's trousers were made with buttons, not zips. Castorina's approach was more practical and clinical. She tried to undo Otto's trousers to free the snake and prevent a possible bite for Otto on a tender part of his anatomy. So now not only was the snake battling to get out but there commenced a battle of the sexes, Otto trying in vain to keep hidden at all costs what he felt should not be seen, yet trying to free the snake, while Castorina was battling to reveal all, with the same purpose. Otto was terrified that more than just the snake would come to light doing things Castorina's way, so he was desperately fighting off her hands, which of course delayed the freeing of the snake.

Eventually the snake got out without injury to Otto. I don't know to this day whether it escaped thanks to Castorina's sensible approach, or simply escaped the way it got in. Castorina still remembers her fight with Otto and the snake with great amusement.

* * *

There came a day when my father told me with a happy smile of almost wonderment, as if it had never happened before, that I had a new baby sister. His joy radiated to me and I felt so happy. I guess because I was the oldest one in the family now, since Nigel was no longer with us, he asked me if I wanted to go and see my mother and new sister. The baby had been born three miles away in one of our other Bruderhof villages, Loma Hoby, where the hospital that the Bruderhof members had built up over the years was situated.

We started out after sunset on foot. My father had a lantern, as torches were few and far between, and as we walked down the trail, he held it up so as to get a bigger ring of light around us. A torch throws out light ahead of you when walking, but a lantern only allows you to see one step ahead at a time.

All at once my father fell backwards on top of me. He had walked into a branch, hidden outside the lantern's ring of light; it all happened in a split second. My father seemed a little distressed at having knocked me over so suddenly and violently, but I was unhurt and we picked ourselves up and continued. We then had to walk over camp land, which is open prairie. This was much lighter and was easier going.

I was so happy to see my beautiful baby sister. My mother seemed to be in heaven, and all was so serene, peaceful, love-filled and joyous in that room. For about an hour I could live in a space of profound beauty, in light and love as close to perfection as it gets on this earth, with my parents and baby sister, yet unnamed, but such a lovely and delightful tiny soul.

Soon after this my mother, whose name was Olwen, came home with our baby, who was also named Olwen by my father, as an expression of his honour and love of my mother. I felt relieved that Mummy and Daddy had got their own choice of name, as others were not so lucky. One of the rules of this authoritarian religion was that when a child was born the parents had to ask the 'United Brotherhood' if they could use this or that name for their child. Some of the moralistic merchants traded in their souls for power momentarily, and would raise questions, and the parents would have to find a different name. One father wanted to name his child Regina, after some queen, and this was turned down by the Brotherhood as being 'too nationalistic'.

During my fifteenth year I began to experience a very dark side of Community life. But there were some happy events too. The year had begun fairly benignly. Christmas had come and gone. The Brotherhood had decided that we could all wear ordinary clothes instead of the peasant costume made by them, which had signified purity to the members before. The women members no longer had to wear their polka-dot black kerchiefs. We could also all cut our hair, which had until that time been an absolute no-no. Females had had to keep their hair long and uncut as otherwise we would even 'tempt the angels', because this is what it said in the Bible. Not that I was bothered about tempting angels as I had not the faintest idea what it meant. Now suddenly this rule was dropped, even though the Bible had not miraculously changed its mind.

So as this was a sort of Christmas present, on Christmas day all the females strode about the place in home-made jeans and with their hair chopped off – apart from yours truly! I felt quietly so rebellious about being told what to do and what to think, but I couldn't say anything for fear of reprisals. So on Christmas Day I walked around in long hair and a dress. I remember my mother saying 'Christine, wouldn't you like to cut your hair and wear your nice new jeans like all the others?' It was the 'like all the others' that made me spit out, "No I wouldn't!" It was a weird experience for me. I was happy to feel angry and tell my mother so – I was safe with her – but in secret I knew that I was very 'evil' to be angry about a holy Brotherhood decision. I guess you could say I felt empowered by my own anger, I was testing the waters, and happy to be 'evil'.

Later I did give in to wearing trousers, as they were

great when riding for instance. They didn't fly up blocking your view as you galloped along, and they prevented scratched legs when walking through the camp land with its long, tough grass. But they only became useful to me after the religious touch had worn off and no one was making them out to be the new God.

One happy memory I have is of a 'Youth Outing' we went on for a few days. I don't know what occasion this was for, but it was exciting to take a few days off from work and school, which didn't happen often. There were over twenty of us youngsters between the ages of 15 and 25. I was one of the youngest. We set off one day with a couple of wagons carrying food and clothing; we also had a couple of horses which we would take turns riding. Otherwise it was a walking holiday. At first it was wonderful walking along, enjoying the flora and fauna, chatting with friends and having the occasional ride on one of the horses. We were headed for a certain place where a river ran and beside the river and near to a very large tree lived a woman who had been named the Flea Woman. She was a very kind woman, but didn't seem to mind living with fleas for company.

We seemed to walk for a very long time and still her place wasn't in sight. It was very hot, being midsummer, so we stopped off at a house which had many mango trees on their piece of land, and asked if we could sit under the trees in the shade and eat mangoes. The owners were more than happy to grant us this resting place and let us eat their fruit, and it was wonderful sitting around in the shade eating one mango after another; they were so luscious. We were used to taking time each day for a siesta, and here was the ideal place to just lie back on the grass and have a kip; that is if you were not afraid of the many insects that might sting or bite.

My friend Katarina was just taking a bite into a mango, but she didn't notice the wasp sitting on it and she was stung on her lip, which immediately swelled up. Some of the boys just laughed at her in their crude, unsympathetic way. Looking back I realise how lucky it was that Katarina was not allergic to wasps, as we were very far from any help. After a while we started off again having thanked our hosts for their very generous hospitality. Still walking along the dirt road, I stepped on a thorn, a long and sharp one from an *espina de corona* tree. I pulled it out and continued walking, but it hurt quite badly and before long there was a little red line running from my foot and up my leg. This began to ache quite fiercely. The oldest of the group, Klaus, had almost finished his studies to become a doctor. He looked at it and smeared some kind of antiseptic on it, saying I should ride on the wagon for the rest of the trip or until the blood poisoning had vanished. He was quite worried, but it didn't get worse and before sundown, it began to vanish. So from then on I had a ride until we reached the Flea Woman.

We had such a warm welcome at her house as she opened up her arms to embrace as many as she could. After unhitching the wagons, we all put sleeping bags and blankets for lying on under the massive tree and set about making a fire to cook the rice and add to it the corned beef we had brought. By now it was dark. Corned beef was very special and hard to come by. When it was fully on the boil some onions were added plus salt. When the rice was soft the corned beef was added. The Flea Woman ate with us and we were well satisfied. It tasted very good, as all we had eaten all day were the hard, golf-ball sized rolls named galletas. Galletas were simply starch, salt and water with a bit of baking powder in the mix. When you haven't much, everything seems delicious and is much treasured and well liked. We had made so much rice that some was left over for the morning.

We laid out whatever we had brought to sleep on with a sheet to cover and shield us from mosquitoes and sat around the still-living fire, singing, chatting and laughing over various jokes and stories. In fact mosquitoes have no respect for cotton sheets as they find their way very easily through material to get at your blood. But smoke they do not like, so we lit several twirled spirals made of dried cow dung and they gave off smoke for hours as the glow went slowly round and round until eventually only a heap of soft ash was left. We used to light these whilst we slept whenever we were without our mosquito nets.

We were soon all asleep or at least keeping our mouths shut and allowing those who slept their peace. Barbara kept me and others awake by snoring loudly, so we tied a string to her big toe, and every time she started to snore one of us would pull hard on the string to make Barbara connect with her brain and stop snoring. This worked exceptionally well, but it left the string-puller without much sleep.

On waking next day we rooted around to find tooth brushes so we could go down to the river and brush up. One of the lads looked hungrily into the rice pot from the night before and loudly announced that it was full of cooked tadpoles. The one who had brought up the water the night before had scooped it from a little shallow pond beside the river and had thus given us extra protein in our supper.

We spent the day swimming in the river, jumping

off the bridge into it and generally fooling around. It was great, as there was no one to watch over us and tell us what we should not be doing. Sometimes the older ones, the over twenties, did try to lay down the law, but no one took the slightest bit of notice.

Towards evening it began to rain. In Paraguay rain is quite comfortable and can give you a good cleansing shower. It was summer time, so the rain was warm. However, we could not sleep outside and get everything drenched, so the Flea Lady invited us all into her tiny thatched house. It had one room at each end of the house; the one in the middle had no side walls and was just like a through way. In this middle room she had her table and a couple of rickety chairs, a hammock and a few other bits and pieces. It also housed a fire in the middle, much like our camp fire outside. The smoke roamed around and up to the rafters and out. The girls were put into one end room, which housed such things as plaited onions and garlic, sweetcorn, sacks of flour and dried meat hanging from a beam, while an animal or two, such as her pig and her rather mangy-looking dog, would wander in and out. In the other room, the one she had allocated to the boys, she had her bed, a single bed with leather thongs strung across a wooden frame over which she put a blanket to sleep on. On this night she slept in the hammock.

It was very hard sleeping on a blanket on the clay floor and it was not easy to toss and turn as it hurt your hip bones and elbows, so I slept for most of that night on my back. I was rudely awakened towards morning by a hen running across my face and as if that weren't enough, several of her baby chickens followed suit, scampering across my nose and mouth to catch up with mother. My breathing frightened them, making their little claws dig deeper than usual!

After this I couldn't sleep any more, so I just lay there taking in everything in the room and imagining how our landlady lived. She wasn't a real landlady as we didn't pay her, except in kind, which she was very pleased about. On leaving we left her some blankets and food and a pair of sandals and maybe more – this meant more to her than the money we use in the West. I think we returned home on our fourth day away, and were soon back in the daily routine.

Not long after this, my father became gravely ill. One day he had stayed in bed and the next he was being rushed off to our hospital in Loma Hoby. Amazingly, no one came to help our family and look after us. My mother had gone to care for our father with the doctors and nurses and we were left alone – very strange for those who purported to 'have all things (including children) in common'. I remember going in desperation to my class teacher and asking what I should do about family and school, as I couldn't do both. She said to just stay home and look after the family for the first couple of school hours. There were by now nine of us children, including a baby and a toddler, so that's what I did. I was 15 and would be leaving school that year anyway, and in fact I was rather relieved that I could care for my brothers and sisters rather than having some old busybody telling us what to do and what was 'right and wrong in the sight of God'.

It seemed an endless time that we were parentless, but I was very glad to be taking the time with my siblings and the wonderful way we grew as a family in bonding and sharing our feelings and hearts. It was amazing – we had nowhere to go with our deep anxiety and worry but to each other.

One night after all of us were back from the various places we went to in the day such as Baby House, Kindergarten and School, a guest to the Bruderhof came in. It was Hela, the mother of the family we had stayed with in Buenos Aires. She asked whether we were getting any care from some adult and when I said no, she was visibly shocked. Thereafter she would visit once in a while, just being kind and giving us all support. Each evening when the younger children were in bed we older ones would go to the adult dining room for our meal. After this supper there would be a pause of about 20 minutes and then all the adults would go to a Brotherhood meeting or a prayer meeting. For all these evening times there were 'watches' walking round on duty seeing that all children were safe and behaving themselves.

One night my brother Andrew was very upset and in tears; he was with me talking about Daddy and saying that he was afraid he might die. I put my arms around my brother and felt his pain acutely, but felt very helpless to console him. As we stood there so abandoned and alone holding each other for comfort, the watch walked in and shouted at us 'what do you think you're doing?' Andrew was five years my junior, so I answered that Andrew was very upset about our dad being so ill. At this she came menacingly towards us, grabbed Andrew by the ear, twisting it so that he bent towards the floor then dragged him and pushed him into bed. I went into the living room and as soon as she had gone I went back to try to comfort Andrew. He was 10, I was 15. We were both shaken and helpless. My heart was racing for the rest of the evening in case she came back. I was only safe from her and her duty towards us when the Brotherhood meeting finished, and all adults went home and to bed.

At ten o'clock the generator was turned off and the whole village lay in darkness, but this meant I was safe until morning, and so were my siblings.

I asked the Isla nurse if I could visit Daddy in hospital, and she said she would ask the Elders. She brought the message back that one of the doctors had said I could not visit Daddy because he was delirious and it would upset me too much. Shortly after this my mother came home to visit us and get some clean clothes to take back to the hospital. I asked her if I could visit my father, and she said I could. She saw immediately how hurt I felt at not being able to see him, and she overrode what the Elders had said. I knew she was being very brave at that moment, but she clearly was beyond caring as to whether she was acting 'in the right spirit' or not – she was following her heart, not her head. I knew also that my mother needed me at this time just as I needed her.

We went on a wagon to Loma Hoby; I could do this in the day as all my siblings were being cared for in communal departments. When we arrived at the hospital, the Brotherhood doctor who had forbidden me to go met us outside the room where my father was. She was furious, saying that my father was dying and I would be very upset to see him. Then she snarled that if I must, I could go in, but we shouldn't blame her if I did not like what I saw.

My mother led me in and I looked at my father, and he did indeed look very ill. As she tried to feed him he was saying things that made no sense. He didn't seem to recognise me. It did indeed hurt beyond hurting. The pain dug deep into my heart. Was I losing the father who had been there forever; my father, who, when the chips were down, could make life all right again, be strong for us children, and keep us safe? My mother's very being gave me strength. I didn't want to run out. I would stay there until someone came to drive me back to Isla-Margarita.

While I stood at my father's bedside in this cool wattle and daub hospital room, my sandalled feet on the red clay floor feeling the Earth's pulse, something strange happened. I had a soft, gentle visit, a visitor of knowing and strength, a visitor of pure love, and it said to me 'your father is not going to die; he's not yet chosen to leave this Earth. He will be back with you'.

I was in a wonderful place at that moment and this love walked with me and above all, stayed with me every time I slept thereafter, for as long as we were alone without our parents. I no longer woke at night in tears and anxiety. I forgave the Sister for her brutality.

Soon after this, while I was cleaning up the living room, my mother came dashing in to tell me that our father was being flown to the hospital in Asuncion, the capital of Paraguay, as medication had just arrived there which my father needed – an antibiotic. She said the doctors had great hope that this would be the answer. She gathered some things together and gave me a hug and a kiss and was gone. Or so it seemed. I did have time to cry with her, but I still knew that Daddy would be all right and not die. I had reassured my mother of this in the midst of my tears. They were tears of exhaustion and loneliness, and relief that at last the answer seemed to be there.

I don't know how long it was, but the day came at last when I was told that my father was better, and that both my parents were being flown home. When they arrived my father looked very fragile physically, but he was back with his deep brown velvet voice greeting us, and so very happy to see us all. My mother too was just one happy person, her face wreathed in peaceful smiles.

It was strange giving back to my parents the responsibility, leading and helping, encouraging and parenting that had been so suddenly thrust upon me, and now was nothing to do with me. I was relieved to give responsibility back to my parents, but felt as if I had been made redundant with no warning. I was no longer needed. I was like a piece of elastic that had been so overstretched that it had lost its vitality and form.

I sat and watched my little sisters looking at Mummy and Daddy with shy love in their eyes and then running to them with sheer joy on their faces. I felt proud of them, but a hurt was in me that I could not fathom. The two sisters next in age to me seemed so strong and a little more vaguely affected. They had also worked quite hard during our parents' absence but had remained in their regular places at school and generally had not been expected to take over. My brothers were enjoying their parents in a new kind of way.

As I sat looking on with deep joy yet close to tears, Andrew came up to me and looking directly into my eyes with the most loving smile, he said, 'It's happened, we made it'. I had shared with him my experience of the Being who had visited me in the hospital and he had understood. His spirit was joined to mine and we were one at this moment. He was the one who joined me back to the family as a sibling, able to leave the parenting to our mother and father again.

For some time my father was at home resting. Whenever I came home I felt the need to check that he was still there, so to say. I felt insecure after all that had happened, I guess. As time passed he was back at work and seemed almost back to strength, although I could see that he would get a little nervy sometimes and not manage all the long meetings. He took a long time to get back to his normal strength. It's my belief that my father had probably suffered something like meningitis, although the doctors never gave us a name for his sickness.

The Bruderhof had a rule that was part of the vow they made when becoming members that said if you had anything against a Brother or Sister you must go to that person to clear it up. You should never gossip about another to a third person. All members had promised in their vows to do this. In practice it didn't work. They didn't do what they had vowed, and in fact the servants and elders spent hours and hours talking about everyone else and what should happen to them if they deviated from the 'Cause'.

I was telling my mother about our time without them, and how we had coped and of course the episode with Sister C being cruel to Andrew came up. A short while later I was taking care of the kindergarten children. I was by now 16 and had left school and was studying at night between 6-10 pm, and working full time during the day.

I was taking care of the three-year-olds when Sister C came down from the kitchen with their dinner. She plonked it down on a table under the trees and strolled over to me, saying 'and who's been telling tales to her mother then?' At the same time she took hold of my ear and twisted it so painfully that I almost screamed. I kept it together simply for the sake of the children all around me.

Now I knew what Andrew had suffered. Some of the children had seen her. How base can you get? It made any kind of honest sharing with my mother very dodgy. At 16 one is still little more than a child, and the comfort of sharing something with your mother that had hurt you is something that you should not have to feel guilty about. Was I the adult who should have gone 'straight to the person I had a grievance with', or was I the child who passes it on to the mother? In which case has it been 'forgiven and left behind', or does it still rancour? As far as Sister C was concerned it didn't just rancour, it made her flaming angry, and she expressed it with cruelty.

The lesson I have learnt from it is that we as humans should never 'vow' to do anything in life. The whole 'vow' thing is very flawed. Let it be 'no' and 'yes' at the moment of understanding. Being true to your own self and honest with yourself is ten times better than making vows to groups, institutions, churches, and certainly to sects and cults. Cults are built on vows, vows where you give power to others, thus leaving your own self powerless. Life is ever growing up and out, broader and deeper, more light-giving, more insight, enlightening. You may be tempted to make a vow to something, but then ten years later the light has given you a broader vision and you are further enlightened. Your previous vow seems childish and even embarrassing.

One vow made by members of the Bruderhof is to be loyal to their 'Brothers and Sisters' for life, even above loyalty to their spouses. If one of a couple 'does wrong' and finds themselves being excluded ('put into Church discipline'), the spouse has to stay loyal to the Brotherhood and not the wife/husband. This has caused endless heartache and trauma to many, yet they still stay loyal to this harsh belief, which of course becomes self-inflicted. My understanding and knowing seem to change and grow wider and more in tune with unconditional love as I journey along on my earthly experience of life, so I can't vow to do anything except to say 'yes' or 'no' in that moment and from my heart.

During my time in Isla-Margarita I seemed to experience many firsts. There was the experience with a huge snake. My brother Michael had a birthday and

I got up early morning to pick some flowers from a field across from where we lived. The grass was long and rough and I had my sandals on. As I went to pick a flower, there lay a huge snake, curled up just where my right foot was about to land. I just managed to move into run mode so that I cleared the snake and kept running, my heart in my mouth. It made me feel sick in my stomach, and it was with difficulty that I made myself stay long enough to gather a bunch of flowers for Michael.

It sounds strange, flowers for a nine-year-old boy, but our lives were very, very different from other Westerners. We lived an extremely frugal life, never seeing sweets, sugar, chocolate and so forth for sure. For birthdays you received a plate of sugar and as many eggs as there were people in the family, so that you could choose to make a birthday cake or have a nice breakfast of fried or boiled eggs. There was only ever one present of a home-made kind, and perhaps a new pair of trousers and a shirt for my brother. To make it special my mother always managed to light a tallow candle and put flowers on the table. The most wonderful presents were cards, all home drawn, with much effort and love, from various members of the family and sometimes from friends as well.

Another strange encounter was one that to this day

I don't quite understand. It was the thing to leave school in December, the beginning of the summer holidays, in the year you became 15. From then on you were a full adult from the point of view of work. We worked all day in the adult world (my first work being in the Baby House), and all evening we became college students, going to school and taking classes wherever they were being given, which meant for some subjects you had to travel the three miles to another of the three Community villages. Three miles is nothing if you have a car. On foot or with a horse drawn wagon, sometimes after dark, it is a different matter, especially when it is intensely hot, or sheeting down with rain and occasionally hailstones the size of ping pong balls, and taking into consideration the wildlife all round, and possibly under foot, such as snakes, or jaguars!

One evening there were nine of us headed for Ibate for evening classes, so we were given a wagon. The wagons were drawn by two horses pulling side by side. There were three boards slung over the wagon from side to side so that three people could sit on each board. We all scrambled up, taking the nearest seat to the front that we could. The slowcoaches always sat on the board nearest the back. On this particular evening I had a seat with a good view of the horses and way beyond. It was still slightly light, yet darkness was falling fast.

The road started on a hill and then descended quickly into a shallow valley and up a steeper hill and round a sugar cane field. This was the view that met my eyes as we started out. Having just pulled away I looked up and above the hill across the small valley was the most spectacular sight. A huge bright, orange-yellow disc hovered over the next hill and just above the sugar cane field. This would have been at most half a mile distant. It was far larger than the sun, moon or planets as it was very close to us; perhaps ten times the size of the moon as we see it from Earth when full. The edges of this disc-shaped 'world' shimmered like a mirage, but this was no mirage, just very real and very much no illusion. We were all awestruck and dumbstruck as we watched in silence.

Suddenly the lad who had taken the reins whipped the horses into a fast run, because we all wanted to get a closer look at this amazing piece of Creation. As we neared the disc on the other hill it swiftly descended and vanished out of sight behind the sugar cane. I had at this time in my life still not heard of 'flying saucers' and the like, but what I did learn on that evening was pure peace, awe and joy from being in the presence of this Being. Since that experience I have had many amazing and wonderful sights, revelations, insights and experiences that are beautiful but which I don't fully understand.

We talked little that evening as I remember us being awestruck beyond chatter. I do remember that the whole evening in and out of classes passed in amazing peace and happiness. I was in a blissful state.

After my father's illness there came a time when the Brothers decided that he was 'in a wrong spirit' and told my mother that she should not make decisions with her husband about the family but alone, that he could not be capable of caring for a family and she should 'take the lead'. This was extremely unusual for a Bruderhof family, as the husband was deemed a stretch above the wife, and outwardly the woman was subservient to the man. Apparently the weakness his illness had left him with was deemed as being an attitude problem, and he was in trouble for basically not being as strong as he used to be. So again I suffered the anxiety of Daddy being on the verge of excommunication.

Several weeks passed, and in talking to my mother about the situation I discovered that in fact she was quietly and stubbornly angry over the state of affairs she found herself in, and confidentially she shared with me that she and my father were ignoring what had been demanded of them, and nothing was going to change at home.

For some while I remained anxious, because to disobey the Brotherhood, or in this case the Servants of the Word, was an offence worthy of the 'great exclusion', which would have meant both my parents being sent away – where? We would never be told! I felt a deep sadness and concern for my father as his body was clearly taking its time to gain back strength. I don't know of a time during my Bruderhof sojourn when being ill was not connected with being sinful. Even to this day I don't take to my bed very easily as there is a strange unease attached; until that is, I make myself aware, and then I can enjoy a very happy siesta.

Being 'put into exclusion' or solitary confinement, was the most fearful situation, and it held me forever in veiled fear. I was also very repulsed that adults could be such low lives, and even imagine such cruel punishment. I was becoming an adult myself and already being asked 'what are you going to do with your life?' This meant that I should start to consider my religious leanings and tell the Servants that I wanted to join the Bruderhof, and the kind of Christianity that they believed in. I knew little about choices where school, college or life commitments of any kind were concerned. For the moment I was going to try to avoid any promises, either to myself or anyone else. I was already sensing a total split between religion and Spirit and felt quite confused about the Bruderhof life.

On celebratory occasions, string quartets and quintets played for us. This was so wonderful to my ears and heart and filled me with a secure kind of peace and love which I seldom experienced at any other time. It could transport me into a kind of heavenly trance. The piano was wonderful, but the strings were more so!

We did a lot of singing, and sometimes the beautiful harmonies and words brought Spirit very close to me. It was so precious to feel this love, peace, harmony and deep joy; it was what I knew as Christ-love. Also, as a sixteen and seventeen-year-old I was often sent to work with the kindergarten children and was left to my own devices – no one there to order me around. The children gave me the same wonderful love connection with the Universe as did music. My violin took me to other wonderful worlds of delight and joy, and I felt totally connected to the Universe. I would join in with others in giving performances, either orchestral or choir, and coped with that quite well, but one day I was singled out to play solo violin, and I was terrified. I got through one evening but when I was asked again I could not make myself play. I told my teacher I had not had time to practise, and got out of it that way. Next time I was supposed to play solo in public and couldn't I found myself in enormous trouble. It was made clear to me that I had only been given a violin to serve the community, and that it was sinful not to use my gifts for 'the greater good'.

From the time I was 15 years old, I had often had panic attacks and they mostly occurred when I was in a group of people, like at a meal time or prayer meeting or a school 'clearing' when teachers would talk about our bad behaviour or how evil 'the world' was. During these panic attacks I would get up and leave the dining room and run home, and only as I neared our family abode could I start to breath without difficulty. It was quite terrifying when this happened. I had not the faintest idea what the problem was or why I felt this way.

One day my violin teacher, who was also the 'Housemother' (the head woman), followed me out and when I was almost home, she accosted me and gave me the most awful dressing down, asking me why I wanted to separate myself from the 'whole', the Church community, and why I was behaving in such a selfish way in not joining everyone for the communal meal. I had no answer as I didn't know myself. I can't remember how it all finished except that from then on life became far more difficult. Now when I got anxious or had a panic attack it was 'evil', so I must be a very 'evil' person. The saying went when someone was being publicly chastised and disciplined that 'we put you into exclusion and hand you over to Satan, cutting you off from God so that your soul may be cleansed unto the judgement day', or another example 'We now give your soul over to the Devil and you are stricken from the Book of Life'. This is the atmosphere in which I was living. Strangely I was never fearful of being condemned to Hell as my husband now tells me he was, because I knew in my heart that this was a very immature 'Christian' way of seeing life. Yet I was very fearful of what could happen to my immediate life if I was seen to be sinful or disagreeing with the Brotherhood. I could be sent into solitary confinement or be shunned by all. At the very least I could be sent to work endlessly cleaning toilets or washing the Brothers' and Sisters' clothes to show how humbly I could serve them for the sake of Jesus and to serve him and those who love him.

I think my fear was of abandonment and rejection, although unrecognised at the time. I now know that Heaven and Hell don't exist in the form that many

Christians would have us all believe. I have a very dear friend who is a Christian who has spent a lifetime believing that his mission is to help all people to convert into the belief that if you die without repenting and declaring Jesus as your Lord and Saviour then you will go to hell and never see heaven. My answer to him at the time was to say 'as I have travelled through life on this planet Earth I have experienced both hell and heaven, and I am at peace in the knowledge that there is no such thing as eternal hell'. Our hell times come from fear and fear stays with us if we let our minds trap fear in us. It is heaven I experience when I can live in the Moment, in awareness and being mindful only of that moment and savouring it. I then am transported into a state of Heaven living, filled with Light, Peace, Happiness, Joy and Love. This state is divine, blissful, true agape love, which I think is Christ Love.

On the other hand, so much happened that was new and extraordinary, and which I am happy to have experienced. I found out one night what it was like to be invited to a termite wedding—or rather when termites take over your space to celebrate their wedding feast, then ending up being feasted upon! We were gathered one night in the dining hall and eating our meat, marrow and manioca (or cassava), when

millions of termites started flying around our heads—
the air was almost black with them by the time they
had all arrived. No sooner had they made their way
indoors, I believe attracted by the light, than their
wings would fall off and they would drop to the floor.
Once in a while I felt a heavy little body fall down the
neck of my blouse; I was horrified. No one had warned
us about these termite weddings; perhaps they didn't
occur very often?

It was not long before I noticed a great big toad by
my mother's foot and I stared, hoping my mother
would not notice for fear she would let out a scream in
front of all the people. As I looked around I noticed that
the original toad had been joined by many, all over the
dining hall. The toads were enormous and simply sat
all over the floor with their tongues shooting in and
out gulping down their feast of termites. Every meal
time a 'Brother' would read something out loud while
the rest of us ate. How I wished this chap would shut
up and let us go home on this particular night. Almost
as soon as thinking the thought, my wish was granted
and the man 'closed' the meal. I was up in a split
second and started to run home. Every step I took with
my right foot I seemed to be colliding with something
fairly soft that emitted a small pop as I ran. When I
arrived all out of breath at our front door, there sat a

big fat toad just in front of me. In my haste to get away I had run, kicking the poor creature all the way from the dining hall home. Termites and toads of the kind that live in Paraguay are both big, juicy-plump creatures.

Horses were the main source of transport, apart from our own legs. One evening soon after my classmates and I had turned 15 we were given the treat of an evening out with the Youth Group so they could welcome us into their circle of young adults. The official names given were either 'the singles' or the 'Youth'. The Youth had somehow managed to get 25 horses together for this outing. The horse given to me had a saddle, although several rode bareback as there were nowhere near enough saddles for all. The young man who had saddled my horse was twenty-five years old and I was very shy of him and in fact I hadn't discussed the horse, or saddling it up with him at all – – he just did it and I was later to find out that he had a purpose for doing it.

It was evening when we all got up onto our horses and left the Bruderhof village for a nice long ride out over the camp lands. The camp was riddled with termite hills, the rock-solid mounds where they led their happy lives, which were quite high in some cases. I believe uninhabited termite hills had often been used as ovens by various Indian tribes. I can imagine that they would serve very well as such.

The flat but rather rough camp lands seemed to go on endlessly, encircled by rain forest. Before we knew it we were riding in the last rays of the sun and with a bright moon already showing. Some in the lead began to gallop and soon we were all drawn to the leaders' speed. After a while I began to feel saddle sore, so I adjusted my sitting position with one leg over the saddle and the other dangling down lower. Thus my left leg was 'sitting' on the saddle instead of the usual straight sitting position. With my weight unbalanced I suddenly found my saddle was slipping, and before I knew it I hit the ground and was utterly winded. The horse stopped dead in its tracks. I had fallen on something hard, hitting myself just below the shoulder blades and in the middle of my back. I was well and truly winded.

Soon folks were standing around me and then when they saw that I was still alive a raucous, rather sarcastic laugh issued from Stefan, the man who had saddled my horse. Later he said, still laughing, that he had purposely left the belly band unsecured to see who would be the unfortunate one to fall off their horse. He found it extremely funny. Needless to say I did not. It could be said that this is what happens when young people are allowed more freedom than they are able to handle.

I lay on the grass for a little while to get my breath back. Although it was difficult getting back up, no injury was sustained and once back on the horse I was able to enjoy the wonderful moonlit night at a slower pace, which suited me fine. It was like riding through a magic world of silver beauty tinged with gold, with no clouds, the moon breathtakingly lovely and a black velvet backdrop to the millions of stars, with the occasional shooting star. The sounds in the heat of the night were many and varied and constant, such as cicadas, frogs, toads, crickets, the night owl and night swallow, the occasional death bird with its mournful cry and the mane wolf's cough-bark. Having lived through the scorching hot day, the night air was soothing and gentle to body and soul with its breezy warmth.

The moon has always been magical to me, as it reflects the sun back to us on our planet Earth. When you're living in a country with only one or two cities, and neither close by, there is no man-made light to muddy the skies, and you become part of the Universe in such an easy way. As I have said, the generators were switched off at ten at night, so reading was next to impossible after this time. Sometimes I was lucky to find a candle, but mostly I had to get used to closing my book, ready or not. I found however that if there was a full moon in a certain direction I could go on reading by the light of the moon, so bright was it. The head of my bed was by the open window and flush with it, so all I had to do was lie there and read – it was absolutely glorious. Of course, as the moon waxed and waned through the month my reading had to be put on hold until the coming of the next month's brightness.

Another pastime at night in my teenage years, when reading was impossible, was to lie and listen for the night watchman to pass by on his horse. Mostly it would be a young man and sometimes one I had a crush on at that time. The crushes didn't last that long, but I went through several lads in my mind and heart over time and I would sizzle with happiness when my latest romantic ideal went by. Strangely they were mostly of an arrogant disposition, and looking back I wonder why I was drawn to young arrogance during my own fledgling days, but this was part of my awakening.

It was all kept secret within my own soul and heart because it was severely frowned upon to show any feelings for the opposite sex. You learn very quickly when living in a cultish situation to keep joys, excess happiness, sadness, fear and anger hidden, as showing any kind of emotion can land you in painful trouble. If you were found kissing and or touching anyone, it would land you in solitary confinement; you would be in the 'small exclusion', shunned, if you had any secret conversations with a boy or were to be found holding hands. And woe betide any poor soul who made the biggest sin of all and had sex with anyone. Sex was a very 'evil-sinful' thing indeed, and in fact we never heard the word. It was something you should be deeply ashamed of, even to talk with each other about. That included talking about animals' sex lives too. It was sinful and taboo, unless you got married, and then suddenly it was holy, from God, and the most wonderful thing on this Earth, so wonderful that again, you should never talk about it! Adults would often say 'would you put your most precious possession on show for any thief to be tempted and steal?' This was to emphasise why it would be wrong to speak of procreation, or not to cover your body with clothing that was hot and restrictive. So either way you didn't talk about sex, before or after marriage!

A group of very young boys had noticed some cows and the activities of the bull on the camp lands. They had worked out that the cows the bull had romped with all had calves later on. One day one of these young lads said to another, 'do you think that is what happens with people?' One boy, slightly older, grassed on them and they all received a thrashing and were put into exclusion.

One day I was followed and stopped by the House Mother, who told me that I should either cut my hair or put it up in a bun 'like Frida'. When I looked puzzled, she said that I was 'bringing all the young men into need' with the way my pony tail swished around as I walked. I was utterly perplexed. How on earth could my pony tail hurt young lads by 'bringing them into need'? I didn't find out what she meant until years later. Apparently she was afraid that they would be sexually aroused. If this happened they had to 'confess' their sin and suffer various consequences. The most frequent was that of exclusion.

The confusions one was put under over the issues surrounding sex were deep. Some years on, I recall some examples of the emotional, mental and physical abuse that two young women underwent due to the attitudes this Christian church community had taken on. Both come second hand, but they were told to me by people who had been there at the time and are very closely related to them both.

The first girl, who I shall call 'A', had been born

into the Christian cult kind of life, and knew nothing different, so she had nothing to compare with. She had become a member of the sect, or rather cult as it had now become. She was a rather innocent person in a very nice kind of way. Not all marriages on the Bruderhof are because there is real attraction and love between the two. If a male loves or wants a certain female he is required to go to the Servant of the Word (Minister) and ask for this woman. The Minister then goes to the girl and asks her. She can say no. But according to the mood of the Minister at that time, or the mood of the Witness Brothers (Elders) plus the Minister, the girl can be in trouble for saying no. However in A's case the happy couple had proceeded through the correct channels and declared in a meeting of the Brotherhood their love for one another, at which time they were considered engaged and there was a celebration put on – a love feast. As a young girl, I was very impressed that on one occasion after the engagement the young man had been away for a few days and when he returned he gave his bride a kiss on the forehead, which was very romantic, and exciting yet slightly embarrassing to me.

A short time later we celebrated their wedding. In the old-fashioned way, their wedding night was to be the happy night, in their case the first experience, of sexual intercourse, and all the wonderful pleasure it can bring. Instead, it was all really abhorrent to the girl as she couldn't reconcile finding pleasure with something her psyche was trained to say no to, because it was sinful. Some time later she went tearfully to her mother and tried to find out how marriage could possibly be a pleasure with sex involved. I guess it maybe never was a joyful pleasure, but she went on to have a very large family.

Young woman 'B' went through the same channels 'A' had gone. So far, so good. When it came to having sex she was utterly disgusted with herself, but of course she permitted it. She became pregnant, but was put into exclusion after confessing to being in 'a wrong spirit' where her husband and sex were concerned. She spent a large part of her pregnancy shunned and alone. I don't know how things resolved for her, but I believe she is back with the Bruderhof community.

A third young mother was treated in the same way by having to go through the exclusion thing, because she didn't want more children—I think she had four at the time—and she was cast as 'being in the wrong spirit'. Another young girl was actually excluded for some time because she had said 'no' to a marriage proposal. When she was invited back into the circle of members, it was because she had 'repented' of being 'superficial and talking badly' of him. Soon she was married to this same man.

I know that men suffered psychological damage too, because of this obsession with 'purity' versus 'impurity' that the Bruderhof has, especially regarding sex.

CHAPTER 7

Between two continents

There came a time when it was decided by the Brotherhood that my future should be considered. Around the age of 16 or 17 we youngsters were expected to know what we wanted to train for, or what profession we would like to follow. This meant going to college to learn a trade or gain a certificate in something that would be of use to the communal Life on the Bruderhof, but something that one would hopefully enjoy and have a certain gift for. There was also the hope that soon a young person would want to commit themselves to the Bruderhof type of Christianity. Although it was always said that this would be a matter of free will and choice, if you didn't make a clear choice fairly early in your life you would find yourself being pressured to make the choice for 'the life', otherwise you could be considered as being against it and could be put out and away from family into the big bad world.

My first choice, had it truly been a choice, would have been to study music. In those days we were not permitted to go to university and I would imagine not to a music academy either. At all events, music was considered no use as an occupation, not practical enough and a little fanciful and egotistical. I was quickly turned down, and so it was that I asked for and was granted permission to enter a college certificate course in child care and as it turned out, psychology. Had the Brothers realised that my course would include a heavy dose of child psychology I doubt I would have been able to do it. Psychology was very much frowned upon during most of the Bruderhof history, although there were times when they would suddenly go very heavily after it and send any young person who wasn't conforming to a psychologist or even a psychiatrist. The pendulum swing that persists in the Bruderhof is very confusing and disconcerting. Where it was a sin to get psychological help, or even recognise psychology one time, it would suddenly become God's gift and a must to us.

* * *

Now the time was close for me to leave my parents and siblings and travel to England to enter a college for my 'training', as it was called. I was in my 17th year.

This was not a college chosen by myself but by the Brotherhood. At first they had decided that I should be sent to Germany and enter the Frobel Seminar, to my utter horror. I had had experience of some German people who had studied Frobel's theories and enacted them later with us, and I most certainly didn't like it. Although I was bilingual and managed German well, I felt easier with the English language and felt German to be very foreign. My Spanish was very weak compared with the other two, but I would have felt happier going to Spain or even staying in Paraguay and going to the Asuncion college, just to avoid Frobel. I was so worried that I told my father, 'I am NOT going to Germany to any seminar!' I rarely displayed anger as it could be dangerous to do so, but on the odd occasion I did let it burst out of me and my parents were clever at translating my feelings to those in charge to avoid trouble.

In some magical way my father managed to talk to the right people in the right tone of voice, and my future was diverted to England, to a humble little two-year course in Bristol. Then news came from a Bruderhof girl who was already in the Bristol college that she could hardly cope with the 'evil' that existed there, being so far from a Bruderhof, so it was decided to send me to another child care course, in Shrewsbury, which was quite close to Wheathill in Shropshire. So my dream of being far distant from the Bruderhof, thus allowing me to enjoy some independence and live in a fearless way, was completely dashed. Again my father intervened. He extracted a promise and understanding from his 'brothers' that I could go and live at the college so as to experience what it would be like to have some independence from 'The Life' (another example of the loaded language they used) and feel a little freedom.

As the time of my departure neared, my heart was very torn, because I didn't really want to leave my parents and siblings. I was after all not yet 17 and England was thousands of miles away, with no direct communications. On the other hand I was excited at the prospect of getting to know the world and the ways of other peoples. Perhaps the biggest draw was the thought of spending time away from the Bruderhof, although at that time I could barely understand what I was feeling myself, nor why. It was both frightening and exciting.

As a farewell gift to me, we were given the chance to go on a day's outing as a family. There were 10 children in the family by this time, but with Nigel still away, by now in Cyprus with the RAF, there were nine children and our parents to accommodate on this outing. This meant two horses pulling a wagon which could not quite carry us all as well as picnic and clothing, so we were also provided with a horse to ride. This horse, called Pussy, was quite reliable but also could be nervous on occasions and needed careful and strong handling if startled in any way. Andrew was given the reins of the wagon with my father sitting beside him to help when necessary and I was given the horse to ride.

We rumbled along past forest and over camp land on a very hot winter's day in late July, but I am afraid I have no memory of where we headed or where we landed. I do remember our parents letting us go into a little shop in a village to buy sweets with the few *guarani,* the Paraguayan currency, my father had handed to each of us. We had rarely handled money before and it was a lovely feeling to give over these dirty little banknotes and receive never-seen-before sweets in exchange. It was amazing that the guarani had such power. Even though they actually stank with the dirt of millions, and ages, they could turn your day into sweetness!

We sat out under a tree for shade to have our picnic and it was a real feast. Someone had prepared it for us with real love and care. The peaceful happiness of the day filled me with emotions that were ready to spill over. I was with my family with no one looking over our shoulders, my parents being themselves, out in nature with the sound of songbirds and insects, frogs and close at hand the cutting ants with their clear 'snip-snip-snip' as they cut through leaves to carry off in their column, down underground where they would make compost to grow their food on.

My brothers and sisters felt more precious to me at that moment because I faced an uncertain future without them and did not know when I would see them again. The love for them, the love for my parents, welled up in me and at the same time loss and separation, seemed to tear at my heart. The sun was bright in a crystal blue sky and gave me comfort and security as I sat holding the love, the moment close to my heart. I remember that my parents and all my siblings seemed so happy being together as a real family with no one else to be accountable to. There was lots of laughter throughout the day, especially from my brothers. At the same time there was apprehension in the eyes of my three little sisters in particular, just as I was feeling.

On the way back home in the early evening the sky suddenly darkened and then turned almost black with rain clouds. I was riding the horse and my father sat on the wagon guiding the horses which were pulling the rest of the family. As big, heavy drops began to fall my father pulled up, and taking a poncho out from our luggage he attempted to rig it up over the wagon as a protection. He did a good job of it, but the hole in the middle let in a stream of water. Pussy was very afraid of the storm, which by now was full on with thunder and lightning, so she dug her back legs in and refused to budge. We tried tying her to the wagon while I squeezed on with the rest of the family, but Pussy still dug her heels in.

So there we were, stuck on the dirt road in the middle of the camp land with water bucketing down from the heavens. I was soaked, and the others were not much better off. My father decided that he would have to ride the horse while I drove the wagon. It worked for a while, but by now the road was invisible. There were a couple of feet of water covering all the land as far as we could see. I knew we were just coming upon a bridge over a stream, because landmarks such as certain trees told me so, but the road and bridge were invisible. I was very scared in case I got it wrong and the wagon ended up tipped over with my whole family out of the wagon and in the stream.

I remember my father shouting something through the noise of the storm and also glancing back and seeing my mother's frightened face. At that moment I gave the horses a gentle slap with the reins to urge them on, then let the reins slacken and left it totally up to the horses to get us over. I held my breath waiting for the horses to do their thing. Heads bent forward and pulling against the wind and rain, those faithful, clever, enduring creatures got us safely and squarely over onto the other side with my father managing Pussy so that she followed suit.

We still could see no land, but the horses knew their way. All around us was brown water. However the sun came out as brightly as ever with its drying heat and soon one could begin to see the tips of the grass and vegetation that belonged to the sprawling camp lands. Before the sun went down beyond the horizon all the water had vanished and we could well see where we were going.

I can't remember anything of the rest of that evening. I do know that we got home and were none the worse for wear. Parting was upon us. I cannot recall my final farewell to my parents and brothers and sisters, either. Hard as I try, the memory is elusive. It is usually my feelings I remember first rather than actual physical happenings. As I try to recall when, how, what, feelings, actions and reactions, I draw a complete blank.

I do recall my ocean crossing back over the Atlantic. Still not 17, I needed guardians to make it legal to leave my parents, I guess. I found myself on board the *Highland Monarch* with a German Bruderhof family whom I knew very little as they had lived in a different village from ours. They had two daughters along with them and another girl of my age, also from a different Bruderhof village. We got to know each other very well indeed over the four weeks travelling. This couple were such kind, fun-loving people to be with and wonderfully trusting, with no religious moralizing or dogmatism thrown in. They looked after me in the best way any parent could with a young teen. They stayed ever the same and became balm to my heart throughout the journey. It was a safe and happy month, albeit with a taste of homesickness on occasion.

So it was that I found myself back in the Wheathill Bruderhof so that I could go to college. It didn't turn out as my parents and I had expected, because the Brotherhood had in the meantime decided that I lived close enough to travel back and forth each day. They even managed to wangle it that the college would allow me to do my 'practice' with the young children on the Bruderhof. So for my first year I didn't get the freedom I had so craved.

At this stage I was given an English couple as my guardians. They were very nice to be with and made no impossible demands of me. They had recently returned from Paraguay having just adopted a little Paraguayan child. Our course required us to do a six-month case study of a child between the ages of three to six, so as I was doing my practice in the Bruderhof Community I chose to do my study of this little Paraguayan girl. This meant that my tutor needed to get to know this child too, so she was a frequent visitor during this period. This excluded the folks of the community who had the responsibility of the younger children from being involved with my college work, which was a great relief.

The only connection I could have with my parents was by letter, and it truly was snail mail as the Bruderhof, at this time quite poor, could only afford mail by land. The letters would not arrive sometimes for six weeks after posting. I had written to my parents that our hoped-for plans had gone a little haywire and that I was not living in college dormitories but on the Bruderhof. I don't know how my parents managed, but my guardian, Peter, came to me one day and told me that my parents wanted me to experience living away from the Bruderhof, and therefore I would be going to live in accommodation near the college. He also informed me that the two girls from the Bruderhof attending the same college would be moving with me. The place found for us to rent was a Youth Hostel, a large Victorian house with extensive and beautiful gardens. It was owned by a Quaker lady and 'friend' of the community, who turned out to be very critical of the Bruderhof members' behaviours and actions later on. However, through her we had very cheap accommodation. She was kind, but the living conditions were very harsh as it was freezing cold, with no heating, and it was like living outside, so permanent and intense was the cold. What a change from the heat of Paraguay!

It was very difficult to do any studying in these conditions. Each Monday morning we three girls were given an amount of money by the Bruderhof Steward to see us through the week, but it was so little that we had to live on bread, margarine and tea for a good part of the time. We did get a cooked college meal most days, but we had to be very selective in what we could afford on our plates. If we wanted to go to the cinema we had to eat nothing all day so we could manage our finances, but this didn't really harm us. We would take a bus to Shrewsbury, and sometimes a train and then stay there until Friday, when we were required to travel back to the community 'to experience the inner life of Bruderhof'.

One of the other girls was doing the same course as I was. When we arrived for our first lecture at the very beginning of term, each person was asked to introduce themselves by name and say where we came from. Elske's turn for introduction came just before mine, and she got up and said, 'I am Elske, and I come from Paraguay and I am Dutch'. There was an awed silence in the class. Elske sounded foreign, was foreign, and no one had ever heard of Paraguay, so this intrigued everyone. All the other students were English.

Now it was my turn. I stood as required and said 'I am Christine and I come from Paraguay and I am English'. There was a split second's silence, and then the whole room of thirty-odd burst into raucous laughter. I had a very continental accent, just the same as Elske's, and then saying that I was English – well, I think the whole room full of people thought I was mimicking Elske, and taking the mick! They howled with laughter so that the teacher had to calm them down. The laughter was not malicious, I was just perplexed. I'll never know if they laughed with me or at me!

As the days turned into weeks they began to know a little about me and I about them, and we were friendly enough, although I always found it impossible to tell anyone of the strange life I really came from, and Elske said next to nothing. By the second year of college I was not only living apart from the community, but doing my practical in another school. Here I had a child of four years as my next case study. She became very dear to my heart. We had been studying Bowlby's Attachment and Deprivation/Privation Theory, and this dear little girl Leslie brought what we were learning very real, and close to my understanding; she seemed to have no experience of loving, deep attachment. I often remember her and wonder where she is now and how her life is, such a dear soul was she. I believed she had had the experience of privation. Little did I know it then, but I think I resonated with Bowlby's Theory at the time because I had experienced being very safe and having an attachment to a main caregiver, my mother, and another very excellent one to my father as a small child. Then suddenly I had had to get used to no attachment – not having anyone to entrust my safety to; a deprivation experience. By now I was a largely non-person, a nobody. Even as I write

I realise that I still have an overwhelming fear sometimes of groups and group activities or lectures, and wonder if this is connected. It makes me feel suffocated and I become again a floating no one, feeling quite alien, even when a subject is involved that I may know and understand very well, and could indeed even teach to the teacher!

Life is wonderful, because when you have had a bad time over something you can look at that side of the penny, then turn it over, appreciating the other side, and you have the capacity to understand others and love much, and in a more complete way. It helps you to be less judgemental and critical and to be able to walk in others' shoes a little more truly and with empathy. If you have walked in the dark, when you see the light it is beautiful beyond words. So I consider myself blessed.

My college tutor was especially pleased with my case studies when they were finished, and I received the highest grade. At the same time I had been taking violin lessons and had received a distinction in my exam too. I was very happy that I had good results, mainly because it had pleased my teachers, but also because it had been uphill work with my English, as my vocabulary was extremely limited, yet I had managed well. Cults which live an exclusive life use their own language, which is often very limited and loaded, and their children know very little of the rest of the world. I said nothing when I got home for the weekend, but I had a young 'Sister' assigned to me to vet my progress at college. She had been sent a few years earlier to Germany, to the Frobel seminar for the same kind of child care course I was on, and had by now graduated. I believe you have to be more academically inclined to have done the German course than the English one.

Soon after receiving the high praise for my case studies and violin achievements, I was called in by this Sister to show her my work. She took it away with her and a weekend later gave it back to me and very angrily and condescendingly rubbished it all, especially my case studies, and told me that I would never have got away with this 'infantile nonsense' had I gone to the Frobel seminar. I remember thinking that perhaps this was the reason I had been allowed to go back to England from Paraguay instead, as I was not good enough for the college in Germany. I felt more guilty than hurt, although hurt was there. It was as if I had wronged the community and managed to bring them into disrepute. After this I never told a soul about any of my college life. I felt a kind of shame attached to it. As the years passed I forgot that I had been to college, and when asked to fill in CVs it didn't appear on my list of achievements or knowledge until some years had passed.

On the whole my college years were a happy time. I was in a completely different culture from the one I knew, a life that I hardly had known existed in the world. It was almost like living on a different planet. It became a safe adventure. I began to be disappointed each Friday when lectures grew to a close and I had to face going back to the Bruderhof Community.

The one nice thing about Fridays was that there was a young man named Jörg Mathis who also was doing a college course in car mechanics. He was coming to the end of his five-year course, but I would see him each weekend, so this added a faint ray of sunshine to my weekly return. He was a few years older than I was and my heartstrings sang a very happy tune whenever I saw him, even if we were not allowed any real or direct contact. His parents were Swiss, people I knew from the communities in Paraguay. His mother I knew only by sight, but his father I knew by character. He was a loving man and this son of his seemed to be much like him. I also knew Jörg's 'Nona' (grandmother), who was one of the dearest souls one can meet on Planet Earth. She was so very gentle, kind, and intuitive – one whose love was truly unconditional. Nona was Jörg's one safe love and rock in his life, as his father was often sent out to Brazil to get, or beg for, medical supplies for our Primavera Hospital. In addition, Jörg's father had suffered the Bruderhof exclusions several times – once for nearly a year when Jörg was nine, so he did not see his father for all of that time. His mother was at the time also excluded but sent separately from his father. Whilst he was still in England his Nona died. Wheathill Bruderhof received a telegram from Primavera and they phoned Jörg at college. Alone, he was so shocked by this news as Nona had been so very close to him. He took the day off from college to go back to Wheathill Bruderhof and went on a long lonely walk up Titterstone, one of the Clee Hills in Shropshire, which was at the time like a wilderness to him. That was how he was feeling, left to the wilderness. I noticed and felt deeply for him, but couldn't say a word to him; I was by now brainwashed enough to know that since I had feelings for him it would be 'sinful' to get close to him. Shortly after this he was sent back to Primavera. He had sat his final theory exam but was not allowed to stay for his practical, so he never had any certificates to say what he had achieved.

At this stage I certainly didn't have marriage in mind – I just was very drawn to Jörg and sometimes felt a sizzle, a sparkle, which I didn't understand or try to.

The question of baptism came up for both Jörg and me, amongst a small host of other young people. The Bruderhof communities have a strong belief in adult baptism and they brought us up to look down on baby baptism – it was one of those things where they considered the 'world churches' had gone wrong. I was approached by the Servant of the Word, who asked if I would be baptised, and I gave it a little thought. I knew that I could never get married if I didn't become a member of the Bruderhof through baptism, though this was not much on my mind at the time. I felt in my heart that any rituals were a little ridiculous, and superfluous for any love affair with the part of humanity that is God. If I was baptised it would only be to make my people happy, not myself. I also had some lovely grandparents of my own out there in the big bad world, and they were Christians. So maybe being baptised would bring me closer to them in some way? I vaguely wondered why the Bruderhof members saw other Christians' ways as inferior to their own. At this point I was utterly unable to even begin to imagine that I could free myself from the Bruderhof and live a normal life, being my true self with the rest of the world.

Finally, for the sake of those who believed baptism was the only way through life, I consented. We were given three weeks of preparation and time off work for this event, which was during the summer holidays. Each day we would get together and listen to the Servant of the Word (Minister) pontificate about life, the Bible, and above all a book called 'Confession of Faith' by Peter Riedemann. We would get to wander out alone and find a place to sit down to read this book. I would go out, incognito, and wander around looking at trees, cornfields, hedgerows, birds, stones, streams, flowers and forget this black book under my arm. When I did remember it, I'd sit down on the grass under a hedge somewhere and open the book. I felt sort of ashamed reading it, as if it was telling me even then that I was not being true to myself. However I couldn't listen to *me* in those days – I wasn't really me any longer.

I remember starting to read it, and it made me feel really sick, very false and uncomfortable. I tried it again later, as I knew we would be questioned on it in the group. I do remember being back and sitting around in a circle with the 12 novices and three Responsible Brothers, one being the Servant of the Word. I went off in my mind to a wild anxious world of my own for a few minutes and realised as I began to tune in again that the others were all eager to add their points of view to the conversation, so I could get away with remaining silent. I listened to those who were only too keen to talk about how moved they were by Peter Riedemann's amazing insights, and realised somewhere deep within my soul that they were on a different level of understanding from me, and that I would be all right.

One very important thing for Bruderhof members is that they remain in 'unity'. If you understood something differently, you were 'in a wrong spirit', you had to come to a common agreement over everything to be part of the whole – you could not be accepted if you voiced disagreement. Yet suddenly I was able to remain with my own Self and it was not necessary to understand their thinking. God basically didn't mind or even care if I was different, although even so, I'd keep it to myself.

After we split up at dinner time I was suddenly approached by the Servant. He asked me very solemnly where I had been for my alone time and what I thought of the book 'Confessions of Faith'. I couldn't find it in me to be a complete liar and for a split second I went numb. Then I heard a voice come out of my mouth which surprised even me. I told the truth. I hadn't read the entire book, but I did not like what I had read and didn't want to read any more (dogmatism, moralists and religiosity have always rubbed me raw). I didn't see the purpose in it. If you have love within your being, you are connected with God. Why would you want to learn how to live from this man Peter Riedemann, who had died long ago, I asked? I left out the fact that I had been disappointed, during my walks about the farm with my book under my arm that I hadn't bumped into Jörg. In the circumstances it seemed wise to keep my own counsel!

To my amazement Hans, this Servant of the Word, looked at me with a broader smile than I would have thought him capable and said, having made sure no one else was overhearing, 'just don't bother with it then'. This was unprecedented. He should have been telling me that I was 'in a wrong spirit'. Instead he said, 'Whenever the others are reading, just go and enjoy yourself in the way that makes you happy'. Then he turned and joined his Brothers.

I remember the day of our baptisms as something I was keen to get over. I have since been to other baptisms that were deeply moving – not mine, to me. It was all very embarrassing to the soul to go through this ritual with water splashing around and making us wet in a very uncomfortable way. My heart was totally unmoved and it seemed cheap. We had no river or sea nearby, so we had water poured onto our heads which drizzled uncomfortably down, making your clothing cling in an 'impure' fashion to your body. I briefly wondered about this and asked myself why God of the Church was so inconsistent – you had to be so careful to dress in a seemly way 'lest you tempt even the angels', yet to show off your faith in front of the whole community you could be bombarded with water which made some parts of your body stand out very obviously. I don't remember anything more of the day; my mind goes into total oblivion.

Yet I do remember one thing more. Hans took me aside from the others just before the baptism, and said 'Don't think this will enable you to get married, you are far too young for that'. I hadn't yet connected the dots, and wondered what he was talking about. It struck me shortly after when two couples got engaged soon after the baptism that he was warning me that if I was in love with anyone I wouldn't be getting engaged just because I was baptised. I was all right – I hadn't imagined I was going to get married just because of baptism – but 'peace comes dropping slow' and it was so in my case. I had felt a lack of peace in my Being, as I had, after all, felt a certain threat in his tone to me, but now I was at peace – for the moment.

One day Elske got some terrible news from

Wheathill, relayed from Primavera. Her little brother had drowned in one of our swimming pools out in Ibate. She was so upset, yet she seemed to hold it in amazingly once we were amongst the Brothers and Sisters. My heart was turned inside out for her. I can't remember what I said or did for her – maybe nothing, but it was a very difficult situation for even me to embrace and understand, let alone her.

Elske stayed at Wheathill for some time after that, and I was alone at college. It was about that time that I received an unwelcome visit from the Bruderhof. As I lay behind some bushes in the Youth Hostel garden, scantily dressed, swatting away for the upcoming exams, the sun beating down in an unusually hot fashion, I heard, then saw through the rhododendrons, a car racing up to the front door at rather an aggressive speed. The drive, long and winding as it was, was made of gravel and sounded the alarm before anyone arrived. As I peered between the bushes from my low-lying position I saw two Bruderhof visitors, two of the Servant of the Word's adult children, step out and give the front door a very urgent knock. Mrs Cox had heard the car arrive, because no sooner had they knocked than the heavy front door swung open and there she stood. I remember as if it was yesterday that Mrs Cox said in a calculated, measured voice 'and what do YOU want?' at the same time folding her arms across her chest as if to defend herself against any unfriendly bullets. By now she had become used to the ways of the Bruderhof and had gently but firmly made it clear to us over various situations that she was not happy with the way we were treated. My hiding place was not far from the front door, so I was able to listen to the entire discourse, with my heart in my mouth in case they discovered me.

'We've come to take Christine back to the community, where is she?' one of them said. To my surprise and silent glee, Mrs Cox said 'I don't know and I wouldn't tell you if I did'. There was more pressure both in tone and word from the two and at last Mrs Cox asked what on earth was so urgent that they could not leave me there, and didn't they realise that I was in the middle of exams. They answered that they wanted to take me home to attend meetings. At this Mrs Cox blew a fuse, and the two Bruderhof members at last got hastily into the car, and laid rubber all the way down the drive until they were out of earshot. I lay there in the sun, my heart's anxiety slowly melting away, my pride in Mrs Cox growing, but still not daring to get up and go indoors least they reappeared, as I knew that no one on the Bruderhof liked to accept defeat from someone who 'lived outside'.

Were they not always right?

When at last I went indoors I met Mrs Cox and she told me all about it. I told her that I had lain low behind the bushes throughout their conversation and been privy to the entire confab. I never knew until that moment what she looked like when wreathed in smiles, but now I did. It was wonderful to share that moment with her. Normally she was a serene, if sometimes quite a severe Quaker. She was still very angry that anyone would jeopardize a young person's future by taking them out of school just before they could complete their last exams and just for the sake of 'meetings'.

I stayed until the end and gained my various certificates, both in Early Childhood Education / Psychology and in my violin playing. Thank you, Mrs Cox!

* * *

It was not that long after this that I found myself once more being sent to a sea port to cross the Atlantic again, this time chaperoned by a man about my father's age who I had known whilst living in Paraguay before. Gerhardt had been on some kind of outreach (more aptly named 'begging', as the

Bruderhof did much of this disguised as outreach, or mission). He was a wonderfully loving, gentle, fatherly person, so different from many others who had joined the Bruderhof. For instance, many adults spoke in sharp language and were cuttingly sarcastic; Gerhardt wouldn't have known the meaning of the word. There were several such treasures on the Bruderhof and it was wonderful when you could spend time with one. He would never have gone grassing behind your back to get you into trouble, thus putting himself into a high place, as many adults did.

I was very happy that I was going to see my family again and he was equally happy at the thought of being reunited with his wife and children. His oldest daughter had been a classmate of mine whilst living in Isla-Margarita. I would see Jörg again, although this didn't excite me too much as he had shown signs of being interested in an older girl before he had left Wheathill to travel back to Paraguay. I accepted this graciously, as I never felt I was worthy of anyone. The other girl was quite naturally 'worthy'. I did feel a little sad at the thought of leaving behind for the second time my two soulmates, Jake and Janet. Janet had been in my class up to the age of 13 and Jake was her older brother. I had a deep connection and love for both and Janet and I were secretly very tearful at the parting. It was not the done thing to really cry. In any case it would have got us nowhere. As I have said before, real emotion of any kind could get you into harsh trouble.

So now here I was travelling back over the Atlantic on another ship, this time the *Highland Brigade.* I remember little of this trip; maybe it had become natural for me to travel these long distances by ship. The thing that stands out is that Gerhardt had a good knowledge of the Universe, which held me captivated as I listened to him. We would go out on deck at night and he would hold forth in quite an animated way for such a gentle quiet man as he told all he knew of stars, planets, the Moon's path and its power. He pointed out the many constellations and the Milky Way, and as we went from the northern hemisphere to the southern, he could tell me why the night sky was changing, and where to find different patterns and pictures in the heavens. It all fascinated me and I was awed by it.

One day Gerhardt found me looking over the railings at the stern of the ship. I was drawn to the might and power of the ship's screw as it powered the ship through the water, leaving a great frothy gully behind; it drew me and repelled me at the same time. It filled me with happy amazement while filling me with fear. This was a dreadful yet wonderful power I was watching. My imagination began to work and I began to imagine what would happen if I fell down from this height into the sea.

Gerhardt quietly came up to me and started to describe my very feelings, saying that when people felt this way it was better just to walk away. This was a strange relief, as it meant I was not unique in having such feelings, yet anyone had the choice to walk away. I looked up at him; we smiled at each other and walked away. He was a wise man.

My departure from Wheathill had been a sudden and abrupt tearing away from my friends, and I felt something 'in the air', something underhanded and manipulative in the whole thing. I had hardly been able to finish my college course; but for Mrs Cox, I would never have completed it. On arriving back in Wheathill I had tried to find out why I had been needed 'for meetings' and what was going on. I never received any clear answers.

I can't remember whether it was on departure or arrival back in Asuncion, where my parents were the 'house parents' to all the young people there from Primavera, but several remarks had been made that I was needed back in Primavera ASAP as there was a young man there who was 'interested' in me. I felt quite perturbed, anxious even, and also felt that I could not be so important to him if he could not be named or talk to me himself. I knew all the young men in Primavera, some well, others very vaguely, just by looks, some by personality. I was not thinking of getting together with anyone at the time. As the Minister had said in Wheathill, I was far too young. Although I had not enjoyed hearing this, I did privately agree, and was in fact very relieved. It made me feel safe from any ministers trying to manipulate me into a marriage. I had left my dear soulmate Jake behind in England and Jörg had gone ahead of me to Primavera – I had forgotten about him for the time being.

After the most wonderful reunion with my parents in Bruderhof House, Asuncion, and with two of my sisters, as well as my new baby brother, now one year old, for the first time, I soon had the chance to chat with my father alone. I asked him why I was needed back so urgently and told him about my near miss at college. I told him that I had been given to understand, in shrouded talk, that there was a boy here who wanted me to come back. What was going on? My father confirmed this. He told me who it was and that this particular lad, Andy, couldn't choose between me and another girl who also interested him. He wanted to see us both to make his decision.

I was absolutely sickened. I felt as if I was just a thing. Imagine being brought all the way back over the ocean on a four-week journey at such short notice just to humour and gratify some young guy's indecision. I was incensed one second, and the next I felt used and helpless. Unfortunately I couldn't unravel my own feelings, didn't understand them. My mouth was dry and my mind and heart froze. Many were the occasions, on looking back on my Bruderhof life, that I realise how manipulated we were by those in authority. Ministers exerted huge power over those who had none. Although we all supposedly 'sat on the same bench', there were those who placed themselves in the 'holy' position of controlling the others, of knowing what was best for them, dropping them high-handedly off the chess board like captured pawns.

I soon learned that Andy and the other girl were both living there in Bruderhof House, she going to teacher training college while he was a glorified houseboy. Andy, who was five years my senior, had had a crush on me and I on him. I used to watch him from a safe distance and wait to see him glance over at me with a quick secret smile. I had felt proud and special to be noticed by him way back in those days, but belong to him – forever? I felt suffocated at the thought. My crush had evaporated. The proud, conceited demeanour which had drawn me back then now repelled me.

I was allowed a couple weeks at Bruderhof House in Asuncion to be with my parents and two sisters and to get to know my baby brother before moving back to Primavera. This time was delightful and scary at the same time; delightful for being with family and scary to see Andy and Frida at every meal time, as all meals were communal. I kept wondering what was going to happen. I thought that maybe a plan had been devised already, should he want me. How would I say I couldn't marry him without being put into Church Discipline, meaning shunned or excluded? We were not allowed to talk to one another; it had to all be done through a Servant of the Word and instigated by Andy.

Soon I could leave this situation behind for a while, as I was being sent on to my destination, Primavera. I knew that at Christmas my parents, two sisters and baby brother would arrive there too, so the whole family would be back together. There were still six of my siblings to meet back in Primavera, and I looked forward to this.

I arrived in Porto Rosario with Gerhardt, having left Asuncion the night before, to find a tractor and trailer full of people there to meet us and take us on to Primavera, the end of our journey. To my joy I saw my brother Andrew amongst the others, who were mostly Gerhardt's family. He made the day look wonderful to me.

After sacks of flour, sugar and yerba tea, plus our own luggage, had been loaded and placed around the edges of the two-wheeled trailer, we all piled on top and started out for Primavera. The tractor driver, Gerald, was an Englishman, fairly new to the Paraguayan experience, who drove in a way that would suit England, but not the earth roads of Paraguay. It was a lovely day and we were all feeling in the best of spirits. As we roared along the dirt road we could see all around from our perch. I noticed that the road took a turn to the left and just on this turn it went steeply up and fell away a little to the right. Gerald revved up with a great roar and attacked this bend at a speed that was far too ferocious. The trailer fell on to its side, and the next moment we all found ourselves sprawled on the ground. The men put the trailer to rights, loaded the freight, we climbed aboard and off we went again. But further along this earthy highway it happened again. This time it seemed to happen more slowly, so I was able to hang onto the edge of the trailer and slide more gracefully out onto the grass feet first.

I was beginning to feel very worried by now, and so were Gerhardt and his family. Andrew was none too pleased either. We began to complain and say we didn't want to get back onto this aggressive tractor-trailer combination, and someone made the suggestion that Gerald should drive on to Primavera and ask for horse-drawn wagons to be sent to pick us up. One other Brother was with us, named Johnny. He was a merry Father Christmas type of person with a positive nature, but this time he got a little too positive. He declared that we should all get back on to the trailer and not be so wimpish. Have faith and trust in God, and Gerald's judgement – that sort of thing.

We clambered back, me with my heart in my mouth, and off we set again. It was not long before we were in trouble again. This time the problem was a large puddle of water, which together with the dirt road and a slight incline made it impossible for the trailer. It slithered and toppled and out we were all thrown again.

I picked myself up and saw Andrew face down in the water and just in the process of picking himself up. There were sacks of provender strewn all over the place and some just inside the edge of the forest. Gerhardt was very agitated, as all his children were accounted for accept his youngest daughter, four-year-old Trauti. His wife was almost frozen with fear as we looked for her. I suddenly spied, under a tree, a sack of sugar and a tiny little hand poking out from beneath. I shouted and ran, and her father and I lifted the sack and there was his little daughter, physically intact but terrified.

Andrew and I stood us apart from the others, and I told him that under no circumstances was I getting back on that trailer. He said that neither was he, and we would walk the rest of the way together. I went over and told Gerhardt the same. He evidently felt the same way and told Johnny and Gerald that we were all in agreement that we would not be safe on the trailer. Johnny went into a state of wild fury for a short while, but we were not budging. In the end he agreed that he and Gerald would drive on to Primavera and send wagons from Loma, the nearest Bruderhof village, to come and pick us up. Horses were a much safer way on these roads, even if far slower.

The tractor and trailer with the two Brothers aboard, plus all the luggage, soon vanished in a cloud of dust. It was a hot September day, spring in the southern hemisphere, and we would be well home by the evening when the night would be chill. It was reckoned that we had approximately forty miles to go, but we knew we would be meeting the wagons within the next few hours. So we all started walking along the dirt road towards home with confidence.

We came to a village, and all feeling very thirsty, we were given water by some very kind Paraguayan folks. In those times the people of Paraguay, although they had little, would share drink, food and even shelter with anyone who was in need. In the West we would think more than twice if there was a knock on the door, especially past dark, about letting a stranger stay overnight. Back then in Paraguay, folks would let you in and offer you the only bed in the house while they slept on the floor, or give you the floor while they kept to their bed, but whichever, the hospitality was great.

At midday, our usual siesta time, we sat on the bank at the edge of the road to rest a little. I remember feeling quite hungry, and Gerhardt produced some galletas, which tasted wonderful on an empty stomach. We sat by the wayside for a time expecting the wagons to arrive, but they didn't, so we set off again. Little Trauti was weary and was beginning to lag, even though her parents and older siblings constantly gave her a helping hand. Time went on and still no help was forthcoming, and we all began to feel tired. I was very glad to have Andrew with me; he gave me courage and I him.

As the sun began to set and there were still no wagons on the horizon, we made our way off the road and toward a little wattle and daub church that we could see not far off. It had a packed earth floor and a big doorframe with no door and square holes all round for windows. I seem to remember that the roof was thatch, very like our own dwellings back home. It was quite tiny inside with several backless benches made of rough wood and stuck into the clay floor so that they could not be easily moved.

By now it was very near complete darkness. None of us had jackets and it began to feel quite chilly as we laid ourselves down on the narrow benches for the night. We had by now realised that we had been forgotten and would have to walk all the way home; we'd continue in the morning. I don't know if anyone slept that night – I dropped off once or twice, but it was impossible to really sleep.

As the day began to dawn we were up and on our way. I don't remember any food. The sun began to feel very good as it warmed us up so quickly. By the time we were properly on our way it felt very hot, and it now felt great that we travelled light.

I remember feeling such relief when someone spied the forest near Loma, the first of our Bruderhofs to appear. As we came close and could see some of the houses, there appeared two horse-drawn wagons travelling towards us. They had obviously not had the right message about our need for transport. I never did hear what had happened. From Loma we all had another three miles to travel as we all lived in Ibate at this point (families were moved around from village to village fairly frequently), so we were extremely glad of the wagons.

The last leg of our journey was completed wearily sitting on a wagon, half asleep and bumping along with a fairly empty mind as far as I was concerned. Just before we arrived at Ibate, the village our family had been moved to whilst I was in England, I spied some small people – my three little sisters! I can't remember now whether they came up onto our wagon or whether we walked the final half mile of our long-drawn-out journey, but the happiness was great. As they approached I couldn't help seeing how beautiful they were, especially their eyes, which shone big and blue, the very thing that at first had caused us so much hurt on our initial arrival in Primavera.

We hadn't long arrived in Ibate when I learned that all my siblings who had been left behind in Primavera when my parents had been sent to Asuncion almost a year ago had been farmed out to different families and situations. The three youngest girls were living in one room with a young, single woman. My three brothers were staying with two different families. I also found out that I had nowhere prepared for me, no room, no bed, no nothing. It seemed as if I was not expected— yet a wagon had been sent to meet me!

My sisters took me to the room they shared with their carer, and soon after this a young woman appeared. She was only about three years older than me. I asked her what was happening to me and my brothers and sisters. I fully expected that I would be with my siblings and we would be a family, but no – she said she would ask the Housemother where I was to live.

At this my dam burst. I told her that she could move back to her own parents' house, as her task with my sisters was done. I would use her bed and see to it that my brothers were given space to live with us. I felt angry and hurt that others would be taking care of my siblings and I would be assigned to the 'singles' group. After all, I had been left to care for them when I was several years younger.

It was quite out of the ordinary for me to be so forceful, but it worked. By nightfall this young woman had gone back to her own home where she belonged, and several short days later the adjoining room in this very long building, a bungalow type, had been freed up for my brothers, and they joined us so that we were a family, albeit with our parents and four brothers and sisters still missing. Our bedroom was both living room and bedroom for us girls and the boys had a smaller bedroom to themselves. Although still only nineteen, I found myself put to work with the kindergarten and pre-school children. I enjoyed this very much and I was soon back into the swing of things.

Christmas was approaching and somehow in the confusion of life, the day came when our parents arrived with the siblings who had spent the year with them in Asuncion, much to my deep delight and relief. Our dwelling space was extended and we looked forward to being a family again.

My life's timeline becomes very disarranged and confused from here on for me. But many very clear happenings stand out as in black and white picture focus.

One thing I know with clarity is that one evening my father took me aside after work was finished and just before the adult evening meal, followed by the usual members' meeting, and said that tonight in the Brotherhood meeting Andy and Frida would get engaged. Several months had passed since I had learned of Andy's dilemma, and clearly he had made his decision. It was always the custom that a couple would ask publicly of the assembled Brotherhood if it was all right for them to become engaged, and only then could it become public and they were allowed to kiss, but never to go too far in their intimacies. It never went further than a peck on the forehead or cheek. Of course it had already been decided by the Servants and Witness Brothers beforehand, so the public consultation was really rather ridiculous.

I was deeply hurt and just burst into tears. not because I was envious and wanted to be with Andy but because I felt used. It almost felt like abuse. No one had deemed it necessary to ask how I felt about Andy, and what I would feel like being dragged back across the ocean and weighed up against someone else in this sneaky manner. I felt like a dirty, useless thing. Because of the power those in authority took over the 'flock', many, many matters of the heart and emotion were twisted, broken and manipulated, over the many years of my Bruderhof existence, and I hear it still happens today. Some folks of recent leaving have confided that married people are even told how they may perform sex. Also the question of birth control is not a private matter between couples. They do everything in 'united agreement'. That is why as a child and young person growing up, you never knew where you were; there was no consistency. There was an abundance of 'clear love' (cold, calculated 'love') and very little unconditional love.

My father put his arm around me, which in itself was very daring, as we were standing outside in full public view, not that I could see anyone around. I believe my father knew very well what I was feeling. He asked me if I would like it if he prayed with me, to which I gave a rather snappy 'no'. I felt really sorry for my father immediately, as for many years it was simply not acceptable for families to pray at home – only in the United Circle of a Brotherhood Meeting or a prayer meeting, *Gemeindestunde* (communal hour), could this happen, and only if you were 'in unity' with everyone else, so my father was being very brave to ask. At that time I would have been very embarrassed had he prayed out there, standing on the enormous lawn of Jesuit grass, right in the middle of the community Village. Daddy's love for me had been daring and fearless, and I had brutally turned it down.

At one point I was sent to live again in Isla Margarita to teach the first and second grade. This meant being away from my family again. I had reached my twentieth birthday by now and was considered a responsible adult where work was concerned. Of course I was not a qualified teacher, but this didn't matter on the Bruderhof. When I had been at school the first language was German, but now it was English. I think this was the reason I was wanted as the teacher for the younger children, because despite the hilarity my accent had brought to my college peers, my English was superior to other young people because of my early beginnings. So I was back on familiar ground, but without family again.

I rather enjoyed being a teacher. I certainly wasn't the usual type one associates with that word. I was apt to break rules, and the children loved it. While I had worked in the kindergarten and pre-school for instance I had not done the usual thing where siesta time was concerned. It was the system for most adults to tie a cloth around the eyes of any child who couldn't or wouldn't sleep so they were in the dark. I would go round and give such children a book to look at or a puzzle to work, or a bit of play dough to squish around. I only found out much later that this was not what should have happened. First and second grade were six and seven-year-olds and a delight to spend my days with. I can't imagine that they learned much, but I know we were all very happy. The greatest delight for me was when I did singing lessons with them, and we learned all kinds of songs, and then I would manage to pick out a few of the more musically gifted to sing a harmony to the main tune.

One day I came to school at seven in the morning when school began to find all the children from my class standing round on the bare earth, either barefoot or in their wooden-soled sandals under the school-wood trees and all focused on something in the centre of the circle. As I approached I saw that the children had begun to sway, with their heads going around in a kind of circle. I hurried up and saw to my utter horror that in the centre of this circle was a snake, coiled up with just the head up and its head going round and round, its tongue flickering fast. I screamed at the children to run away – I was very afraid for them as I had no idea what kind of snake this was and it could be highly venomous. They took no notice and continued to sway. I grabbed the nearest children and with a big shove sent them off. They were so unused to me shouting in fear that they snapped out of their trance and all ran for the school house. I saw a Brother down near the kindergarten buildings and yelled for him to come. I showed him the snake and vanished with the children to the safety of the classroom.

It was during this fairly short sojourn in Isla Margarita that I met up with Jörg again. We both had family in Ibate and worked in Isla. We also spent time in the young people's group of 'singles'. I liked him a lot and found him to be special. On weekends a duty rota would be posted for all to peruse in case one had to work on the weekend. The weekends we had no work, those of us with family in other communities could go home to them. It was a three-mile walk, or if you were lucky you might get a mule or horse to ride. If you were female you had to find a man to accompany you, as it was deemed unsafe to walk alone. So here was this wonderful excuse for me to ask Jörg if he would 'take' me home on the weekends we were both free, as his family also lived in Ibate. For a Bruderhof girl, being so imprisoned where a normal life of interaction with the opposite sex is concerned, this was an absolutely wonderful opportunity and such a delight to me. However, Jörg would often be given a mule to ride as he was one of the few who could control this creature. This gave us a dilemma. He felt awkward letting me walk while he rode; at the same time he was afraid the mule would bolt with me on its back. In the end he decided that I should ride and he would take the halter of the animal in case it became difficult and wild. Jörg told me later that he was dead scared that someone would see us in this fashion 'playing Mary and Joseph' as he called it. I hadn't thought of this, but I told him I liked walking because

I was afraid of the skittish mule. One try had been enough.

So this was the way I really started to get to know Jörg. I loved those times being together; it was amazing being alone with a young man, especially this young man, with no one to tell us off about anything. Although they were short-lived, these times were precious. I can't remember what we talked about, only that I felt very easy, at peace and happy with him.

I was moved back to Ibate to work in the kindergarten again after a while, and our lovely freedom was ended. Jörg was also moved to Ibate some time later, but of course now there was no legitimate reason to walk off together.

Little did I know it, but I was soon to face an experience that would be most injurious to me. There had been much communication by the upper echelons between the now thriving and affluent Bruderhof communities in the USA and us very much poorer ones in South America. Some years previously various folks from Primavera had gone to the States on a mission. They had planted communities in the States and now there were three run by American members, with several members still there from Primavera. Given that we were 'all one' and had 'all things in common', various brotherhood members resident in Paraguay felt they could speak up and ask their Brothers and Sisters in the USA to share a little more, so to speak. I guess one could say that we in South America were quite deprived. There was for instance absolutely no refrigeration in this very hot country, no freezers, still no hot running water. Much of our clothing was still made out of sugar sacking. The hospital often struggled without the right medication and equipment. It had one small family-sized refrigerator, the only one in the whole of Primavera, and that ran, I am told, on kerosene. There still were no flush toilets and no running water to the houses, but of course it is much easier in a hot country to go down the garden path in the middle of the night to visit the outhouse, or carry buckets of cold water to wash at home, than it is in the West. However things were tough and everyone believed in sharing. To cut a long story short, the American Bruderhofs felt that the ones in Paraguay were in the 'wrong spirit' to be asking for help. Several Brothers in Paraguay had said that it was a bit over the top that the head woman, the founder's wife, who lived in the luxury of the USA Bruderhofs, was being sent from country to country by air to visit family and friends, while in Paraguay, Brothers, Sisters and children were living such a hard physical life.

It was announced that the community that housed the hospital, Loma Hoby, was to be closed down, making two to three hundred people homeless. This would have a huge practical impact. There were Bruderhofs in England, Germany, North America, and South America by now. Every so often the Bruderhof would go through a religious 'crisis', which felt always as if it was contrived by those running the show, which is what happened now. Many families were sent away into the Great Exclusion. This was very conveniently manufactured and executed by those in power because it meant less people to have to accommodate in another community. It was announced to us that those hand-picked for exclusion were rebellious, or in a wrong spirit. It was decided then that a planeload of people should be sent to the Bruderhofs in England and Germany and in some cases to be expelled back into the big bad world. My parents were on the brink of being in the latter group, because my father was one of the folks who had asked for financial help from the USA Bruderhofs. In fact he had shown me the first draft of his letter of appeal and asked what I thought about it. I sensed that it was too direct, too honest, and that he would be in trouble when it was received at the other end. I feared he could be excluded. He agreed, so he changed it before sending. Nevertheless, his 'attitude' was judged wrong. I don't know what happened but there was a reprieve, and my family was suddenly on the list to go to a Bruderhof in England. I was delighted, but this was very short lived as I was reprimanded for my delight and told that I was old enough to stay in Paraguay and live independently of my family. After all I was almost 21 years old by now and the two remaining Bruderhofs would need me to look after the children! I was also reminded that I had been lucky enough to have been sent to England to college, and now I needed to give back in gratefulness for the sacrifice others had made for me in sending me there.

CHAPTER 8

Outcast

The day came when all my family departed for England and I was left behind. To say it was grim is an understatement. It was a crystal clear day, but for me the sky was covered in slate grey the day they left. I felt as if the end of the world had arrived. I couldn't cry, I couldn't protest. My deep sadness was so forlorn, and the darkest sense of abandonment set in. With the flick of a switch my family had gone, and I might never see them again. There are simply no words to describe my feelings.

I do remember that my parents said a hasty goodbye and that as the children were loaded up onto the lorry my mother seemed to have lost one of them,

I believe it was Olwen. She was still only about six years old and all I could see from where I stood amongst the crowd on the dirt road was that my mother was very flustered and hunting feverishly around amongst the crowd on the lorry. All at once, just as the lorry started to pull away, she found her. I could see the relief on her face, but it was too late for her to look up and wave a last goodbye to me. The lorry turned the corner of the dirt road in a cloud of dust and they were gone.

Hardly had they left when a Sister, the Work Distributor, came up to me and said that my day's job would be to clear out my family home and clean it for the next occupants. I don't know how I got through the day – it was so very difficult and only served to magnify my pain and loneliness. My heart was torn out of me with an empty black hole in its place; I was left hollow and working on automatic.

I have no memory of the following days, but I know that somehow I functioned. I worked with the kindergarten children; they always gave me joy and lifted my spirits. They were so free and intelligent in spirit, compared to the adults, and were so non-judgemental and kind. They were so thankful for all one could give and take. We had fun despite my pains which were kind of covered over by my happiness with the children.

It was not long before another crisis loomed. I was, by invitation, taking the breakfast meal with the Minister's family each day. We 'singles' were invited, usually arranged by those in prominent positions, to be part of a family for the breakfast, being the only meal in the family. At times there was a change, and we were to eat in the singles' group. Those in authority and dominance (for instance, those responsible for who worked where, for doling out what folks needed, such as soap, toothpaste, clothing, those being considered worthy of being Elders, and of course the Servant of the Word made these decisions.

I was soon to understand that this Minister was very nervous about something. He confided in me in his anxious way that Brothers were coming down from the communities in the USA to have meetings with us, to kind of 'sort us out'. He conveyed to me that this was 'a very serious time'. Soon afterwards he brought the subject up again, and this time he was quite angry, saying it was entirely my brother Nigel's fault that they were coming. I could not understand what Nigel had to do with it. He knew no one from the communities in the USA and very few in Primavera.

Nigel had come from England to visit our family some months before they had all left, but he had stayed in South America when the family departed soon after, and at this time he lived in Asuncion. Later he was to move to Brazil. He had come across several families who had been excommunicated from the Bruderhof, living on practically nothing, having had no help from them. At Christmas he had bumped into a family who had been friends of my parents prior to the Bruderhof days, the very people whose son had so annoyed Nigel when he was a small child in the sandpit at home. They had invited Nigel for Christmas dinner and to Nigel's shock they had nothing but a watermelon to offer for the celebrations and they had five children of their own. Nigel tried to get the Bruderhof to do something for these folks, but to no avail, so he took it upon himself to go to the British Consulate. He explained the situation as he saw it, and the Consul decreed that either the Bruderhof were to set these families up financially in Paraguay or pay for them to go back to Great Britain and get established, whichever they chose. Of course there are always two points of view to every story, but the Bruderhof did not take kindly to Nigel's interference and my parents in England were both denigrated for having such a son.

At the time I didn't know what my brother had done, but I was told later. For the moment, I realised that things could turn nasty. The atmosphere became vibrant with fear, but hidden beneath a cover of artificial exuberance. Many Brotherhood members seemed to be artificially high, but acting manically, rather like a bunch of people suffering with ADHD. I was threatened by the Minister, who told me I had better be ready for anything because of what my brother had done. It was all a scary mystery to me. Why was this Minister so angry at me?

Then the announcement was made that three Brothers had arrived in Asuncion from the USA and would be with us at Primavera very soon. We were going to have 'a wonderful time' celebrating their arrival with a customary love-meal – and this would take place in Isla Margarita!

On the given day we all gathered in Isla. Those of us in Ibate were either carted there or took a ride in one of the lorries. As I remember it, the wonderful celebrations turned into absolute bedlam. The days blur into one massive inferno in my mind. There were several joint community meetings, and most of the time the three Brothers from the USA shouted their lungs out at the Brothers in Primavera. They would shout and scream at various individuals, asking them 'Why did you say that?' or 'why did you do this?' It was public humiliation for one soul after another. It was expected of all, and time was given in these meetings, for each one to confess to all their perceived sins. Then one of the Brothers from the States (by now two more had travelled down to Primavera to 'help' them) would suddenly change tactics and open up a story book with some kind of dripping religious thread running through it, and it would turn into an artificial all song and light and holier than thou atmosphere. We would all have to listen to these 'moving' stories read by these hard, manipulative men. I remember a woman of about forty, a mother of four, being verbally dragged through the dirt in one of these public meetings by a couple of these worthy Brothers. She was crying out loud, trying to justify something she had supposedly done or said which was deemed by these men to have been 'sinful'. The fear factor was enormous. People would get up in the meeting, unable to make eye contact with anyone, and say things like 'I am guilty of such a wrong attitude, I have been so selfish and now I want to make a new beginning' or 'I am so guilty of jealousy' or 'I was guilty of wanting my own way and I don't deserve being a part of the Brotherhood'. Occasionally one of these three Brothers would bark out, 'Yes, you ARE unworthy, you don't deserve blah, blah, blah'. So instead of the poor soul finding an empathetic listening heart to forgive them, they would vilify her and lower themselves even further by standing up again and saying even more harshly what evil souls they were. They would try confessing more sins so as to ingratiate themselves to these men, their 'Brothers in Christ'.

These men took such power, and we in fear gave them more of it. This was a Christian community? Although I was up to the hilt in fear, I stubbornly was not going to 'confess' anything in front of this enormous assembly. I kept my mouth shut and quivered with drawn-out anxiety and fear for the moment when my name would be called upon to give account. I remember at times being caught up in the emotion of 'confessing' in fear and being on the brink of standing up and confessing right there and then, and then suddenly wondering what I had to confess, and remaining silent. I would then think something up, some horrible sin like 'being proud of myself', only to find that my spirit would not lower itself to such degradation or declare what wasn't there to declare. Later I was to find out that partly because of not confessing, I was given the label 'Liar'. My very silence perhaps, made me a liar to others. The label sticks to this day amongst the Bruderhofer. Whenever they are asked why I could not visit my parents or siblings (most of whom still live there), the answer seems to be 'because she is a liar'.

Even thinking about that time, I can feel the confusion that reigned. My mind stays tied in knots, and it tells me that I still have not unravelled the emotions of the time to sufficiently describe and understand them all. But I am free! I am happy! I have a wonderful life! This freedom of spirit came about through a visit to the most wonderful and insightful counsellor; he helped me change my life. It wasn't a quick fix, and it took a long time to gradually open up to the light; the light I had known as a very small child and indeed, before I was born. So even if not all the knots of my life are completely unravelled it doesn't matter – I am content and at peace and free.

One thing I learned in my counselling sessions was that I can be proud of myself; that is no sin. I think it comes very close to loving yourself. Back in those Bruderhof days it was the worst thing to love yourself. Now I know the beautiful light that fills the soul during the moments when you have love for yourself. Then are you complete and serene and filled with such peace, the peace that truly does pass all understanding. When you have love for yourself, you have such all-embracing love for others, it is quite beautiful. The treasures of the heart spill out to all those you meet; life, light, love, happiness, all these sparkle outwardly. During such moments you feel one with others. These are moments of sheer bliss, when you are united fully with the Universe.

But to go back to my story, I can only say that chaos and panic reigned supreme during those weeks of the 'clearing'. All of a sudden I was given to understand that I was no longer invited to the meetings. All Primavera Brothers and Sisters were officially 'in the exclusion'. The only members that remained 'United' brothers, and part of the Brotherhood membership, were the five who had come down from North America. These five had taken the power, encouraged by the Bruderhofs in the USA, to exclude everyone in Primavera, leaving themselves in total control, 'in unity' with God and each other. All the hundreds of others had to repent of their sins, and when the few saw fit, the many, one by one, would be invited back into the unity of the Church, the Brotherhood.

There began a sorting of the goats from the sheep. Ibate was emptied of those who were likely to make good sheep, so many people began to pack their few belongings and move to Isla Margarita as possible sheep.

During all this time, as we all walked around with our heads hanging low in deep depression and fear, the American Brothers spent the evenings feasting and drinking, roaring with laughter. They then had the audacity to report to the Brothers and Sisters in the USA how hard their mission with us had been, as they had had to carry the huge burden of our sins.

There were several young people, couples mostly, who had the knack of ingratiating themselves to the American Brothers and finding favour with them. These young adults flattered them, smooth tongued and smarmy, or so it felt to me. They would go night after night and sing to these strangers and praise them for the wonderful soul-saving insights that they were bestowing on us all by shouting at us and, in their 'clear love', telling us what evil people we were and thus giving us all the chance to repent so as to live a blameless and pure life, so that when we died we would join the Upper Church and be in Heaven. These boot-licking individuals would also take special food to the US Brothers and treat them like kings. So it was not surprising that these younger people were the first ones to be accepted back into the inner circle of members, thus giving them power too, to make judgement over the rest of the lives of the now excommunicated ones.

During this confusing time I woke one morning to find my room-mate Beate packing her few belongings and on the verge of walking out. I asked her if she was going somewhere and she replied, 'Yes, we are all moving to Isla'. Although I felt something sinister afoot where I was concerned, I asked, 'Am I supposed to be packing too?' It took me great courage to ask, because I knew the answer. Her first response was to say yes, she thought so, but at once she corrected herself in an embarrassed, sheepish way, and suggested that I should ask the Servant of the Word.

No way was I going to go begging. I was also very fearful of what he might say to me. I felt for sure that I was in the Black Books for some reason, though what it could be I had no idea. Now I waited to be summoned by someone of the Brotherhood to either receive a dressing down or be accepted as good enough to go with the others to Isla Margarita. I certainly wouldn't be ignored. Everyone had to account at some point for their inner state, account for the 'evil spirit' they were in, and find some terrible attitude that they had been living with to confess to. I was barely twenty-one and still rather innocent of the fact that folks who 'had been chosen by God' to 'lead others on the path of righteousness' could be so manipulative, devious and power hungry. At that time of my life I did not know how human nature can turn a person who has been badly hurt in their past and has no self-esteem into a pain to others. Now I know this of the men from the

USA. I was unaware that if some people don't deal with their dark side and turn it into sunlight it will remain more heavily in shadow, so that they might find their way out of the darkness by treading on others. They end up desperately hanging on to all they know, which is taking power over other people, to keep themselves high and safe. Our American brothers clearly had unacknowledged problems of their own. They had brought arrogance and selfish power, with seemingly no conscience where hurting others was concerned.

As I think back it seems amazing how in everything in life, there seem to be two sides of the coin. I was at this time incredibly trusting, yet absolutely unable to give in and trust when my intuition and instinct wouldn't let me. So now I was caught in a trap, between my head and my heart. My head was telling me I should trust those in authority and admit that I must be in the wrong. Yet my heart was telling me that I was not wrong. Somehow my soul felt as if it was being ripped apart. Now I understand so much more; then I was in a dark and foggy place.

I can't remember Beate leaving. I only remember waking up to a beautiful early morning dawn and finding myself in an eerie, silent world, a void. I was alone in the one room that was for the present, mine.

I looked out across the village green, with its thick dark green Jesuit grass intact as always and still faithfully growing, but there was not a soul in sight. I could see half a dozen buildings, including family dwellings and the communal dining hall. There was an early morning beauty of peace surrounding me, and yet this began to be bombarded with fear and apprehension. I was alone and forgotten.

I soon found I was hungry, and went in search of something to eat. If I went to the kitchen I might find someone there who would give me food. As I came nearer to the building I could see that it sat in loneliness too, not a person to be seen. The kitchen was built with a low wooden wall surrounding, and the upper half had shutters kept open by long poles, except during storms or during the few days of cold in winter, in June and July. I could see the whole place from where I stood outside, all the table tops, the dented and blackened pots and pans, ladles, enamel plates, bowls and cups, with their many chips making unique patterns to each, and the open-fire oven, dead, cold and uninviting. From where I stood just outside, I spied a half piece of bread on the counter top, so I went in to take it for my breakfast. I was half scared in case I would be seen and half scared in case I was not discovered, since I felt forgotten.

I picked the bit of bread up and found it was brick hard. This does happen easily in hot countries, so I figured that maybe it hadn't been abandoned that long ago, and there could be someone around to come and work in the kitchen as usual. I tried the bread and suddenly wondered whether I was stealing and would be in trouble. However, since no one came there was no one to get upset with me either.

After a brief hesitation I walked around the dirt road a little way and saw some orange and lemon trees in the garden area. Pushing myself through some undergrowth, I saw that there were two oranges and one lemon within my reach, so I picked them. They were the last fruits of the season, so they were precious to me. I have no memory of eating either the bread or the fruit, but I do remember feeling anxious on several counts; was this the last food I would find? Was I stealing, or did I have a right to this food as everything belonged to everybody? How long would I have to fend for myself here alone? I can recall being back in my little room – at least I had a bed – and looking out over the village and not knowing what on earth I was to do; how to spend my time, my life.

One day, or maybe two days, later, I was so hungry that I started wandering through the village. It was still so silent. Birds were cawing, cackling and singing, so wonderful and friendly to hear. I could hear crickets and frogs and the many creature noises that fill the Paraguayan air. But no humans were to be seen or heard.

All of a sudden, out of the corner of my eye, I saw a movement across the way. I stopped in my tracks, almost afraid to breathe. Then again there was a movement, and as I stared, I saw a woman I knew called Phyllis almost running from house to house. She was a sweet little English lady who was not one to be harsh or cruel, yet I dared not call her name. I made my way towards the spot, but when I got there she seemed to have vanished. I sat down at a picnic table nearby and waited fearfully. I thought she might not want to see or know me, but I desperately wanted to see and know her.

I hadn't long to wait before Phyllis came out of the house. Before I could say anything, she exclaimed in a joyous yet guarded way, 'Christine! What are you doing here?'

I do remember that before I could think I said 'I don't know'. I truly didn't know! That broke any awkwardness there might have been. She asked if I had had anything to eat and I told her no. She explained that she and her husband and three children were in exclusion and should not be speaking to me, but she told me to go into their living room and wait while she would go and find me some food. After what seemed an age she returned with a piece of bread and an egg which she had somehow managed to boil. She also had a mug of yerba mate. I guess she had run to the other end of the Bruderhof village to find the hens and back to the kitchen, lighting a fire to boil water. I will never know. I was so glad to eat!

So now I knew I wasn't alone. In fact Phyllis encouraged me to bring my few possessions and move in to the empty room next door to her family, which I gladly did. It was almost identical to the room I had vacated. It had one window that was very low and went across the entire wall at one side of the room under which stood a bed, and at the other a big wooden door that went straight out onto the grass, overshadowed by shade trees. The floor was of stamped clay and the roof of thatch, with no ceiling.

It was so good to be close to someone, and I was especially lucky that it was Phyllis. Her husband wouldn't talk to me, and she also tried to be silent around me as these were the 'holy' conditions under which they acted, so the occasional 'disobedient' word from Phyllis was priceless and very welcome to me.

Again, I have no memory of the following days. I guess I did nothing, and where I got my food I will never know. I do know that Phyllis came to my rescue once more with egg, bread and yerba, because I remember opening the egg with great joy to find it was still quite raw and lukewarm – difficult to eat, but hunger will allow much!

One day I took myself on a walk, daring to go further afield. On my way back I heard noise coming from the laundry. I went in and there was a woman I knew very well. She had been a doctor for all the years she was a Brotherhood member, and here she was washing clothes in the laundry. It took much courage, but I asked her if I could help her. She snapped at me quite harshly, saying 'My husband and I are in exclusion and what are you doing here?' Again I could only say I didn't know. She snapped that I must be in exclusion too, and told me to leave her alone. I expect she only spoke to me like that because she was fearful, but for me it hurt deeply, and quite threw me. She was my mother's age and I had trusted her; it had shocked me that she would speak to me in this way. She was the same person who had been rather harsh when my father was so ill a few years earlier; however I had still dared to trust her again. Maybe my trust was borne of desperation.

I made a quick exit and never ventured back to that area. I can't remember bumping into anyone else during the six weeks or so I spent almost alone in that ghost village.

Now I realised that all those deemed by the American brothers to be 'in unity' had moved to Isla Margarita and those that weren't had been either sent to Ibate or away from the Bruderhof. I couldn't imagine why I had been left behind.

One day I was aware that Phyllis and her family had gone. I don't know what happened to them. I do know that some years later they went back to the Bruderhof and rejoined. I have so many blanks over this time in my life. There are situations and happenings that stand out like black and white photos in my memory, very stark and clear, but the in-between bits had been buried even as they happened, and I don't seem able to unravel it all.

There was one night that filled me with terror, one which for years I buried. It was only a few years ago that I believe I must have been led by an angel to meet the counsellor I have already mentioned, and with his help I was at last able to look at, and finally hold (embracing the truth, even though painful) and then let go of this particular night. Now I can stand apart from it, and it is not me, I am not that experience.

It was a very dark, moonless night and I had gone to bed and to sleep at 10 pm as I had no means of reading, otherwise a favourite pastime. With no moon it could be very dark indeed, especially as there was no electricity as the generators were switched off at ten. Because of our habit of very early rising, one felt quite tired even that early. Ever since the departure of my family I had found myself in a sort of empty sadness, a time of nothingness, a void but with pain mixed in, around the time I dropped off to sleep. Now however, during this period of confused isolation and abandonment, it was a wonderful escape to just fall off to sleep, a place that I could be without thought, feelings, anxiety; an escape from the pain of lovelessness.

All of a sudden I was awakened by a rasping, rustling noise coming directly from my window, and saw a dark human figure step over the window ledge and land by the head of my bed. Before I knew it this person was on me, totally overcoming me, taking possession of my body, with a quick, rough force I didn't know a human had. I felt as if I was being torn apart, suffocated, totally controlled and completely helpless. My body and soul were violated in the extreme. Then, as suddenly as this person had arrived, he had gone. In paralysed fear of a return, I got off my bed and hid under it, and there I remained until sunrise. I was absolutely freezing by morning, even though it was the height of summer. So hard was I shaking that it was quite an effort to get up. I had lain on the red earth floor, my heart racing and not daring to move, but maybe it was the fear that froze me.

The sunrise brought me such comfort. I will never forget as I ventured out of my room, what secure warmth I felt standing in those wonderful rays of the sun as it crept up in the east and heralded the day. The sun embraced me with its rays, kissed and hugged me with its warmth and glow and I kissed and hugged it back with a grateful, loving heart.

Time passed, but how, and for how long after this event, I don't know. My main feelings at the time were of shame, self-loathing, fear and almost constant anxiety, but on a low, taking-it-for-granted level. I took for granted with my mind that everything was my fault, leaving no room for anger towards any other being. For some reason, even though I imagined everything was my fault, I couldn't be angry with myself (maybe because I really did know deep down that I hadn't done anything wrong), and so fear and anxiety were my companions.

One evening I decided that I couldn't live this way any more, and my rebellious nature came to the fore. I pulled out a small brown suitcase that I had brought from England and packed it with my few bits of clothing, sandals, one pair of shoes, very precious, which I would never need in Paraguay, some books to read, and any other useful bits and pieces I could find, and decided that when morning came I would walk to the first Paraguayan house I came to and beg them to let me live with them. Anything would be better than living this lonely, godforsaken, useless life.

We girls had always been warned that it was not safe to go alone amongst the Paraguayans. Inside I became angry at that thought and those voices ringing in my mind, and answered back, 'nothing could be worse than what you perfect Christian Brothers and Sisters have left me to, with all this religion that is such a farce'. My mind was saying that I would find love within a Paraguayan family out on their little *chakra*, even if there was no food. This is one time I recall venturing into anger, but only within myself; I didn't know that I felt angry at the time.

Next day I was ready for my hunt for a family that would take me in. I knew that this family would be totally non-judgemental and if they took me in, it would be out of genuine kindness. I indulged myself in a little anguished fury, imagining how the Brothers would feel when they found me gone, eventually, when they remembered me and wondered what I was doing, if they ever did. If they were sorry it would serve them right! They would never know where I was.

I sat taking farewell of my past, farewell of my present existence, and gradually, as I remember, an element of peace began to grow in me. If only I had not sat and allowed myself those moments of almost happy peace...

I was jolted out of my peace by the most awful happening. A wagon with two people in it was coming towards me from the dining hall in the centre of Ibate. Before I could think straight, I saw one of the two point at me and soon they had arrived in the place where seconds before I had been about to start on my new life. A young couple were sitting on the wagon and without any greeting whatsoever, they said to me that they had come to take me to Isla Margarita. There were conditions, and these conditions would be outlined to me on arrival.

This couple, Juliet and Alfo, were well known to me; in fact I had been in the same school class as Juliet. They had recently become engaged and were two of the darlings of the visiting American brothers. This did not bode well for me. They had been nice enough as single young people but had become absolutely brainwashed, and it is my belief that they could not really think for themselves, but went along with the tribe, the Brotherhood conformity. This also gave them status and 'worth'.

I hesitated when they told me to get up onto the wagon, as they wanted to go straight back. I still had enough energy of my own to think fleetingly that I wanted to go and find a Paraguayan family, not go with these two. However this resolve was fast melting away and I was starting to freeze again. Even as they looked at me with clear cold expectancy, I became a slave again, my soul was enslaved to others, and I was lost to myself; and all this through fear.

This couple didn't seem to wonder why I had already packed my case even though I hadn't known of their coming. I hardly had the energy, but I managed to shove my case up onto the wagon. I hauled myself up and sat on one of the seats well behind Juliet and Alfo. For the entire half-hour ride to Isla Margarita, they chatted together, laughing and joking around with each other, totally ignoring me. Not one word was spoken to me, nor did they involve me. I was absolutely of no account. I didn't exist. I couldn't help but feel that I was truly worthless. I truly was a non-person!

On arrival in Isla they didn't stop until they had arrived at one of the dwellings on the very edge of the village. Alfo jumped down off the wagon and called outside the door. He had a few words with the Sister, who was called Margrit, and she came and told me that I was getting off there, and I would be under her care. She wasn't unkind, but she certainly wasn't kind either. Alfo flung my case off the wagon and was gone with his Juliet.

Margrit told me that I was to live in Isla only on the condition that I lived alone, ate alone and worked alone. She would bring me my food and bring work from the sewing room for me to do. I felt an outcast, a leper, despised, but why I was treated this way I knew not. Margrit seemed totally indifferent to me. She didn't just seem indifferent, I believe she was.

I can't say how long I existed as an outcast, almost fearful of my own shadow. It was not living, just existing. By the time Margrit had made the long walk each day from the kitchen to my little room with something to eat for me, the food which had started out as a hot meal was more often than not covered in cold cow fat which had separated from the gravy as it cooled on its long, slow journey. I was often hungry, but such was my anxiety that I found it hard to eat. I would sit on the edge of my bed and mend socks for Brothers and little shirts for the baby house children. Time seemed to have stopped.

One of the three original American brothers,

Henry, had left and gone back to the States, which was a shame, as he was if anything the most sensitive and had a greater capacity to be gentle than the two who had first arrived. The other two seemed not to know the meaning of the word 'gentle'. Henry had been less prone to shouting at folks in public meetings and telling them they were sinners. He was in fact not American at all but had some years earlier gone from Primavera to the States to help build up 'community life' there. By now he, with others, had planted three Bruderhof communities in the USA. He was also the one in command, and it is my belief that flattery from the young Americans had gone to his head and replaced much of his real nature of compassion and caring. Now he struggled between the love of power and the truth he knew in his heart. Mostly at this point in his life, being liked by the beguiling, flattering young people of the new country and maintaining power was irresistible, and more important to him.

Now I heard murmurings that Henry was returning to us all, as he was deeply unhappy at the many that were being excommunicated and sent away from the Bruderhof. At the same time as this news reached my ears I was inexplicably told that from now on I could go to communal meals. I was also allowed the privilege of walking around freely again.

One day we were all told to gather outside the kitchen under the trees there, as we were awaiting a surprise. Quite a few folks got the news in time, and there was quite a large gathering of people when the lorry rolled up and a huge wooden slatted crate was lifted down. The young woman who had been elevated to Housemother in this new 'united church' of all those who would appear whiter than the driven snow screamed out as she peered between the slats of the crate, *'Ein Schwein, Ein Schwein!'* (a pig, a pig!) At this the lid seemed to rise, and out stepped not a pig, but Henry. There was a split second's silence and then a roar went up – I think it was happiness – which was very loud indeed. I stood at the edge of the circle of people and was silent. I still felt I was not acceptable, and unworthy of joining in, but deep down it felt scary, as if a degree of madness was upon the people. There was definitely a hysterical element to this welcome.

I was ironing clothes in the sewing room one Saturday, it being the only place that housed irons, when I heard a girl asking someone outside whether they knew where I was, as Henry wanted to speak to me. I was really terrified of what this would mean, so I hastily closed all the shutters so that no one could see and find me. Time went by and just as my heart had stopped racing quite so much, I heard the voice outside asking passers-by where I was, then again, and again. Eventually I realised that they would catch up with me sooner or later, so I thought I had better face the music, whatever it was, so I stopped what I was doing and went out.

The girl whose voice I had heard was one of Margrit's daughters. She soon spied me and told me that Henry wanted to see me in his hut, which would translate as 'in his office'. I made myself walk over to where I was told his hut was, but my feet seemed to be holding back as if magnets were in place and not allowing me forward. Eventually I arrived and was very warmly invited in, which surprised me. I was invited to sit down and then Henry said in the kindest, really concerned way that he had noticed me, and seen that I was very unhappy and wondered what it was all about. The change in his tone was real – at least for now. He was not speaking in the same tone I had been hearing during the past eight weeks. I felt safer and yet not quite trusting of this turnaround. I didn't know why things were as they were, and I had no idea how to answer his question. I do remember wondering what he might want to hear, which I guessed would be some kind of confession.

What had I been guilty of? What could I say to him, and what was I blind to about myself that needed to be forgiven? Was it something to do with the man who had asked to marry me? Digging around in my mind for something I thought Henry might be wanting to hear, I told him the story, thinking I would at least get a lecture on how proud and conceited I was. Nothing was forthcoming, but this conversation did make me realise where my true heart lay – with Jörg. All of a sudden I realised that I more than liked him, and had done for a while. I was much too shy to say this, because we girls always had to wait on being asked, and he had not asked – – or so I thought. Henry did some more probing as apparently 'other young men had asked to marry me'. He named a couple of them, but not Jörg.

Henry asked me if I would like to leave this place sooner rather than later and go to another Bruderhof, either in the USA or England. By now we had all been told that Primavera would be given up and we would all eventually find new homes in other communities on other continents. This would take time. To his question I eagerly answered in the affirmative, thinking that now I would be sent to England where the rest of my family were. When he told me that it would be one of the communities in the USA, my heart sank like a stone. However I knew the policy of keeping families apart (once you are deemed old enough,) which seems to still exist to this day, and I hadn't the courage or the self-love to ask to go to England.

Henry kindly shook my hand to say goodbye, and I walked out, still with fear my biggest enemy, but holding this small bit of kindness in my heart.

Sometimes we still have surprise visits from Bruderhof members, and one came a very short time ago. I brought up the question about why they were so afraid of emotional ties to family members, and why our own families could never visit us, but contact is always through some representative, sometimes folks that are unknown to us. The answer was that our families didn't want to come as they wanted to put Jesus first and their loyalty to Jesus was paramount to them. My family wanted it this way. I knew from my experience of Bruderhof life that being 'emotional' is a grave sin and is not the 'clear love' which they all aspire to. They were unable to answer my question honestly. A young girl who had recently been sent away from the Bruderhof and had nursed my mother while she was ill told me that my mother had told her about my husband and me and our three children. During my mother's illness she had shown this young woman photos of us, and said with longing and sadness in her voice that these were her daughter

Christine's children, and she couldn't understand why the Brothers wouldn't let her see them or talk to us. Nevertheless she was obedient to her Brotherhood.

In forty-one years I saw my mother only twice and my father once. Both have since died, and I was not informed about this until after their burials, and then not by family on the Bruderhof but by a third party, because it would seem that we were not wanted at the funerals. We were given to understand that they felt we might pollute the atmosphere because, in some strange way, Bruderhof members seem to think they are in special contact with their 'Upper Church' and that we could somehow spoil this as we are not 'in Unity' with them. I would think that this 'Upper Church' has precious little to do with love, as love makes no barriers. They would seem to believe that all those who have died 'in Unity' with them form a Church in eternity which they will be part of when they die.

CHAPTER 9

America

Now to go back to a life in time, my life. It didn't seem long before I found myself on a tiny plane to Asuncion to begin my journey to the States. It had four seats, including the pilot's. I remember standing with a bunch of other people on the grass strip that counted as the runway and waiting for the plane. I was to travel with two elderly gentlemen, one of whom turned out to be not so gentle. As we waited, someone had the idea of picking tangerines from a nearby tree, which was wonderfully loaded, to take to the Bruderhof people in Asuncion. By the time the plane landed we had a lovely sack full. The one man who travelled with us was a guy from the States who had been looking to buy Primavera from us on behalf of a group he came from called the Millikens or some such, I believe – maybe a sect of some kind.

The Brothers and Sisters who had come to say farewell to us were taking their time about it and the pilot was very troubled about this as he had warned several times that a storm was brewing and then he would be grounded; we would not reach our destination. Finally he was taken note of, and we were soon taking off. I had never flown before and to me the engine seemed to roar as angrily as a hornet. It was sharing the pilot's mood, I thought.

We seemed to be on a smooth ride to Asuncion when suddenly the plane began to roll about. I trusted our pilot knew what he was doing, but Friedel, a Bruderhof Brother who was handicapped, seemed very ill at ease. I knew him well and knew him to be a very sensitive, intuitive man. We sat side by side in the back seats and I tried to reassure him that we would be all right. Finally we were surrounded by black, fierce-looking clouds and the pilot announced that he was going to land. We landed on the open camp land in the middle of nowhere. Before long the rain was coming down in sheets as it tends to do in South America, and the water was rising fast. We were stranded, and we watched from our plane as the water came higher and higher.

As we waited to see how things would pan out I noticed that a ragged bunch of children were beginning to surround the plane. They were quite happy to be deep in water, and were laughing and happy in the warmth of it. It was not often, if ever, that they were visited by a machine like the one that had just dropped out of the sky, in which humans sat. Their eyes gleamed with the wonder of it.

The rain had stopped, but the plane could not take off from such a mass of water, so we sat some more. The man from the USA became impatient in the extreme, and wanted to get out and go to the nearest shop to buy some food; maybe he had other needs too. However in Paraguay you often had to put needs to the back of your mind. The pilot told him not to leave the plane, so he started to eat his way through the sack of tangerines. I was surprised that he felt so free to do this as they were for our folks, the smaller Brotherhood community who lived in Bruderhof house, Asuncion. But I did think he must be starving, and kind of brushed it aside. He was throwing all the skins out of the window. This in itself didn't matter as it was good food for the camp land, but it hurt to see the children watching him and receiving nothing. Finally

Friedel and I dropped some tangerines out for the children, as the plane stood too high to actually give them to them, and they were delighted.

All of a sudden our American friend lost his cool, and became quite angry at our situation and the 'stupidity' of the rest of us. He said he was going to the nearest village while we waited for the water to recede, and with that he jumped out of the plane. As we watched, a truck came by full of recruits and this guy managed to stop it and climb aboard and they vanished from sight.

The road was dry enough by now to travel on, as it stood very much higher than the grassland we were sitting on. By now the sun was burning down and the water was quickly vanishing. The pilot shouted down to the little children to step back, and as he was revving up to take flight our American friend appeared, very disgruntled that there was no shop in the tiny village he had managed to reach. We took off at an angry speed and as we ran down the camp land it felt as if we would never rise up. We were heading for forest and the water was splashing up in great sheets. Just before we hit the forest, or so it seemed, the plane rose, and next thing I knew the trees were just below us. I heaved a sigh of relief.

In Asuncion among the Bruderhof folks there had

been much worry and they had begun to think that there had been a tragic accident. I was glad when we landed in Asuncion just before sundown, because I had understood that the planes didn't fly in darkness.

Next thing I remember is that I was on a plane bound for the USA with an old Sister by the name of Maria. I don't recall a thing about this flight except that it was a huge machine and I vaguely wondered how it had lifted off and how it flew at all, as it was so ungainly looking. My brother Nigel was a licensed pilot by now and had told us about the countries he had been to and of his adventures, but never did I realise from him the size aeroplanes could be, this being the first of many flights to follow. Most of the flight we were over land and it was breathtakingly beautiful. I was absolutely mesmerized, but that is all I can recall.

My next memory is of Maria and me going through customs – I was ignorant of the existence of border controls – and being asked questions. It was as if these customs officials spoke a different language, although it was English of a sort. They were clearly high-ranking. One question asked in a lowered, secretive tone was 'are you communists, or have you met any communists?' It seemed so ludicrous for a grown man, an official of the US government, his status blazoned across one side of his chest, to be asking such a question in this babyish, secretive way, I considered he was making a joke and I laughed and said I didn't know (I didn't know if I had ever met a communist!) At this he became very angry and almost shouted, 'This is no laughing matter, it's deadly serious!' At this it flashed through my mind that we were to be sent to prison, or at least back to South America. Then Maria, who spoke no English, was saying *'Wir sind Christen'* (we are Christians), which I translated into English so that the official should understand her. I had no idea why she said this, but it seemed to be the key that let us through the door. I have wondered about this each time I think back; what did this mean to the officials? I will never know. Maybe to them a Christian should never meet a communist! Also, if we were truly Christians we weren't communists, so we were safe to have in their country! The Americans, I was to discover, were scared out of their minds of communists and communism. In my innocence and ignorance I had no knowledge of such worldly complications. All I could see was a childish man doing the job that should have been done by a wise and kind man. I felt a vague sorrow and compassion for him as we left, but I didn't know why.

It was mid-April and in New York State, where the

Bruderhof 'Woodcrest' was situated, it was the beginning of spring. Trees were only just about in leaf, some still bare, sparkling blue skies and birds nest-building and in full song. Woodcrest was very posh. By this I mean the physical structures and the lay out of the village; a sumptuous environment, replete with electric kettles, electric skillet, toaster, hot and cold running water, a bath tub or two in every house, cups that were of the finest quality and unchipped, wonderfully soft mattresses on the beds, all the scented shampoo one could wish for and flush toilets – and you could take your time in the toilet as they were indoors and warm with no snakes visiting you at just the crucial moment! Greatest of all, you could eat your fill of the food offered, unlike in Primavera where one mostly left the table still feeling hungry. Here in this land of milk and honey you could gorge on biscuits between meals, unheard of or imagined in Primavera. You could make cakes and sweets for yourself and family because there was so much sugar, butter and flour it seemed as if it must all grow on the trees.

On the first full day in Woodcrest an old school friend of mine who had travelled from Primavera just six weeks before took me down a long track and up a bank where we hung over the wooden fence that was the barrier between us and the throughway, or motorway. I gasped; never had I imagined so many thousands of vehicles all racing in one direction while another snake of cars and lorries raced along in the opposite direction just yards away. Two lanes in each direction – it was spectacular! My friend Hanni laughed at my amazement in a 'happy to show you' but smug kind of way as if she had been used to this all her life. She then took me up a hill within the Bruderhof confines and up there was a reservoir. She told me to lie on my back as she was doing and look at the wonderful view upside down. I did so and was rewarded with the most magical view across valleys and mountains, woods and river, all 'above' the most perfectly blue sky. It was just as magical the right way up!

We stood for ages enjoying this amazing world we lived in. Creation was simply magnificent, glorious, majestic and perfect. For that day, excitement, happiness and love, the love that is in tune with all creation, pushed out completely all anxiety and worry for the future. I didn't need to worry, as I was living in the moment, which was beautiful. Just Hanni and me, with below us in the Bruderhof village all those people, most of whom I didn't know, and for now was not bothered with. This planet was a perfectly exquisite

place to be part of. I was in love again – for the
moment.

* * *

From now on for the next twelve years, I will revert to
snapshot memories of my life, because that is all I
have. So much came tumbling head over heels to
challenge me over these twelve years that I have still
been unable to place all events in order. However I try
to unpick the garment, I am unable to find all the ends
of the threads to match up the stitching so as to give a
timeline of events.

Because I had come out of an excluded position in
Primavera, and was excluded by the American
Brothers who had come out of Woodcrest (their
membership had in theory excluded me), no one knew
what to do with me, which pigeon-hole to put me into,
or what my place was in their society. They didn't
know what I had done wrong and I didn't know myself,
so I didn't belong in any form or convention. I felt like
a fish out of water, but quite often I was able to jump
into my natural habitat to refresh myself when some
Brother or Sister actually accepted me as a complete
and whole human being. I still was not allowed the

honour of going to meetings, be they members' or prayer meetings. If you had been excommunicated you could not go to a prayer meeting because you were only allowed the privilege of prayer if you were in full 'unity' (conformity) with the Brotherhood.

So there I was, not belonging anywhere but being inexplicably accepted to work and eat with everyone else. I spent my breakfast times with two different families who each had a small horde of young children and shared me between them. I was not there as a joy to them, as a friend invited, I was not there to be happy with them, but as a person they had to 'carry', which in Bruderhof loaded language means that you are a problem person, and you become their task and mission to bring back into Unity through your repentance. They are there to judge and measure your repentance and how 'deeply' you are sorry for what you have done wrong. They then report to the Brotherhood when they deem you humble enough to ask forgiveness, with broken heart, for your sins. So I didn't enjoy breakfast times, and my anxiety would rise with the sun each day. Even though these two couples didn't know me at all, they were there to judge me and weigh me up. Their living rooms were filled with self-righteousness. I felt like the fly in the ointment. But in defence of these two families, there never was a lot of love lost between Bruderhof folks as they were definitely against showing happy emotions as well as negative ones, so perhaps they were simply being normal. When Wheathill in England was started, there was much happiness amongst the English folks, but when people started to arrive who had been part of the founders' first Bruderhof to teach our parents how to be a good Bruderhof member, the happiness was stamped out pretty quickly.

Now my initial joy at being on American soil was fast disappearing. I was surrounded by heavily critical people, and panic attacks began to plague me again. There was happiness amongst the children most of the time and I was given the job of caring for the one-year-olds, of which there were ten, all between almost one and getting on for two years of age. The joy was taken straight out of it when I was watched over and my every move was dictated by the woman in charge of the baby house. I was to get all ten of these babies on to their pots, change them all and then take them out, warmly dressed, for a walk, while dragging the three who were yet unable to walk along in a wagon. If anyone has ever tried this in deep snow, you will know that it is impossible with such very young children. Putting ten pairs of wellies on ten little pairs of feet takes an age in itself, yet I had to make sure that this woman in charge of the whole baby house didn't keep complaining about me, so the pressure started mounting and I thought that I would never again want a toddler to care for. I had to get everything done within a certain amount of time, otherwise I got a talking to.

It was fashionable at the time in the USA to let small children eat finger food, so I had to sit these 10 children down around a semi-circular table and when their food arrived from the kitchen, dump a mound of spaghetti or whatever was the chosen menu for the day in front of each, and expect the toddlers to eat with their fingers. Of course there was gleeful smearing around of the spaghetti as these tiny humans had fun trying to paint the table with the colourful mess. They were all tied into their chairs, which was a mercy as otherwise chaos would have reigned supreme. The problem was that I had to do all the tying, which took time, and the responsible adult was always hurrying me along so that all children had eaten, were potted, washed and on their little bed rolls in time for the person coming to look after them during their rest time, while the rest of us went to dinner at twelve-fifteen. It was a nightmare. Although I was well trained in upbringing education and help of children between the ages of zero to six and loved being with them, one to two year olds are, and were, a nightmare in a group situation. My theory is that they are better with Mum or Dad at home – that is then the most beautiful experience and lovely time of bonding and love. During this time I began to quietly start to think for myself, and come to some of my own conclusions, which I kept close to my heart as it would not have profited me to speak out.

One morning at breakfast my 'foster parents' informed me that I was being sent to a Bruderhof by the name of Oaklake, in Pennsylvania. I had been in Woodcrest for six weeks. Now I was to move on again to another place in this new land that I didn't know, and without being consulted. I was after all an unworthy thing. I silently heard, and made no remark – one didn't remark, especially not in my position. I was upset.

After a three-hundred-mile journey, driven by a young man of my age whom I knew from my years in Paraguay and accompanied by two old ladies, I must have arrived in Oaklake. I have no memory of my arrival whatsoever. Usually the Bruderhof custom is to have a 'love meal' when someone departs or arrives. Maybe this happened, maybe not.

This Bruderhof was a much freer, happier place to be and for a short while I began to find real happiness as I worked with the four and five-year-olds as my day job. My breakfast family was really lovely. They had about seven children, and the mother, Jane, was a very gifted poet. I loved being with them as they were so kind in the way they welcomed me into their family.

It was not long though before I was asked by the Housemother of Oaklake to switch to another family. I felt very insecure with all the moving around and could never get used to any situation for long, but the second family turned out to be absolutely wonderful. They were completely accepting of me, and clearly I counted to them as being valuable in my opinions and thoughts, which they would ask after as I never freely gave them, and there was much fun and laughter during our breakfasts together. Dick and Dot, as they were called, took me in as one of their own children, and I began to be expected to drop in whenever I wanted and was not on duty anywhere. They had five of their own children and I became the sixth – I was in fact already a young adult, but was so happy to belong.

The Servant of the Word at Oaklake, Mark, came to me soon after my arrival and asked me why I was not part of everything, such as prayer meetings and so forth. I again had to say that I had no idea, but related to him my story, from my perspective of course; of how I had been in the Exclusion and I assumed still was.

Mark assured me that it was time everyone forgot about it, and invited me to take part in anything I wanted. He wanted to bury all of 'that nonsense', so with no explanation for all that had happened to me I was accepted into 'Full Unity' with no questions asked. In this way I was able to enjoy one full year of fun, and happiness, working with the pre-school children.

Soon darkness began to descend again. We were in a time of 'crisis', which was a term used by the members, the Brotherhood, and indeed in my opinion was instigated and set up by the Witness Brothers (Elders) and Servants (Ministers). We had visits from the Elders and Servants of other Bruderhofs. The one leading Oaklake vanished with his wife and children, and all of a sudden I was back in trouble. During a meeting one night a young woman suddenly verbally attacked me, saying that I was in a wrong spirit as I had asked her why young people seemed always to be unable to leave the community and enjoy our times together whenever a Servant of the Word was away from the community. I was stunned. I did indeed wonder at the tightness put upon us, and it did seem to happen whenever we had no Servant resident at the time. Apparently it was really evil to question anything those in charge did or said. This young woman had never come to me to share her displeasure at anything I was supposed to have said, even though all on the Bruderhof make a promise that they will always go to the person concerned when there is a dispute. She had always pretended to be quite happy with me, but now she could lick the boots of the Servants by telling on me. During these 'crisis' times, they spent much time in 'clearings', meetings where people stand and confess all kinds of bizarre 'weaknesses' and 'sins', sometimes true, a lot of the time made up, so that they will again be acceptable and be this wonderful purified spirit, 'forgiven' and accepted back into the Brotherhood.

Then I remember being in exclusion again. I was told to stay in my room, so I did. Day turned into night and night turned into day, and I was still in my room and very hungry, and worried and depressed. No one visited and no one seemed to miss me. When I thought everyone was asleep in their beds after midnight, I took to going down to the communal kitchen and raiding the fridge to satisfy my hunger. There was plenty to eat, but it was all very cold and had to be swallowed fast in case someone came and found me. I would stand there swallowing cold cooked carrots or a handful of mashed or boiled potatoes, and if I was lucky there might be something in the protein line, although this was unusual. I managed for a week.

Some time and somehow I was sought out and invited to go to work again, but I was told 'not with the children'. I figured this was because I might defile them, but they said I was needed in the laundry. Because I worked amongst the people, I figured I would be OK to eat again in the communal dining room. This I did and was not sent away. Now I was back on the slow miserable way up the ladder to being acceptable.

There was a day when I overheard the Housemother say to Mike that he and his wife Shirley should take me on as their responsibility to extract from me my sins, to get me to confess. Mike made a remark that indicated to me that he was not pleased to be given this task. Mike was a Witness brother and was therefore deemed trustworthy for such a task. Just as he consented he looked up and saw that I was within hearing distance, and he looked very uncomfortable. I was glad to have the power to withhold or disclose that I knew what was going on. I chose to leave them wondering if I had heard them speak about me. This gave me a little strength.

Soon after this I was invited to Mike and Shirley's home and they tried, through unconvinced hearts, to get me to confess. I didn't nibble their bait because I hadn't the faintest idea what I had done wrong. I told them I didn't know what they wanted of me, and Mike said with a wry smile, 'I don't know either'. We then started to get together once in a while, and the same question would be asked of me; I still had no answer and it would turn into a laughing session, neither of us able to find any point to these confession sessions. Shirley was, I felt, a wee bit uneasy, but Mike was a full-on joker, and he it was who enabled me to stay fairly sane during this lengthy 'clearing crisis' time. Coincidentally Mike was again accosted by the Housemother within my hearing – they never saw me – and asked whether I had confessed anything yet. Mike answered in the negative. She shook her head, said something I didn't catch and moved on.

Times of general crisis and 'clearings' were usually followed by the good people celebrating the Lord's Supper, or Communion. I never made it, but by the look on everyone's face it was literally a dead serious event. All members, in unity, would file into the dining hall wearing long dark clothing and come out an hour or so later looking like cod-liver oil in winter, with faint saintly smiles on their faces as if it was quite an effort to smile. Once I was invited along with several others who were on the fringes of the community to sit on the outskirts of the dining hall and watch the proceedings. I didn't want to go because it made me feel sick to be treated as a lesser being, but my curiosity got the better of me, plus I would be asked to give an account of my reasons for not wanting to go, which I had no strength for. I have never found that rituals of the religious kind sit very comfortably with me.

This particular night made me feel somehow ashamed of the human race – I don't rightly know why. All the Brotherhood members sat around a huge oval of tables. They were terrifyingly serious. On one table were several jugs of wine and loaves of home-baked bread. They started by singing a very serious song in a very slow tempo. Then there was a lengthy reading from, I believe, the Founder of the Bruderhof. It was difficult listening material, and as I was a creature below the rest taking part (much like a downstairs maid being invited to the upstairs dinner with the master), my concentration kept leaving me, while I considered running out as panic would set in. On the other hand, any thought of getting up and leaving in this dark situation would panic me too. So I sat, every muscle in my body taut, waiting for the end. There were distractions that came to my aid such as another serious dirge-song, a change in tone of voice as the Bible was read, someone sneezing and trying not to, a prayer or two that was very lengthy. As everyone had their eyes shut or was looking up at the ceiling, they were locked away from me for the duration. All these served to keep the level of panic manageable.

Then came the big moment. The wine was poured by the Servant of the Word into two glasses and he handed it to the persons to his left and his right. Slowly, very slowly, and without a sound (it was as if all life had stopped), the wine was passed round until it came to its painful end since by now, all had had a sip. I was vaguely grateful that I was not permitted to take part as I didn't fancy drinking from glasses that a hundred others had added their saliva to.

Now it was the turn of the bread. The Servant took a loaf in his hand and with some difficulty, broke it in half. He ripped a bit off for himself and then passed the halves to left and right. Another long silence ensued while those worthy souls chewed their way through their bits of bread. When this was over I breathed a sigh of relief, as I figured it was all about to come to a conclusion. A song was suggested and a hearty volume was forthcoming as the whole congregation carolled forth, their lungs acting like giant bellows. For these folks and for me too, the song was the highlight of the evening; for them because they seemed to feel some kind of victory, and for me because it was over.

Now they all rose from their seats and still in

serious mood, they went round greeting each other, the men kissing and embracing one another and shaking hands with the women, and the women kissing each other and giving their hands to the men. This was seriously spooky to me, but I could now escape incognito.

While Mike and Shirley were still supposedly helping me to repentance, all our little get-togethers came to a sudden end. Nothing more was said.

One day I was trying to look busy folding clothes in the laundry when I was advised by someone that the Elders wanted me to go to their meeting. I arrived at the door in near panic. Next thing I remember is sitting on a straight-backed chair with 12 men in a circle. A quick glance told me that these were the ones who held authority over all others. They were twelve Servants of the Word and Elders. Here I was, not much more than a girl, with twelve eagle-eyed monsters looking down on me. Again, I hadn't the faintest idea why I was called in, but I knew it wasn't good.

The head man started to say in a very loud but bearable voice that everyone knew about birth control and that it could be read about in the papers, heard about on the radio and seen on the TV. Since we had never had access to any of these, I hadn't got the vaguest idea what he was on about. It has to be understood that most of these Brothers were either American or had been in the States for some long time, and were all very worldly wise, while I had not long come from Paraguay. I didn't respond to this Brother, so then began the baying of the dogs. One after another, they started shouting at me. They couldn't scream loud enough. I couldn't even hear by now as I was in such terror, so full of fear that I genuinely could take little in. I did hear some say that it was high time that I confessed. I said nothing – what could I say?

Gradually the shouting subsided and I heard the head man again speaking in a slightly gentler tone. This was Henry, the one who had got me out of the crisis in Paraguay. It was as if he had to take on a role when in front of his Brothers, as he had not been aggressive in this way when alone with me. He too was shouting, but in a contained sort of way. I listened as he told me that he knew I had given a young couple a magazine to read whilst still in Paraguay and in it was an article about birth control. I was surprised at what was in the magazine as I knew nothing much about this subject, but I had certainly given a whole pile of very interesting magazines to Janna and Pete to read. I had received them each month after returning to Paraguay from my very kind tutor back in England. I had loved receiving them as we had very little current reading material to hand in Primavera, and I had happily shared them with Pete and Janna, as they were newly married with a baby, and they were about child care and psychology from before birth to 6 years of age. I had had no idea an article about birth control was within these pages. Apparently this whole subject was 'evil' and certainly not to be advocated by a young single girl.

This then was what they had been after me for during all this time when treating me so inhumanely and trying to get me to 'confess'. It became clear that Janna had gone with her evidence to the Brothers who had arrived in Primavera from the States, and all this time they had been waiting for my confession of the sin of spreading the idea of birth control. I had never read the infamous article and certainly knew not of its existence. Was this why I had been left in Ibate for so long alone? Was this why I had been left with no food or human connection here in Oaklake, and was this the reason for Mike and Shirley's efforts with me – and now this?

I was not given the chance to reply or explain, as these Brothers told me what I had done, told me what my thoughts were and what a sinful person I was. I have no memory of what followed.

* * *

How I achieved this, I have no recall, but I next remember finding myself in 'full unity' with the Brotherhood. I was accepted as a whole person. But for how long?

I have no recollection of how this came about, but I was told by a Minister that a certain young man had been flown over from England and was interested in marrying me. It was the boy I had been so close to as a child, my best friend's brother. I was asked whether I felt I would like to see him again and whether I might consider him for marriage. I was stunned, but quietly excited. I had loved this lad, but I really was confused at how a person would feel if they wanted to get married. What was love? What was love in marriage? I had given up with Jörg; it was sad, but so much had happened and maybe he never did want to be with me, as no Minister had asked me about him. I had accepted this.

I had heard of three types of love; one was Filos, (brother/sister, friendship love), one was Agape (divine/spirit love) and last, and in Bruderhof terms less than least, Eros (erotic/physical attraction/sexual love). The Eros kind was seriously frowned upon by Bruderhof folks. So why was it so seriously wrong if it came under the general term of love? Jake had been a soulmate, but what did I know about these matters?

One day he arrived, and I was joyous. It was like having the happy part of my childhood days back. He was still the same old soulmate, the same young man I had met again whilst going to college in Shrewsbury. I was happy at the thought of marrying him and when I was asked shortly after he arrived I said 'yes'. He was told of my answer and the usual engagement love meal was celebrated. I was filled with happiness, yet there was a niggle which at the time I didn't recognise. Once we were engaged we had the freedom to go out together. We could hold hands and kiss, but kissing of the French kind was not permitted. Certainly sex was absolutely out of question until after you had married, and vowed before the gathered Unified band of Brothers and Sisters, that you would stick together through thick and thin until one of you would die, and this was all made legal by going first to a Registry Office, after which there was the 'real' ceremony in the community. Only then were you married before God, and then God and the Bruderhof people were united, and satisfied that the newly-weds could have sex, which now was abruptly and instantly holy. It was as if one minute you were eating a sloe which you would have to spit out because of its bitterness, and suddenly it changed whilst in your mouth into a lovely sweet ripe plum. Your mouth can deal with a sudden change like this more easily than your psyche can.

The newly-weds also promised in the ceremony that if their spouse was disobedient to the Church and landed themselves in any sort of discipline which should separate them from it, then the other one would stay loyal to the said Church and not follow their spouse out. This was the only condition that they could separate on, even though, for some, it meant a lifetime's separation. If one of the pair was separated by exclusion, the one left on the Bruderhof could never divorce and remarry.

Thankfully I never got the chance to make these vows. When we had been engaged for a little while I was walking through a long corridor within the main building when the main Servant of the Word accosted me. He informed me that Jake had been sent to another Bruderhof, as he had been excluded. Only a couple of hours before, we had been enjoying ourselves and climbing up a local mountain. Jake had apparently exhibited 'spiritual pride'. He needed to take time and repent of this.

Once more I found myself unable to grasp what this man meant, and I was quite stunned and felt as if the breath had been knocked out of me. I was not permitted to say goodbye, so to make it plain sailing for themselves, they had sent him before informing me. On asking the Servant what he meant and what exactly Jake had done wrong, this man was unable or unwilling to explain more. I was expected to trust him and his puny god.

Some time later Jake was reunited with the Brotherhood and with me again. Not much time went by before I was sent into exclusion and into the 'Outside World'. I never have found out why. No one was able or inclined to give me answers. All my guesses and suppositions could be way off the mark.

Next thing I remember was being in Morgantown, West Virginia with twenty dollars in one hand and a suitcase in the other. Someone had transported me in a car and dropped me off, I assume, but my memory is a blank. I do remember that I held on to the twenty dollars as if my life depended on it – and it did at that moment, though I doubt I had a purse to put it in. Maybe this is why I found it in my fist and seemed unable to park it anywhere.

I was quick to find accommodation and a job. Again I have no recollection of how I went about this. One thing I do know is that I have always had a guardian angel, or perhaps many angels, by my side, otherwise I dread to think what might have happened to me.

I do have a vivid memory of the flat I had found for myself, and the hospital where I easily found work as a nurses' aide. For the next eight years memories are sketchy, fragmented, but as before, that which I do remember stands out very clearly.

The hospital I had landed myself in was a Catholic one. I hadn't known that until my first shift, which was from eleven o'clock in the evening to seven in the morning. When I entered the hospital I was taken to the floor I was assigned to, and there the Charge Nurse gave me instructions and a little guided tour. Although I had never worked in a hospital before, nor ever worked for pay, I found it easy to catch on, and worked quite hard as I was happy to do the work and learn. One positive result of being brought up on the Bruderhof was that we were indoctrinated in hard and conscientious work ethics. I never dreamed that I could be otherwise, so laziness would never be a temptation, or trying to shirk and leave others to the dirty work, so to say. I began to enjoy the work very much and folks treated me well and as an equal.

On my first early morning I heard a little tinkling bell coming from down the corridor and sounding louder and louder. I also got my very first whiff of what I now know was incense. It was only five thirty in the morning, so I was startled at a noise that could wake patients at such an early hour. One nurse nearby said to me, 'quick, turn your face to the wall'. I thought for a minute that she was making a stupid joke. 'Why?' I asked when I realised that she was serious. 'You have to do so because the priest is coming by, we do it out of respect.' I swallowed hard not to retort. I was in rebellion yet again; would religion never stop dogging me? I just stood with my back against the wall so that I could watch this new theatrical production. The incense smelled quite nice and it certainly helped to subdue the languid-sickly smell that pervaded the hospital.

Round the bend of the corridor there appeared a man in a long gown swinging a lantern that gave off smoke, and he was whooshing it all over the place. As I stared I noticed two nurses with their faces pressed against the wall, hands behind their backs. This made me feel very embarrassed for them; it was a kind of degradation to themselves and humankind in general, and it gave me a rush of anger. I said nothing. Later the nurse who had spoken to me before said something along the lines of wishing she could be as brave as me, and she hoped I wouldn't be called into the Head Nurse's office. I never was.

From then on I never stood with my face to the wall. Gradually I got to know this priest, and he turned out to be the gentlest man, although humbly arrogant. There must be a word for humble arrogance – sanctimonious perhaps. I wonder what people feel when they are honoured in this way. Perhaps it's taken so much for granted that it never becomes questionable. I don't think it has much to do with love, and I got to thinking that if Jesus came down the hall, or Gandhi, or Martin Luther King, the last thing I would do is turn my face to the wall!

I noticed one very wonderful thing had happened for me since leaving the Bruderhof. For years prior to my expulsion I had felt ill. I felt sick very often on waking in the morning, and eating was something I had forced myself to do. I had persistent headaches, and on many occasions I had the most severe back pain, sometimes forcing tears to my eyes, so sharp it was. Added to this, anxiety, and panic attacks which made me think I was about to die came upon me fairly frequently. Now, the headaches, sickness, and back pain had totally vanished. It was really marvellous. On the rare occasions when I hadn't felt able to go to work on the Bruderhof due to my apparently ailing body, I would be severely told off, and it was said that I was putting it all on. So it became a thing of the past fairly quickly to allow any illness to prevent me from going to work. On the rare occasions when sickness had prevented me from working, I would feel the guilt almost suck my insides out. The panic attacks and anxiety became less frequent but they did not leave me entirely for a long, long time.

I don't think my work in the hospital went on for too long. The doctor on the Bruderhof had given me some medication, two kinds, but had not told me what they were. He had said, if I remember, that it would help prevent pain. It was probably during one of those rare occasions when I missed work due to pain. I took this medication obediently as the order of the day was not to question but to 'trust' and 'accept'. The doctor was also a 'Witness Brother', or Elder. Ours was not to reason why, ours was but to do or die, so to speak.

As I was about to leave for my morning shift I grabbed a bottle of medication from my apartment and rushed to work, as I was only just going to make it on time. Once there we had to gather around the nurses' station to hear what had transpired during the night and be given our assignments for the day. As soon as everyone had dispersed, I innocently shook a pill out of the bottle, but before I could swallow it the nurse in charge said in a very indignant voice, 'what do you think you are doing?' She snatched the bottle of pills from my hand and made it clear that she was more than displeased at me having them, let alone actually taking one. She asked me what they were. I said sheepishly that I didn't know, which of course was true. I think she thought I was being facetious and taking the mickey. She went ballistic and said that I should have told her at my interview that I was taking antidepressants. So now she had given away the secret: antidepressants! I was sacked on the spot, although I did finish my shift. I felt very small and very guilty, but couldn't quite work out why.

I never swallowed another of those infamous pills. It transpired that the other medication, also 'banned', was a contraceptive. In a Catholic hospital, for a young girl in those days, I was advised that taking them too would be a dismissal offence. It gave me no problem that I discontinued them so abruptly.

My next memory is of a new place of work and a new home. Morgantown was a university town with a hospital attached to the university. I somehow managed to get a job looking after five children between the ages of six months and eleven years, who belonged to two of the doctors working in the hospital. This job came with a bedroom and bathroom of my own in the basement of their house, which was large. As the house was built on a split level, my window looked out on a lush, green lawn of gigantic proportions.

The Gilberts were a very nice and appreciative

couple. They didn't get on with each other at all, but they each got on with me quite happily. He was a gruff, shy man, and she was a gentle airy-fairy woman, both of the intellectual type. The children were my only responsibility and neither parent interfered. I was supposedly off duty at six in the evening when the parents were meant to come home, but very often one or the other would come much later and my time would be dragged out. My working day started at six in the morning, and I would get all the children up, including the baby, around seven. The husband owned four cars, and I could take my pick when I needed to drive. However, I soon learned which one was his favourite and not to be touched by myself, even though he never verbalised his preferences. I would give the children breakfast with Mrs Gilbert, who would then vanish off to work and I would take the school children to school with the two youngest in tow as well, all packed into a big Oldsmobile. It was easy work for me as I was very used to children and could manage them quite easily; on the other hand I had never driven any children, let alone five at once. Driving lessons were the first thing I thought of after leaving the Bruderhof, as America had little public transport, and I received my driving licence soon after.

The Gilbert cubs were all nice children, even if two

of them, Jimmy and Elisabeth were full of mischief. The parents were certainly not particularly cut out for children, and seemed to have no appreciation for the time it takes to help a child to grow into an adult.

Being with the Gilberts was a happy healing breath of fresh air for me. Both parents were so appreciative of my work. Mrs Gilbert had a tendency to pile more and more work onto me that was not strictly taking care of the children, but I didn't really mind. I loved the children dearly and absolutely. Even though I was still extremely young, at 23, to be responsible for a big family, it was one thing I could do, and do very well.

Down the road, in an equally large and beautiful home, lived another doctor's family, from Scotland. He was a university hospital doctor too, and she was a lady of leisure. They also had a live-in girl for their three children. Her name was Geneva. We soon made friends and would arrange our one day off at the same time so that we could spend it together. Geneva was very large in all ways, and ebony black; I was very small in all ways, and very light and fair.

Geneva and I would go to a coffee bar in town and enjoy a good laugh and some better food than we got at home. We had frequented the same bar several times when I at last put expression to my curiosity over something. Each time we had been there a very fashionable, well-made-up, elegant lady sat in the same place, with a cigarette holder balanced between her long, highly-manicured fingers, puffing delicately whilst sipping her drink through (in my opinion) too brightly-painted lips. She was always looking around with a vague, yet pulling look. She clearly wanted to be noticed, yet didn't.

I whispered to Geneva, asking if she had noticed that each time we were there, this lady seemed to be there too. I also said that she made me feel rather freaky and asked whether she felt that way as well. Geneva burst into raucous laughter and said, 'Don't you know? It's a transvestite!'

That was one more step towards educating me in the real world. I didn't know what the word meant, and of course Geneva explained. I had a long way to go in this world, and so much to learn.

Another time I was walking down the high street with Geneva and as always when in her company, it felt like all heads were turning to stare at us. On the Bruderhof all heads would turn away as I passed, which made me feel like a leper. This happened so much that I almost thought I was imagining it. I mentioned this to her, asking whether folks were truly staring at us or whether it was my imagination. She was always ready with a very substantial laugh that would shake the very mountainous person she was, which she set going at my remark. Giving me a dig in the ribs, she said 'Of course they is all lookin at us'. When I asked why, she roared with laughter again and said, "Cause you is white and I is black'. I had had no inkling of prejudice and racism in my bones, so now I had learned something new. I had watched Martin Luther King and all he had done to free his people down south, and naively thought that this attitude of the whites towards black people was miles away. Here where we lived near the Mason Dixon line in the USA there was still huge prejudice and racism, after all. Now I felt that Geneva and I were in a secret warm world together, one that only we could enjoy entirely, as others looked on and wondered. It was a strange thing that people were unable to see the soul of my friend, to enjoy her wonderful company, just because she had a different colour skin. I was incredulous. It was sad that folks seemed not to see and know each other's spirits because of a different-coloured outer layer, which was after all beautiful! But maybe we were both outcasts of a kind, outcast but not forsaken; we were blessed with joy together.

CHAPTER 10

Standing up to the bullies

Over time I began to feel the warmth and strength of new spring sunshine beginning to overtake me. Light was starting to shine and warmth to grow over the dark cracks and crevasses of my life.

One day baby Becky was asleep and Jen in kindergarten, and of course the other three were in school. It was a bright sunshiny day in spring, so I went and dug a garden all along the front of the Gilberts' house, near the bare wall. I sowed a massive amount of morning glory seeds in this garden bed and by the time I was finished Becky was awake.

Those seeds grew wonderfully well and seemed like nothing I had seen before in strength and depth of green. They grew into a massive thick border, creeping up against the white wall of the building. Around the middle of June, early in the morning, I got up and went outside and there to greet me were masses of deep azure blue morning glories looking at me. I was spellbound. That wall of the house was facing south east and the happy early morning rays of the sun shone on the flowers, helping them to radiate back their glory to any onlookers' eyes and hearts.

I stood there drinking in the beauty, peace and wonder of this work of creation. I had been part of creating and was also part of creation. As I stood there I became part of this circle, the circle built in light and love, and I fell into a trance, into another world so to speak. In this world was the love of creation. I heard the most beautiful voice tell me the oddest thing, which was not to be understood with the mind. The voice was as music, filled with beautiful volume yet gently quiet. All at once I could see a being to my right, but higher than I stood; a regal, loving energy was surrounding me and this being appeared like a native American. It said that one day I would have a son in my life and I would call him Jonathan. I didn't understand with my head at all, but my being, my heart and soul understood, and I knew perfect joy and peace and love.

I seemed to be in that secure world for a long time, yet to this day I do not know how long I stood. I have no memory of going back indoors. Of course I must have continued with the day's work. I am reminded of that wonderful world every time I see morning glories, even the small white ones that grow wild as weeds. Believe me, they are never weeds for me. They are fashioned in love.

Many, many years later I had a son and called him Jonathan. When we named him I had forgotten about that being, the voice and my taste of heaven all those years earlier.

I am not sure how I filled my time after six in the evening in that period, or what I did when I had time off. I have sketches of memories such as dancing in the university and taking lessons in dancing, with a whole bunch of other people. I just loved to dance and there I had no one from the Bruderhof watching over me and finding that there was a 'wrong spirit amongst the young people'. The dancing helped me to start on the road to finding carefreeness. It was like dipping my toe in the waters of life, so that gradually I would be able to immerse myself in life and real living.

I remember being introduced to a man called Carl Rogers. When I say 'introduced' I don't know that I ever met him; perhaps he was on the TV. I certainly read much of his work, probably not understanding half of it. Whatever, I was schooled somehow in psychology and counselling, and felt at home in the Carl Rogers theory and what he brought through talking therapy and psychotherapy's way of healing. My memories are annoyingly sparse. Perhaps much time was taken up in reading. I do know that I attended classes in the university and also remember that much of the time I was disjointed from my real self. I always felt like an alien amongst other normally brought-up people. More than likely I was not quite in touch with my real self.

At one point I have a very clear memory of a professor called Roman Aquisap, who brought me a step towards my truth with a bang. He called me into a meeting of several professors and told me it was regarding a job vacancy that he felt I was well suited to. I walked into the room and saw before me the same kind of gathering as I had last been called on the Bruderhof. They were all men, sitting around a large mahogany oval table. However, rather than the shouting I had endured last time round, they told me very respectfully about a government initiative. The universities were being asked to set up 'Head Start' programs. The universities would be giving the work over to people such as me, trained in the care of young children, and it would be government funded. These were programs to give pre-school children day care and to teach the poor and unemployed how to care for children, giving them training in child care and immediate employment.

To cut a long meeting short, since I was so terrified about being there, I heard hardly anything. I only heard that they were asking me to take the position for one area of West Virginia. It was impossible to grasp the fact that they not only trusted me but believed me capable of carrying out the position to the highest standard. As I walked back into the sunshine with Roman I was thinking, 'They don't know what an awfully bad and incapable person I am, they don't know me. What do I say to explain?'

Roman said, 'So, what do you think?'

Here was my chance, so I made it clear that I didn't think I was qualified or able to fulfil such a position. He turned on me and the very peaceful, calm Roman said very sternly and with raised voice, 'You are always putting yourself down. Of course you are qualified! This job is just made for you, and you are going to the interview. They will offer you five hundred dollars a month and you are not accepting that. You will tell them that you only accept the job for six hundred.'

I was completely blown away. He had turned this thing on its head. I went to the interview, did exactly what Roman had said and got the job and the 600 dollars a month. I did catch an askance look between the Interviewers when I told them I wanted 600, not the offered 500, but it was agreed. While I sat in that interview it was as if someone else was speaking through me, someone powerful and sure.

During my time in this job I was really happy and set up 14 centres, each with the equipment needed plus three teachers and a cook, drawn from the unemployed bank. The centres were in different counties, all within West Virginia, and quite far apart, which meant much driving. This I loved, as by now I had a Dodge Dart. Roman did me such a favour and this was a really strong step to finding my self-worth, even though it remained wobbly for years. Roman had believed in me with genuine and absolute knowing and kindness – and he a professor! I felt safe.

I remember the first car I owned. When I was still with the Gilberts I saw this Rambler sitting at the edge of a field, and it looked good enough to me. I still had only a little money and it only cost seventy-five dollars. Dr. Gilbert took me out to see it for himself and contact the owner. We noticed a great hole in the floor on the passenger side, but Dr. Gilbert reckoned it was worth buying, so I did. It never felt good when I glanced over to the passenger side of the car when driving to see the road rush by underneath me, so the best thing was just to not look. I was proud of my little car. Later I acquired my Dodge Dart and I loved driving it – it felt so powerful. It's amazing how a powerful car can help you to find another step towards a healthier self-esteem – my Dodge Dart helped me there.

At one point in this maze of my personal history, I received a phone call from a Brother at the Bruderhof. It was one of the Servants/Ministers calling, and as soon as I heard his voice my heart started racing in anxiety. My heart bumped so loudly that it seemed like it could be heard several blocks away. He asked me in a very calm voice whether I would mind Jake visiting me. I was taken aback, as I had been left in limbo over the whole issue of my relationship with him. I had not been allowed dialogue or communication of any kind with any person on the Bruderhof for an extremely long while, let alone Jake. I was in the 'great exclusion', the big lockout.

I managed to tell this Servant that if Jake wanted it, then I was happy to meet. Arrangements were made and he came and visited me in a restaurant as it was unacceptable for a man to come to my flat.

Jake seemed as pleased to see me as I was him; however I knew that it had been set up, and it would not be something just between the two of us, but rather an arranged get-together, with ulterior motives. Sure enough, after we had eaten, Jake asked what I wanted to do about our engagement, saying that the Brothers felt it was better that we broke it off. I asked Jake what he wanted, and told him that I wanted only what would make him happy. I did desperately want him to find happiness, but I was really not at all sure about us becoming man and wife, and even if I had been invited back to the Bruderhof to live, by now I was realising that I was happier away from all that. On top of this, I felt I was not up for marriage within what could now definitely be defined as a cult.

He was unable to express his desires and didn't speak with any conviction and clarity. When he eventually drove away I felt very sad on the one hand and relieved on the other. Sad because he had been a kindred spirit since childhood (there was a love between us that I didn't understand at the time), and he seemed so unhappy, but relieved as I knew deep down in my heart that I wanted to stay free, and also that I did not really want to marry him. It took some while to work this all out though.

Sometime later I received another phone call

telling me that Jake might marry someone else. I felt confused, hurt and relieved at the same time. I now know that the hurt came from the power the Bruderhof assumed they had, although I was relieved that as I didn't want to return to 'the Life' I didn't need to explain to Jake that I couldn't get married to him.

During those years, around 1965-66, I was also contacted by a Servant of the Word to invite me to go and visit my family, who lived on a Bruderhof in England. The Brotherhood's pendulum had swung towards the kind side. The man said something to the effect that it was sad that I hadn't seen my family for so long and therefore he was offering me an open-ended visit to them. This could have been seen as a ruse to get me back, as these upswings were often used that way for those who had been excluded. However I will never know the true motivation of this 'kind' offer. I had been forcibly separated from them for most of my time from the age of 17. That had meant, by and large, no contact at all. This was something that needed some serious thinking. It was during my time with the 'Head Start' program and I was at last doing very well financially and experiencing some enjoyment in my work, which helped me start to build some self-respect. I was also finding more peace in my heart and soul.

I was terribly torn. It was a huge temptation to

visit my family, whom I missed terribly, but they had dared to reject and abandon me for the sake of the Bruderhof's religious beliefs, sometimes termed 'the Cause'. In the end I decided to take up this seemingly friendly offer. This was braving it to a large extent, as I was well aware of the pendulum swing of attitude that seemed second nature to the Bruderhof. It was quite possible for them to change with the wind and tell me I was not welcome just after I had got my tickets, for instance. My anxiety levels seemed to reach right up from my feet through my stomach and throat and up into my head every time I heard from them or even thought about them. But I decided to go, and break off with Head Start.

My next memory is of being in England and finding myself living on a Bruderhof with all the Bruderhof hallmarks in place. My anxiety had been almost unbearable as I set foot on their land, but it was turned into great joy at seeing and being with my parents and siblings. My parents were entirely genuine and showed in their actions how happy they were that I was 'home'. From them I received trusting, real, loving hugs and kisses. My siblings, however, were a different matter. I could feel very strongly that they had absolutely no trust in me, and were weighing my every word and move. When I went to embrace one of my sisters she visibly drew back and put a weak hand out to me for a hesitant, insincere handshake. I knew I had been openly vilified on the Bruderhofs and I believe this had infected them deeply. Andrew, the oldest of my brothers who was there, was the only one I felt some genuine welcome from. All the others acted as if under a spell of darkness.

My youngest sister Marcella was an exception. She had been born in England while I was in the States, and I had never met her. By now she was approaching four years of age. She was naturally shy yet drawn to me, and I of course to her. We both had something to overcome, but the bond would be there to make us natural sisters in time, I thought. I had felt very hurt that when she was born I had had no offer from the Brotherhood to go over to England to have at least a little contact with my family and to know Marcella. She had been born on my birthday. I had been told of her birth, which was something I was supposed to be grateful for, as I was told at the time. However family counts for little on the Bruderhof, even though they proclaim the opposite. It is very hard to account for my very deep pain, despite the joy at meeting my family. Such paradoxical feelings!

Over the years, Bruderhof members have been in contact with several of my friends who are also

Bruderhof exits and have warned them off me, saying I am a liar and they should not have relationships with me. These friends know how the Bruderhof brotherhood works, and have never stopped their friendship. However, one of my younger brothers, who left them, and whom I helped to get on his feet, has been so affected by their slander that he has cut off all kindness and closeness, cutting me out of his life, and has sadly become a very hard man. Yet he was a man of such wonderful love and sensitivity beforehand. Hopefully one day he may become his wonderful self again.

This is what the arrogant mind of a cult can do; it can turn a heart to stone. I do know that as humans we are all capable of lying sometimes, but this does not happen to be one of my shadow sides, and certainly doesn't represent who I am.

I know that as counsellors we endeavour to listen and hear where those who entrust us with their stories are coming from, to endeavour to walk in their moccasins. We promise ourselves to be congruent at all times, equal in all respects, to be true to ourselves; I promise myself not to be haughty or a 'know it all' in the way of the ego, and to transcend any 'dislike' of anyone to be one with them in a circle of love – this means humility within myself. We promise ourselves we will be empathetic and not judgemental. Above all we promise to have unconditional positive regard, which for me translates as unconditional love, for all our visitors seeking help.

I do wonder though, if I can ever entirely know what someone else is really feeling. In my experience as one who needed help, it is extremely difficult to find any human words to express those finely-tuned deep tendernesses of emotion that waver between consciousness and unconsciousness. We are weird, supernatural and wonderfully made. Each one of us is separate and unique, yet we are one. The One is the All and the All is the One. Despite this we often come upon difficulty as we try to work our inmost emotions and meanings to pass on to a well-meaning helper. At such times I have found great consolation, love and trust in Spirit, which comes and unites through beautiful light, one with another. I have been the lucky one, and very blessed in being given the most wonderful counsellor when I went in search of one, albeit very late in my life. He turned out to be not just a counsellor but one with me in Spirit too, so this great combination of a man who had studied, and was still in fact studying psychology and counselling, and yet gifted so deeply in intuition and instinctual understanding, combining this with Spirit and wisdom, was a great gift for my life's journey.

The time back in England with my family is something that until this moment I seem to have pushed like dirt under the carpet instead of looking at it for what it was, embracing it and then letting it go. I have no words or understanding to describe the complete and overwhelming pain I felt at this time. I can relate my story, but not my feelings. What transpired during what should have been a happy time became the very opposite.

I did get to spend time with Marcella, and being so young she was trusting and loving, putting her little hand in mine and taking me outside to show me all that excited her about creation, which turned out to be to gather sticks, stones, flowers and show me the rabbits and the family dog, Lassie, a golden Labrador who liked swimming in the lake. All my other siblings treated me with disdain and, I should add, contempt. I tried to become liked and loved again by them, by asking them about themselves and sharing with them what I had been doing at work and with the people I had met and so forth, but there was always this cold silence. They were simply not interested. Equally they didn't want me to know what was going on in their lives, as the Brotherhood is a very secretive group, arrogant, judgemental and so sure that they have the only true way of following Jesus, and that they are acting most truly and faithfully to deliver what God wants of his people. They will sometimes say they make mistakes, and every so often they ask forgiveness in a general way, but never will they be specific and say what it is they have done to us that they are sorry about. My siblings were clearly ashamed of me and were so brainwashed that they believed me to be an 'evil' person. I became a leper again, as this is how all the adults who were members of the Bruderhof treated me.

This visit started to shift me back into feeling unacceptable, feeling that I was a leper who no one could get too close to in case they became infected, not good enough to be called a full person.

Then suddenly I realised what I was doing – I was allowing myself to be brainwashed again into becoming a non-person. With this realisation I became strong, and although I would not have confessed to it at the time, angry. I was boiled up and ready to speak my truth. I had been given the experience of knowing that I was acceptable to the rest of the world. Roman, the professor who had helped me get my Head Start position in West Virginia, came to my mind and heart, giving me courage and enabling me to get myself back.

About a week into my visit to the Bruderhof, I was

called into a meeting in the Servant of the Word's Office. Dom, the Servant, sat there with my parents present and several others, sitting in a circle. With a watery, heavily-guarded smile he told me to take a seat, and started questioning me about Nigel. I remember wondering what the dickens Nigel had to do with him, as he had been gone from the Bruderhof nigh on 10 years and before Dom's time.

I glanced at my parents and detected fear in their eyes. Dom was playing with me, a cat and mouse game with my understanding, emotions and spirit. Something had been going on prior to my joining this unholy nasty meeting that I had not been privy to. However, a picture soon began to unfold before me and I could understand very clearly what was going on. Dom had been trying to get my parents to confess to dirty tricks that, in his mind, had happened years before in our family. Since no such happenings had occurred, my parents had denied any thing such as sexual deviation between their children, and now Dom was trying to twist some confession out of me, thus trapping my parents! Had I never lived away from the Bruderhof I would not have understood what he was talking about, so alien was it to our family to have had any leanings towards deviant, perverse sexual games. Living in the real world, I knew a little of such things.

I was simply outraged, and I told Dom in no uncertain terms that he had a bad and dirty mind, and that in our family it had never been even a thought to play sex games, so it could not have been a temptation. I was simply furious with him. Why was he bringing this up, and what was his purpose in trying to break my parents, so as to tell lies against themselves?

Dom suddenly broke down in tears, and said no more. I could see my parents' relief when I spoke. As with the toads in Paraguay, they had been holding their breath in fear, but now the fear was released and they could breathe easy again. I don't remember how this meeting ended, but I felt strong and clean, even if I was still angry and deeply insulted and humiliated on behalf of my parents.

Why would someone want to act with such disdain? The whole unity aspect that lurks on the Bruderhof may be part of the answer. It is the belief amongst the members that you miss out on purity and wholeness, and on being worthy of God's Kingdom, if you don't live 'in unity'. It would be claimed that you can't live 'in unity' if you had any skeletons in your closet, evils unconfessed to your Brothers and Sisters. If someone had suggested that our family had acted in a 'sinful' way and told Dom, the Servant of the Word, it would be his duty to bring us back into the unity of the spirit of the Church. They are constantly digging up the dirt. You have to bare your soul and speak out to a Servant or Witness Brother anything that is a bad thought, or as they would say an 'evil' thought, a negative thought or action, anything that you have done 'wrong', and in so doing entrust that person with your soul. They speak much about forgiveness, but in reality there is no forgiveness, or very little, amongst or within the Bruderhof regime. In fact they would record every confession and to my knowledge, some have been filed for future reference, apparently kept for eternity. Whilst I lived on the Bruderhof I sensed a sadistic streak in their ways and living. It felt as if many of the Brothers were spending their days hearing people's confessions, then bringing the stuff of people's emotions and confessions to be chewed over in open meeting in order to expel folks for their 'sins'. In fact this was giving these men, with their power mania, a fiendish, perverted satisfaction.

One could ask how Bruderhof members interpret 'unity'. I believe we should really be calling it 'conformity'. Unity is the idea in the minds of Bruderhof members that all should be in agreement over any issue, be it practical or of an inner religious or spiritual nature. This, in my experience, doesn't work. As human beings we will never all be able to agree and think the same thoughts, act similarly over any given thought or do things the same way.

As we walk in God, Spirit, Universe, light, love, or source – call it what you will –-then it would seem that we can experience absolutely, a Unity that is Divine without agreeing on anything. I have known this on rare occasion whilst on the Bruderhof, and experienced it very, very often during my life's journey since leaving the Bruderhof.

I have no recollection of whether I worked in any of the community's departments whilst on this English Bruderhof, and if I did, where, or what it was like. During the short time I was there, they went through a huge amount of upheaval and unrest as yet again Brothers arrived from the USA to help them through a 'crisis clearing' time. I remember that my little sister was very fearful living in the atmosphere this 'crisis' afforded, and as if sensing that I was not part of it all, being only the 'guest' that I was, she would tag along with me quite a lot, so I would take her out around the park and over the fields to sort of shield her from the chaos and unrest in the ether.

To add to my anxieties, one of my sisters had complained that I wasn't singing in the right way and in the right spirit as we sang together. We were a very musical family and we had for as long as I could remember sung many and varied songs, many in harmonies we had either learned at school or made up as we went. I had been absent from the family for so long that they had mostly grown into more mature voices and tended to take up the learned tenor, bass and alto parts as prescribed by the choir leader of the Bruderhof. I was innocent of this development in the family and tended to harmonise in a syncopated fashion whilst singing the light-hearted songs. This sister evidently didn't approve at all. To give her her due, she spoke up right in front of the family assembled and said she didn't like the way I sang. I was most surprised and taken aback. I don't think I took this lying down, as I remember trying to find out what the dickens she meant. However, mine was not to reason why, mine was but to do or die – I was only a guest!

This same sister had several serious chats with our parents after the rest of us had gone to bed at night. I could hear the cadence of their voices from upstairs and instinctively knew this was bad news for me. I could bear it no longer and was drawn downstairs in my night clothes and bare feet to stand outside my parents' door and listen in. Sure enough this dear sister of mine had put on the mantle of the dogmatic, authoritarian religiosity, and was having a full-on talk with my parents about my wrong ways and what a bad atmosphere I brought in to the family. She couldn't put up with it. 'We mustn't tolerate it' she said. Our father calmed her, and I could hear his soothing rumble in and out of the conversation. I heard my mother say something in support of myself. That pleased me and made me feel safer. I began to feel the cold so much that I had to take myself off back up the stairs and into my warm bed. Still this sister went on down below me.

I had known her as the most wonderful, loving, bright-eyed and clever girl. She was very gifted in almost everything she put her hand and mind to. What had become of her? I had loved her dearly all my life, even when so cruelly parted. This was not her! But whoa —she was now a Brotherhood member, and if that wasn't enough, she worked for the Servant of the Word, and in the general office, and was much liked by him, the Elders and the Housemothers. So she was in the cream. I need to say that I don't hate her because of the situation I found myself in whilst on this Bruderhof; when we are revered by others, any of us can allow an arrogant pride to envelop us, and soon we are swamped in it. I'm sure she has had her ups and downs in life, and maybe she would not even remember this episode after all these years. I haven't seen her for at least 36 years, as we are still not allowed any family visitors from the Bruderhof, but I love her with a love that is beyond expression, beyond words, and always will do.

The whole time I was on the Bruderhof with my family was a huge pain to my heart. I was right there in the midst of them and yet so very distant. It was as if we came from different planets. Yet these were my brothers and sisters, the ones I had cared for with such depth of love when our father had been so ill. The ones I had let eat when food was short and gone without myself – I had been so happy to do so that I had not even missed my food. Whilst on the Bruderhof with family again, my love was hurting terribly, my very heart pained, it ached and ached! Love can make you ache.

Not many weeks into my visit, I was again accosted by Dom, the Servant. He said he needed to have a chat with me. He announced in a quiet but forceful manner that the Brotherhood felt I didn't belong on the Bruderhof and that it would be better I found a position 'outside' again.

My father advised me how to apply for twelve childcare situations, and to my surprise all twelve answered, accepting me for job with their child care teams. I assumed that I would be able to visit my family whenever I wanted, so I accepted the position in closest proximity to where they lived, which was in Buckinghamshire.

I have no memory of my departure from my family. I just remember that, true to form, once a decision is made that someone must go, they are not allowed to hang around for long. I believe I was packed off the following day. It was hard to gather my thoughts, and I found myself wondering what had happened after I left.

It had been painful to leave my family; I also had a huge feeling of guilt, of abandonment, and rejection, but knew not what I had done to deserve this. There was shame because of being an outcast from my own flesh and blood; this could only mean that I was unacceptable to mankind in general, the Brotherhood, and my family too. On the other hand I was accepted by the staff of the children's home as if I was as good as they all were as a human being, and surprisingly they didn't judge me – certainly not as an unfavourable one! This made me feel whole and peaceful.

Soon I slipped into the work and routine of the place. I had a room in the staff house, a stone's throw away from the children's house. We had a nice dining room within the staff house, but there is little I recall of the physical layout.

I soon learned to love the children in that home. There were forty little ones from newborn to five. The babies were divided into two separate rooms, but the rest were divided into three different groups so as to mimic family groups. It was a very long day we worked, and not all staff were really cut out for working with children in my view, but I must say they all gave it their best shot.

One girl, Irene from Swansea, quickly became my friend. We had great fun and laughed a lot. I felt very impressed by all she told me about a boyfriend she had had, and I felt a twinge of envy for her freedom, and embarrassment when I had to tell her I had never had a real boyfriend. Irene was the most wonderful friend anyone could have, and when off duty, we got up to all kinds of high jinks with the rather stern Superintendent of the home. She was very old-fashioned and said we had to be in house by ten-thirty at night. All staff had separate bedrooms.

Irene and I decided to sleep in the same room and use the other as our little living space. We went ahead and moved things around. But someone must have snitched, because just as we were settling down to our first night together, one on the floor mattress, the other in the proper bed, there was a knock on the door and Miss Steel came in uninvited, shouting in a shrill voice, 'What do you think you are both doing?' I was incensed to find that at the age of twenty-five I was being ordered about in this fashion. However I was so used to freezing in fear over this kind of tone and attitude that I just got up and we both did as we were told and moved everything back.

Miss Steel had a Deputy Head who was very lazy, and she acted as if she didn't know one end of a child from the other. It was the custom while the staff ate their lunch that one of them would watch the children were safe while they all had a midday nap. It was hoped that all forty would sleep so that one person could cope. Of course this never happened. It was a case of going from baby to baby, from a two-year-old here to a four-year-old there, to comfort and cajole in whispers, so as not to wake all the others up. At the end of this hour you were expected to go from room to room getting children up, changing babies and putting all the beds away in time for the rest of the staff to come back on duty, so as to release you to eat. No member of staff managed this midday duty perfectly – it was an impossibility, but I certainly did very well given the organisational skills required. Interestingly, neither the Head nor the Deputy Head ever managed to put themselves up for this concentration of responsibility.

One day I was on duty and had managed to get all babies changed and the green room children up and drinking their juice on the veranda when the Deputy stood before me, stopping me in my tracks. She was a very big woman in her early thirties. She immediately began criticising me heavily, asking why was I not out with the children on the veranda. I responded with the obvious, that I was about to get this little lot up. I couldn't be in two places at once, and neither could she for that matter. I could see all the children through glass partitions. She went on, and I got angry, something which had happened very rarely in my life. Suddenly I heard myself spouting forth about the fact that the Deputy never lifted a finger to help, always just walking up and down while the rest of us worked, and we did many extra hours with no thanks from her, and if I was not good enough then I would leave and find a new position. I almost looked back over my shoulder to see who was talking, hardly able to believe it was me.

Expressing my truth by painting my picture in an explosion of words like this had made me feel so good, so strong and whole. At the same time I was filled with a strange compassion for the Deputy, because her face turned bright red and with a tear in her eye she turned on her heel and left me to get on. I didn't consider saying I was sorry to her. From then on she showed me respect for all I did, and I respected her.

One day I decided to phone my parents. On phoning the Bruderhof community's switchboard to ask for them, one of my sisters answered, which made me very happy. It was the sister who had found me to be a thorn in her flesh over my singing. We had a little chat and she seemed quite happy with this but slightly cautious, and quiet in tone. I don't think I ever knew why, but she never did put my parents on the line.

CHAPTER 11

Atlantic crossings

Shortly after I had spoken to my sister, a call came from Dom. He said in a measured tone that he was coming to visit me at the home. Immediately my heart raced and I felt sick to my stomach. It was a statement, not a request. He told me he would come at 6 pm on the coming Thursday.

I made sure that I would be off duty, and soon the day arrived. It was a dark, cold November evening. I was too embarrassed, as he was a Bruderhof Minister and not a relative, to invite him indoors, so I went out to the car, which he had parked just under my window. As I went out the door of the car opened and his wife appeared, inviting me to sit inside their vehicle as it was pouring with rain. I sat in the car, very relieved that they didn't want to be invited into the staff house.

They told me the purpose of the visit was twofold. One reason was to ask me why I had had the audacity to phone my sister to try to reach my parents; they made it clear to me that this had been very wrong. The other was to tell me that the Brotherhood had decided to close down the Community in England, and all the Brothers and Sisters were to emigrate to the States. I would be free to stay in England or go back to the States, as I pleased. He reminded me however, that if I stayed over a year in England I would lose my immigrant's status in the USA.

Even though this was a repeat of what had happened in Primavera, it was shocking news to me. It felt as if yet again the new American communities were taking over and their control was complete. They seemed all powerful, with little respect for the many people who had spent so much in building up the Bruderhof under very difficult world conditions. But on the other hand, who was I to bother? I was no longer one of them.

Most of the time I sat in the car with Dom and his wife he was shouting aggressively at me that I was wrong to have phoned my sister, because I was excluded, so I should not have been talking to anyone, especially not to my family. All the way through his tirade the skies were emptying furiously, thundering on the roof of the car.

Finally they left and I got out and scurried round the building to let myself in through the front door. I was very embarrassed in case any of the off-duty staff had overheard all the shouting. It appeared not. Irene asked what they had wanted, and I do remember that I couldn't explain to her, being so ashamed of the extraordinary attitude of these people towards their own, so I fobbed her off with some lame tale about going back to the States.

I realised that if my family was being removed to the States with the whole of the two English Bruderhof communities, then if ever the pendulum swung back to kindness it would be prudent to keep my immigrant status by returning to the USA. I let Dom know this, and it wasn't long before he had arranged a ticket for me back to the States. They were paying this time, and so they should have. Dom didn't tell me where he was sending me, but he did say that someone from one of the Bruderhofs there would pick me up from the airport. I didn't even know whether I was being sent to New York, Connecticut or Pennsylvania. I reflected on my stupidity in believing the call I had received back then offering me the chance to see my family in

England, and felt I had been conned by the sweet voice telling me it had been a long time I had been parted from my family and they had somehow wanted to make good this situation. I think now that it was a way of trying to get me back to become a member, but since I didn't 'fit in' it had collapsed. I will never know.

I think it was around ten at night when I arrived back on American soil, and true to their word I was met by a couple who I had known in Paraguay, who had by now risen somewhat in the pecking order. Jack and Julie met me out of customs right on time and took me silently to a car in the parking area. By their silence I knew that they saw me as under Church discipline; that meant no talking to me, the sinful one. The telephone was now the means of communication within the Bruderhof, to tell other communities of the state of another's 'soul' and how they were to be treated. Jack and Julie had obviously received the message. Many years later Jack was to apologise to me about this time. He is the only one who has ever said he was sorry about any specific incident of painful treatment, although he is still within the Brotherhood. I was very touched by that, and wondered why he stood alone in this attitude. Was he being very brave? Yes, I think so. His heart overrode his head and his orders.

Around midnight we arrived in a town, and they took me to a house with a veranda. They opened the door and we stood in a hall. Now at last they spoke. Jack told me that the house had been divided into three apartments. There was a couple downstairs and a single elderly lady on the second floor, while they had rented me the attic rooms. We went up and I was quite impressed to see that they had kitted it out to a large extent for me. It was very warm indeed considering that it was freezing, with deep snow and icy cold outside. I noticed that all the windows were covered in a type of plastic outside to act as double glazing. It was centrally heated, and I had no input in regulating the heat which was controlled downstairs by the couple.

Jack told me that they had paid the first week's rent and from then on it would be down to me. I asked about job possibilities, who the landlord was, where to find him, and asked where I was. He said I was in Brownsville and that I could ask the director of the old hospital for work, saying he knew him. Julie opened a cupboard in the kitchen, showing me that they had put provisions in there to last a few days until I could earn some money.

Of course the children of the Bruderhof understand little of the workings of the real world. By now I had learned quite a lot, but Jack and Julie had not. They didn't appreciate that once I had found work, I would have to work for a week or a month in hand, and I wondered how I would feed myself. Having known what it was like to be seriously hungry on several occasions in my life, I wasn't overly worried, rather hurt that they didn't seem to care. They said quite curtly that now they would go, and left, before I could ask what state Brownsville was in, or whether I would ever be considered worthy of contact with them or my family, or anyone else I knew in the Bruderhof.

So here I was, completely and utterly alone in a world I didn't know. I couldn't place myself as I had no idea geographically where I was. I had no car and knew nothing about public transport, as I had never encountered it in the USA when I had been there before. I was to discover that it didn't exist in and around Brownsville. I didn't have a single address of any of my acquaintances and friends who had left or been thrown out of the Bruderhof and were scattered all over the place. Brotherhood members made very certain we had no such contacts. I was utterly alone. I was in a black hole, but my heart and resolve still had a flicker of light to sustain me. That Light must have come from pure love, unconditional divine love, which, if we would but remember, never leaves us.

I was very hungry, so I opened the cupboard, which

revealed the bread, cheese and jam and the few tinned goods that had been left me. There was tea and coffee too, and some artificial juice crystals for making drinks, called Kool-Aid. I gazed at the food, and had no appetite. The sight of it made me feel sick. It was not the kind of sickness which goes with fever, it was the kind where when we are at rock bottom, a nobody, rejected and forlorn. Your stomach tightens up and rises to your throat, and you can't swallow; even drinking is difficult. I shut the cupboard door to hide the food, opened my case to find my night things and went to bed.

Around three in the morning I awoke with a start, my heart racing. Sitting up, I noticed that I was sweating; it was mercilessly hot in my attic apartment. I tried to open the window, but of course it was sealed. I tried another, and it too was stuck shut. I couldn't get a whiff of fresh air—I was stifling. I felt I couldn't breathe; I was suffocating.

I walked out of the flat in my night clothes and went down the two flights of stairs and to the front door. Opening it I breathed in a deep lungful of fresh, clean, crisply cold air – it was wonderful. To cool down and indulge in this fresh freedom nature offered, I stepped out onto the veranda. I had never heard of automatically closing doors, but now I was to find out that they worked. For a minute I stood enjoying the icy night in total silence all around, and then quickly the icy cold crept up and over me as I stood in my bare feet.

On turning to walk back inside, I found I was locked out. Now I knew I could freeze to death, as the temperature was much lower in this place than anyone could imagine. I stood helplessly staring at the door, which on the upper half was made of glass, and suddenly noticed three little round knobs one above the other beside the door. What were they doing there? They had clearly been set for a purpose.

Suddenly I thought of an explanation. I figured that they were buttons connected to the three apartments. Which one belonged to which? Maybe I was the top one, as I lived under the eaves, so the lowest one belonged to the couple. I was too afraid to wake them, so I would try the middle one, which I hoped belonged to the old lady, who surely could do me no harm.

I pressed the middle button warily. I heard nothing, but in a minute or so, I saw the feet of a person appear on the stairs, and as the person descended she became whole and real – the elderly woman from the second floor. I was saved! She walked quite slowly, and I had time to feel very relieved but highly embarrassed. Did she even know that I lived here?

As she opened the door she stepped back a little to allow me to enter. 'Who are you, and what are you doing ringing in the middle of the night?' she said. I told her that I was the new tenant and had just moved in. I apologised that I had needed to wake her because of my ignorance of the workings of automated doors. She introduced herself as Mrs Marker. Through her toothless gums she said, 'you're a Limey aren't you? Why don't you come into my apartment?'

I had heard somewhere that the English were 'Limeys' to the Americans, so I agreed to both question and invitation. Mrs Marker's front door entered her kitchen, which was long and narrow and despite her age she had a bar and tall bar stools along a wall. She made coffee, filling a big mug for me, and plied me with doughnuts. She seemed to have boxes of these delicious doughnuts and no sooner had I finished one than she offered another. Even as I reminisce on this occasion, my heart swells with comfort and happy love at the memory. Mrs Marker was my angel.

She asked questions while she ate and drank through her toothless mouth, and I answered as best I could as I drank and scoffed hungrily through doughnuts. She was very direct with her questioning and I tried to answer truthfully but without giving the Bruderhof a bad name. Nevertheless she hadn't a good word for 'The Brothers'. I could tell that she was scandalised at the way I had been dumped, even though I tried to dress it up. She was a canny old lady. She told me proudly that she was German. She sounded very American to me, but at that time I didn't realise that most Americans are proud to call themselves after their European ancestry.

Mrs Marker did let me in to the fact that I was in Brownsville Pennsylvania, which was a 'ghost town'. She said it had fallen into utter disrepair with no job prospects since the mines had closed down. Now there were no jobs for anyone and many had left town; those left behind mostly lived in dire poverty. It didn't look good for me. The hospital in town was no more, but there was a hospital, newly built, four miles out of town. No public transport existed.

I looked around a little when daylight broke and it was indeed a dreadfully shabby sight that met my eyes. An enormous river ran behind the house, the banks of which were unkempt and very muddy. The whole town looked as if it was dying. I felt much like the town seemed. If it had not been for Mrs Marker and her kind acceptance of me, I don't know where I would have been.

Somehow I found myself in the hospital, begging for work as a nurses' aid. I walked up to a nurse station and asked for whoever was in charge. A middle-aged woman met me and sharply told me she had no work for me. Looking back I understand her attitude entirely. I was desperate, but I expect she found me to be quite odd, and if not odd, then very impertinent. I turned away, feeling very down, with a lump in my throat and a knot in my stomach.

As I walked back through the enormous hub of the hospital, with its dining area for staff, I noticed a passage with doors leading off. I saw that over one door was the word 'Director'. Walking up to this door, and with my heart in my mouth, I knocked on it. A kindly-looking man opened it, and with a surprised face asked what he could do for me. I told him my whole truth. I couldn't afford to be careful about protecting the Bruderhof in what I said. Of course it is quite unbelievable that someone should be dumped in Brownsville the night they land from England, with no relatives or friends to meet and care for someone of around twenty six years of age.

I can't remember the conversation, but I do remember that he gave me a job working as a nurses' aid on the maternity wing. I was to work the night shift. Even though I had no way of getting to work and back, I wasn't going to let that stop me from accepting this job – it felt like a lifeline to me.

I soon got to know someone at work by the name of Jackie, another angel sent to me. She gave me a lift to work each day and also invited me in to her and her husband's apartment for a chat and coffee and sometimes for meals. She and her husband lived very close to my apartment. Soon the attic above her became available, and I moved over. It was a cheaper option and also nice to be near Jackie at the time; we could synchronise times of going to and from work more easily.

I loved working where I was constantly in contact with the beauty of innocence and love-dependence of a newborn baby. These lovely little angels gave me much to healing my battered heart. It was a time of happiness at work. Living alone and being barred from contacting those I loved was a great pain and constant reminder that I was 'unworthy' of love. I took it for granted that I was an unworthy person, but that didn't lessen the pain that constantly dogged my heart. I rarely fought the feelings of being a lesser being; I accepted it but this didn't still my pain. There was much fun and laughter amongst us as workmates in the hospital, but every time I laughed, something reminded me that I didn't deserve to be happy.

It was a time of learning, as all time is, but for me it came as a time when my ignorance of the world was lessened and I began to understand how things worked. One example of this was that one day when I was walking down the long medical wing, to where I had been assigned in my new position on day duty, and encountered a tall man in a suit whom I had never encountered before. He stopped me and asked 'have you insurance?' To me he was speaking a new language. I must have looked puzzled. He continued in a slightly annoyed voice, 'have you got life insurance? I can insure your life'.

I was amazed at the arrogance of this man. Did he want to insure me against death? How could he possibly be so full of himself as to claim that he could insure my life? He was telling me that he had the power to prevent me from dying? No one could insure life! I was beginning to get annoyed at him accosting me at work and promising me such rubbish. I told him he could never insure my life, and added that he could not ensure anyone's life. This poor gentleman looked nonplussed, and we passed each other by. I looked back at him, and he looked back at me.

Much later I learned what life insurance was. I figured in the end that I wouldn't put money I needed now into a funeral fund – I still couldn't imagine my own death.

I always made sure I worked during national holidays as it was too painful to be alone on such occasions. At Christmas time I was on a night shift. Everything was quiet and around midnight some of the doctors on duty invited some of us, during our lunch break, to share a drink with them. I knew of no rules that said there should be no drinking on duty. In fact I had hardly ever had an alcoholic drink. I trusted the doctors, as they were the ones in authority. I was used to doing whatever those in authority suggested when it came to the institutional. Some of us went and joined the doctors, and when they offered me Scotch whisky, I took a sip, found it revolting and offered it to someone else. All the doctors were very kindly toward me because I was a Limey and they liked the English, or that's how it appeared to me. They laughed in a friendly way that a girl from England didn't know whisky. We had a nice break time together. I was feeling very happily accepted by all the staff, and had a glow in my heart, but not from whisky!

The following day we were called into the Head Nurse's office, the one who had refused me a job, and she gave us a tremendous row. She made it clear that if we were ever found drinking on duty again, we would be dismissed. Needless to say the doctors were not called in. I had learned another lesson that day for me, about the ways of the world.

One day another phone call from the Brothers broke into my comparative peace, and as ever it made me feel sick and made my heart race. This call was simply to tell me that if I wanted it, my father would come and pick me up to take me to the Oaklake Bruderhof community for a weekend visit with my family. It was very hard to trust this Brother because it had been ages since I was with them, and I hadn't known that my parents and siblings were actually living in Pennsylvania. I also sensed that there could be an ulterior motive in the invitation – i.e. to lure me back forever. They would start by finding something I could repent of, with more than likely more yelling and shouting and being put down by the men in power. But with a quavering gut and a thumping heart I said yes. It had been well over a year since I had spoken to or seen any of my family.

The day arrived very soon when my father arrived and we shyly greeted each other. For unknown reasons I felt guilty and ashamed before him, and knew that in some way I had let him down – yet had I, or did he know me better? My parents seemed to accept that this daughter of theirs was continually 'in a wrong spirit' and needed the constant discipline of exclusion. Yet they were never angry on the rare occasions of meeting. Daddy probably didn't realise that I had no intention by now of returning to live forever under the painful load of being a 'leper' within the community, even though I knew I wasn't the only one to be treated as such.

The weekend went all right, although I was constantly in an anxious state. I was invited back on several occasions and somewhere during these times I was asked to give violin lessons to several children. I loved doing this, and as I was not playing at the time at any other venue I left my violin in my sister's bedroom under the bed they had reserved for me on my visits. I guess after some time it was found not to be the 'right' policy to have someone such as myself to give their children lessons. On one occasion I decided to take my violin back with me on the Sunday night as I left to go back to my digs and work. On reaching under the bed, I found it was gone. My beloved violin that had travelled with me all over the world, my constant, and very often my only, companion was not there. With foreboding in my heart I went into the living room where my mother was, and told her that my violin had vanished, and did she know where it was. I could see that she felt awkward as she explained that the Housemother felt I didn't need it any more, as I was no longer giving lessons, and that she had given it to someone else who could give lessons in my stead. I later found out that the 'someone else' was one of my sisters. So the Housemother had stolen my violin and given it to my sister!

I acquired another violin some while later, but it was never dear to my heart – it had a rather proud, forceful tone to it. My own violin had had a tone and breath of gold and silver strands; lush yet sweet, deep, yet with a nightingale's ability. Its sound was sublime. The new one was hoarse, stiff and awkward in tone. I felt somehow sorry for it, so I started to play it. But I think it knew where my real heart lay!

Time went on. Each time I was at Oaklake I would see Jörg somewhere, mostly working on cars within the community. He never spoke to me and I did not speak to him, except to say hello. We were both under the influence of fear, the fear that kept control over all Bruderhof life. I could see that he was constantly in the small exclusion and my heart longed to relieve him of this degradation and unhappiness placed upon him.

One time I was at home on a Saturday evening with only my two youngest siblings and my parents. All the others were out on an evening with the young people's group of the Bruderhof. When eventually they came home it was near midnight and they all came laughing in, full of what appeared to be joy. One of my sisters started telling of what they had been doing for the evening and showed my parents a card they had all signed to give to a Servant of the Word in welcome, as he was to arrive the following day. This particular sister started talking about Jörg, and several of my siblings joined in, in mockery of him. The one sister criticized heavily the way he had signed his name, saying he had written in tiny letters to show off how humble he was. The rest had laughed. I knew that he wrote in such small writing because he felt a nobody. I didn't expect he even realised this himself.

I couldn't get angry on behalf of myself, but I exploded with anger on behalf of Jörg. A stream of anger at my sisters' and brothers' attitudes came out of my mouth, and I didn't let up until I ran out of steam. The entire family were stunned into silence. But then I heard Daddy's firm, warm voice back me up, and say he was glad for what I had expressed. It was my turn to be dumbfounded. My siblings were no worse or no better than anyone else on the Bruderhof. This was just the way Bruderhof people seem to behave, weighing up everyone else's beings, characters, and what they would term being in the 'wrong spirit'. Arrogance would seem to be the second name of the Bruderhofers in general. Yet as individuals, they can be quite different.

There came a day when I received another phone call. This time it was to announce to me that the Brotherhood had decided to start up a new community in England. My father had been amongst those who had journeyed to the UK to find and purchase a place. Eventually they had decided upon a situation in East Sussex. After his return it had been decided that my family, amongst others, were to move back to the UK. The question was whether I would like to go back with them, and help them set up in England. Again I was offered the temptation to be part of my birth family again by going. Would my siblings accept me? I knew my parents would. How far would the Brotherhood interfere with family life? Had my siblings become even more overshadowed and infected by the dogma of organized religion, the controlling, ideological arrogance, that the Bruderhof seemed to use, or were they older and wiser now? I didn't know. To be separated by thousands of miles yet again, from the family I so longed to be close to, was one too many for me. I capitulated and agreed to leave my job, which at the time was in Parkersburg USA, and join the family to travel by ship to the UK.

It took us about five to six days. It was amazing to

be with my family and experience them all as a normal free family. Any fear of getting it 'wrong' seemed to have vanished, and all of us were happy with one another. Big Brother was not there to be accountable to; he could not watch over us and see what we did, and the free spirit in each was tangible, one could almost scoop it up and hold it close. My mother, having money of her own in her hands for the first time in almost thirty years with no Bruderhof steward to watch over her and account to, went to the ship's shop, and bought me two gifts. One was a Hummel figurine of a little girl, the other a gold pendant. As she gave me these gifts her whole demeanour was one of love, and she said to me that I wasn't the terrible human being I had been made out to be by the Bruderhof brotherhood, and that she accepted and loved me as wholly as any of her other children. One of my daughters has always loved the pendant, and now I have passed it into her safe keeping. It represents great love to me.

We docked in Southampton and were met by some Bruderhof people who had travelled ahead of us. The buildings and land that had been purchased by the Brotherhood turned out to be a disused TB sanatorium. It was in a beautiful setting and the buildings were not in too bad repair.

Over the next week or two, four more families joined us from the communities in the States, with a few single people as well. There was none of the stiff religiousness of a mature Bruderhof community. No one was boss. Everyone worked hard to get the place clean and in ship shape order, ready to become a fully-fledged Bruderhof. There was as yet no Servant in residence. It is perfectly obvious that this was why there was such a free and happy atmosphere in all that we undertook in work and play. It was a very happy six weeks.

Then a message came from America that Rich and his family were being sent to join and lead us. Rich was our Servant of the Word, and our six weeks of free and happy fun came to an abrupt end on his arrival. He was forceful, loud and commanding. Humour and laughter were not his bent (he did possess a humour of his own, but it was sharp and cutting). The familiar words about the Bible, unity and love were delivered through teeth of steel. Every night a Brotherhood meeting was announced, and they spent much time talking while I, plus one of my sisters who I believe was also in disgrace at the time, and one other girl, a very unassuming and quiet lass, spent every night between the hours of eight until eleven o'clock painting one room, apartment or house after another. This was hard work; we were used for this in readiness for more Brothers' and Sisters' arrivals from the USA. The three of us were always tired as we had worked since eight o'clock in the morning.

I felt that my parents enjoyed being back in the country of their birth. As a family there seemed mostly happiness displayed, and I was fairly well accepted, although still treated as a lesser being whenever anyone else from the Brotherhood was present. I felt sad that my siblings, most of whom by now were members of the Brotherhood, used to leave my mother to do all the work at home. They would come in late and eat whatever they could find, leaving the mess for my mother (or me) to clean up. My brothers would not even make their own beds and never did my siblings get up and make breakfast ready, even though by now they were all in their twenties and my parents were nearing sixty.

As I observed this I was very perplexed. I remember saying to Mummy that I felt angry at how she and Daddy were treated by them, and why did they put up with it? She said sadly that my siblings were all working for the community, for the Kingdom of God, and family came second. Work for the community was more important than family and mother. I could see that she didn't have her heart in what she said, and she appeared to be very weary, almost depressed at this knowledge. I made it my business to stay and help my mother and if I was late for the job I had been assigned to do for the community, then tough! Since I was not an acceptable human being any way, I would not allow myself to feel guilty about not helping the community in their work schedule. Of course I did go and work in this or that department as soon as I had finished helping at home.

A year slipped by, and the usual Bruderhof celebrations went on, the usual crises were lived through; the pendulum went forever on its back and forth ding dong, up in the sky, and then suddenly plummeting down into the depths of darkness. Nothing could be counted upon to stay peaceful and stable, ever. There were excitable ups and huge, dark downs.

There came a day when another Servant of the Word arrived from the States and again all hell let loose. I was upstairs above what was called the Brotherhood Room with my little sister in our living quarters one night, and I could hear this Brother yelling at my parents. Not just the visiting Minister, but more and more Brotherhood members jumped on the bandwagon and started at my parents. I could hear every word squeezing up through the floorboards.

One of my siblings took up with the Servant and sided against my parents. This gives more 'Brownie points' on the Bruderhof, when you 'stand up for the right' against your own family, especially if it's your parents.

The issue had been that Nigel had made a visit from Brazil. Whilst with us he had discussed one evening such topics as what we thought about flying saucers, angels, the cosmos, in depth. At the beginning of our discussion there were only my parents, Marcella and myself in the room. It was wonderful for me to share in Nigel's thoughts and experiences. He had seen UFOs and watched them fairly frequently in Brazil. My parents listened very peacefully, and were I think, quite intrigued, putting in a thought here and there. Soon we were joined by those of the family who had been busy with Bruderhof community work. Lastly we were joined by one of my siblings who had just become engaged, with her partner and a single Sister who took breakfast with our family at the time. As they walked in, Nigel was talking about angels, and his thoughts that there were probably angels of light and possibly angels of darkness. All this had been passed on to the Servant by our religious couple, and my parents were now being brought low by the Brotherhood for not 'standing in the right spirit' and for allowing Nigel to speak in this 'blasphemous' way, and not challenging him.

The end result of this was that the entire family was torn apart. Some were put into various types of Church discipline, exclusion or solitary confinement. One adult brother and I were the only ones left in the family apartment, neither of us 'decided' for. It seemed as if one day we were all in the Darvell Bruderhof, and the next there were two of us, the two that did not belong to the Brotherhood.

Yet again I was asked to clear and pack up the family home. Everything was to be taken to the Housemother. Since I had resolved to leave them all again, I hid some precious music records in my room until such time as I could escape from the Bruderhof again.

I was to find out that my parents, with my youngest brother and sister and several other siblings who were members or novices, had been shipped back to a Bruderhof in the USA. I had not been given the opportunity to even say goodbye; nor was I given an address for them in the US. As there were several Bruderhof villages in the US it would take some time to find out where they had been put, in their state of Church discipline. The Brotherhood would keep this from me, so I had to wait to hear through the grapevine, whenever their lines opened. It took a long time. When I did hear, I found my father had been separated from my mother, he being sent 'outside', away from any Bruderhof community.

I wrote to an aunt of mine about my situation, and asked if I could visit her to get myself together. I had lost my American Green Card by staying too long in the UK. I was no longer an American immigrant, so I would need to establish myself in the country of my birth, the United Kingdom. I received a letter by return of post and after packing a few things together and leaving a couple of cases for my brother to ship after me I left, and arrived with great joy to the fresh air and fresh spirit of my aunt's home.

My aunt lived in the family home of her parents, which she had bought for them years before. This was in Stratton, near Cirencester in Gloucestershire. There was plenty of space for me, but so as not to be a burden on her, I went job hunting the next day and was accepted as a nurses' aid in Cirencester Hospital, where a cousin of mine was a nurse. It was absolutely wonderful sharing time and home with my very dear aunt. She was like salve poured on a much-wounded heart in the way she spoke, and in the way she accepted me as a whole and valid human being. When she laughed it was like a clear-running brook tinkling over pretty stones of different colours and shapes. Collis, my Auntie Col, was so dear to my heart; I feel her presence even now as I think about her, gentle and unassuming, yet clear and firm in her faith and knowledge of life. She was my rock, my angel, my friend and my substitute mother.

Over the next few years I worked mostly in child education, having many and varied interesting experiences. My brother Michael, whom I had left behind on the Bruderhof community, had left them for good, and also found work within the social care institution in England, and he lived not far from me in Oxfordshire. We would meet up from time to time and it was wonderful to have one sibling to enjoy life with. I was beginning to be happy to belong to the world, the 'outside world' often so despised by Bruderhof members. At least in their speech it was despised. I think that deep down, if individuals had allowed their inner god to speak for them, it might have sounded different, but they were toeing their party line.

I began to love Planet Earth immensely, and found love and joy in so much. The children I cared for became so dear to me that not a one was left out from my heart. However, I often found that I could be at loggerheads with those in positions of Authority, especially where truth and justice were concerned, despite my new-found freedom. This mostly occurred in my mind and heart, as I said nothing. I would just quietly follow my own initiative and allow myself the freedom to hear my own instinct and intuition, and act upon it. I was beginning to feel like a bird freed from its cage.

For one reason and another I moved rather freely from job to job and from one county to another. Maybe this was partly due to trying out my newfound freedom. If I didn't feel easy with any given situation I could move from it; in my earlier life I would have just bowed my head and forced myself to fit in. Perhaps now I was swinging too far in the other direction, but I was footloose and fancy free and enjoyed being so.

CHAPTER 12

Finding Jörg

Over the next few years many situations occurred which taught me new ways, opening my mind to dare to new concepts. I began to spread my wings and learn to trust them not to collapse and let me down.

Once, whilst working in Buckinghamshire, my very dear friend Sina, who hailed from Sicily, asked me to go to church with her. We had spent much time together and had enjoyed laughter, fun and hard work too. She was a very trustworthy and honest person, gifted in childlike love. I was amazed at first that she was part of a church. I was afraid at her question, because it was deeply set in me that churches were wrong and superficial. Deeper still there was set in me from the Bruderhof dogma the idea that it was very wrong to 'come to prayer' with anyone you were not in unity with (suggesting unity of spirit, but this really meant conformity, as I've said). Such was my fear that it took me a few minutes to answer. Then in a flash I knew – I would go to church, the most feared place, with her because I trusted her, and if I fell down dead when they began to pray then I would know that the Bruderhofer were right. If I was still alive when the prayer finished I would know that they had it wrong, and the rest of the world was a safe place to be.

That Sunday we went to her church in Chalfont St Peter. I wasn't familiar with what happened in a church. In this one, everybody just sang and sang their hearts and lungs out. The singing went on for ages and I loved it. Just when I was beginning to relax, the singing stopped and we heard a man begin to pray. We younger adults were all seated up in the gods on benches, as I remember, with no backs. I edged to the front of the bench, hands holding on tightly to the seat, knuckles white, staring at them and past them onto the floor. It was now or never for my exit from the planet.

All of a sudden I was in peals of happy laughter, and I felt as free as a bird that flies. I was full of joy. I looked round at Sina, head still quietly slightly bowed. She hadn't heard my laughter, and nor had anyone else. The man was coming to the end of whatever he was praying, and then his voice faded away like silk. I hadn't heard a word he said, but I knew my sojourn on Earth was not ended, and I also knew that the Brotherhood had lied. I had faced a fear and overcome it.

I remembered the only other time I had been inside a church. When visiting my grandparents at age seventeen, my grandfather had said on rising from the breakfast table on Sunday morning, 'Well now, let's get off to church'. I had been taken aback and filled with fear. I said I couldn't go and he said 'and why not?' I tried to say I wasn't 'in unity'. He said, 'Rubbish, you're coming!' On that occasion I had simply put myself in a bubble, distanced myself, and was deaf to all that transpired so as to keep the fear at bay. Now, ten years later, I was free of that particular gremlin.

On one occasion, whilst working in a children's home in Oxfordshire, something happened to open my eyes. This particular home comprised three cottages, each housing twelve children of various ages. The idea was that it helped them feel more family likeness. I was hired as the supervisor of one of the cottages. It was a fabulous job and I was very happy working with the staff and children. Each child was like a precious jewel to me. I worked hard, but was quite happy to do so. The supervisor of another cottage, Mr Jackson, was also the head of the entire children's home. He used to hold a weekly meeting of all staff, just to keep everything on course and let us know of any new rules that social services had agreed.

One day I had a call from the Director of Social Services asking to see me. At the meeting, he told me he would have to let me go. I was absolutely dismayed. He was a very kindly man, probably nearing the end of his working life, and quite well known to me. I got in touch with my brother Michael and told him what had happened and said I didn't know what I had done to deserve this dismissal. He actually laughed, and said that I was too good at my job, and that no doubt someone was jealous. At this time he worked for the same social services department. I was quite disbelieving at first but spoke to the Director again asking why I was being sacked and what had I done wrong. He sat with me with a sad kind of smile on his face and said, 'Well the honest truth is that this is a jealousy issue; Mr Jackson knows that you are more capable and able than he is with the children and your work in general, and he wants you out as he feels threatened.'

We had a discussion as I tried to grasp why the

Director would give in to such unfairness. Mr Jackson had never complained or confronted me. All I had to lift me was the thought that I must be good at what I did, and that I was therefore a worthwhile person. But still, this was grossly unfair. By the end of the conversation I had been offered another position in Oxford City. This chapter in my life gave me much to think about. Where was fairness, justice, and why could this happen to someone, me?

One day I was sitting in Michael's garden on a very bright, sunny day, writing a reply to a letter from my father. He had asked me what I was going to do with my life, and what my goal was. Since I had never asked to return to the Bruderhof, nor asked forgiveness, I guess my father was beginning to get concerned that they were losing me to 'the world'. Despite having felt the burden of guilt for much of my life I still had no idea why I had been sent out into 'the world' in the first place; I didn't know what I was guilty of, so I didn't know what to ask forgiveness for.

That glorious spring May morning filled my heart with delight and I felt free, freed from the Bruderhof, and happy to just meander along finding out what life was all about for me. I realised that I had no goals, and I was not beholden to the Brotherhood. In fact I wasn't beholden to anyone or anything. I was just me, a tiny speck in the great cosmos, yet as I became just me, I was also growing in confidence and happiness, and a vague excitement was starting to grow in me, making me feel safe and strangely loved. I sat in this beautiful garden, the river flowing at the bottom, just beyond the small hedge, and flowers, trees and grasses all round me, birds singing and utter, and perfect peace wrapped around, and filled me.

So I wrote back to my father to say how I felt, and told him that I had no goals, no idea what my future would hold, was not striving for anything in particular; but one thing I knew, and this was that I would never belong to the Bruderhof again. Putting this down on paper to my parents gave me such happiness and freedom – it was a wonderful day!

* * *

I was now working in London, in a children's home. The children were aged between three and 18 years of age. It didn't take me long to fit in, and I was into the full swing of things. Over the next couple years my life was to take a huge swing into happiness of the most wonderful kind, but I did not know that yet. There were also times of difficulty, but now I was better equipped not just to survive but to make my own way through life.

At first I was on the staff of the Child Care Department. On Saturdays we were expected to 'special' a child. This meant that one child would be assigned to you, and you could spend much of the day doing something nice with that child. This included going to the cinema, or to a musical, going to see the Christmas Grotto at Harrods, going to Biggin Hill to watch the goings on there – anything within reason that this particular child would choose. One Saturday I was assigned to a lad called Derek. He was fourteen, and really quite shy. I asked him what he would like to do and he said he wanted to go to the fair that was to take place in the grounds of a private school not far from where we lived.

The grounds were extensive and really beautiful. We had just walked into the entrance when Derek spied a round tent which offered 'Psychic Readings' displayed on a board outside it. I gave him his pocket money and told him I would sit down at a coffee place close by while he did whatever he wanted to. It was a lovely sunny day and I was sitting daydreaming when someone flashed out of the psychic's tent like greased lightning, and before I knew it Derek was at my elbow, white with fear and breathing very fast. I calmed him down a little and asked him what he was scared of. At the time I had no idea what a psychic was, and if they were as I guessed, human, what they did. I had gathered along life's way from various Christians that mediums were doing evil – were psychics similar, were they doing evil? I vaguely felt they might be.

But now my responsibility was to Derek, and I needed to know what had happened to make him so fearful. He said there was a woman in the tent who had told him he was a thief. I wondered why she had said this, and he told me that she was talking all about his life and then had said he was a thief. At this he had jumped up and fled.

I asked, 'So are you a thief?' I knew of the exploits of some of the older children. Derek said that the previous night he had joined some lads to steal alcohol from the corner shop just across from where the children's home was. They had taken a crate of soft drinks.

After this confession he calmed down a lot and after a chat about how he didn't think he would be into stealing again for a while he went off to find what else was out there for fun!

I meantime headed for the psychic and her special knowledge. In the tent sat a very pretty young woman, very human, very ordinary, with a smile to stretch round the world. She indicated a seat in front of her and sat shuffling away at some cards. I hadn't come to play Canasta or Strip Jack Naked, I hoped. She explained to me with a smile that she would read my past, present and future. I grinned back and said I didn't think I believed she could do that but I would give her a go. She didn't 'read' that I was doing this to see what could have possibly given such fear to Derek. He was not unused to stealing and being caught out by one of us staff; had she threatened him? I was about to find out.

After a shuffle of the cards she took them and laid them out in the pattern of the feathers of the Prince of Wales. She then asked me to turn one after another over, beginning with the ones to my left and telling me what each was saying. To my utter amazement she had my past so perfectly described that I sort of sucked in air. How could someone know so exactly how the Bruderhofer had dressed and describe it all to a T, the multilingual background, the moral harshness, the culture?

Then it was time for the present to be revealed. This too turned out to be so perfectly accurate that I was again flabbergasted. As she proceeded with the present she turned up a card with a little man on it, bag over his shoulder, running fast and away and above his head read the word in huge letters, THIEF. I smiled a little uneasily, as I was still prone to thinking I was a bad person, and said 'so I'm a thief too'. Before I could continue with my thoughts of what could I have stolen, the woman said, 'This means that you are stealing yourself away from something, some situation unwanted, some life experience that you don't want'. That was exactly what I was in the process of doing, and it was taking quite a lot of 'stealing away' as I became a freer and more whole and happy person. Wow! She was amazing.

Now she came to the future. She read that I was going to get married and have three children. I broke in and said that I had no boyfriend and was already 36 years old. She smiled and went on. I would get married and we would have three children, one boy and two girls. Although this seemed impossible, I felt lifted into happy wonderings. We would move out of the city, she said. We would never want – we would always have plenty; I wondered how. My life would be more and more satisfying. Gosh – it was all too wonderful, but too impossible.

I had learned much. For one thing psychics were not evil. I realised that mediums were probably not evil either. I had understood that I still needed to open my heart, mind and understanding, and not be closed to others' ways of being and thinking. I needed to get even further from my brainwashed state. It was all quite exciting. Had I not been penned up and isolated for years within a religious Bruderhof, I might not have been quite so naïve about life. We all have our individual paths to follow and now, as a free thinker, I know that I had chosen my path before I even came back here. In some ways I was more mature than some of my colleagues, while in other ways I was still very young.

I would love to meet that lady who was my psychic reader now and tell her how wonderfully my life unfolded, in much the way she had foretold. By the time these things came to pass I had forgotten about her.

When Derek rejoined me with his hands full of goodies and a smile on his face, I could chat with him about my experience and he opened up to me about his.

On a day off from work I was invited to visit some ex-Bruderhofer who lived in Didcot. They had managed to connect with quite a few ex-Bruderhof 'children' and when I got to their house I found I was in a room full of old friends from childhood. My cousin Roger was there, to my enormous delight. It was such a wonderful thing to be reunited with children I had grown up with. It was also very encouraging to realise that I was not the only one to be picked on and be sent away from friends and family by Brotherhood decree. At that moment it felt very good to be just one of the many. How Ursel and Reg Lacey ever found out where we all were I will never know. The Brotherhood had for many years put great effort into not giving us addresses and information as to where others were.

There were so many of us in the Laceys' living room that there was only standing room. The chatter was very animated and loud with loads of laughter sprinkled in.

It was here amongst this happy reunited crowd that over my shoulder I heard Jörg's name mentioned. I pricked my ears up and heard someone say that he was in Nigeria. If Jörg was in Nigeria, he was certainly not with the Bruderhof any longer. My heart started to race. I swirled around and asked Ursel if she knew how I could find an address for him. She advised me to phone his aunt and uncle, Wilhelm and Lini, who had been excommunicated from the Bruderhof and now lived in Winchcombe.

She produced their phone number before I left and I phoned that same evening. They said they didn't know where he lived but gave me the address of his brother Christoph, who lived in Sweden. Christoph answered my letter by return of post and included his phone number. I phoned him forthwith. He gave me an address in the USA and said that Jörg was only doing a drilling job out in Nigeria for a limited time with another of their brothers, Andy. All of these were people who had long ago been tipped out of the Bruderhof boat. Gradually we were finding one another!

I asked Christoph if he thought Jörg would be going back to the Bruderhof, as I knew that if he did this, I could not be with him. I also asked whether he thought Jörg would mind me contacting him. I knew the Bruderhof mentality too well, and if Jörg was still utterly brainwashed he would not want to leave them for good and might be more reserved about contact.

Reassured by Christoph, I wrote to Jörg at his USA address. Shortly after posting the letter I was off on my annual leave and left with my brother Michael for Brazil, to visit Nigel with his wife and children. We were the only three out of twelve siblings, at this time, not to be part of the Bruderhof (later one of my sisters also left). Life was becoming happily exciting.

I spent a wonderful four weeks in Brazil with two of my brothers and Leonice, Nigel's wife, with their two beautiful little daughters, Sheila, who was around four, and Jeanne, who was just about a year. This time was more wonderful than anyone could imagine. As family we had been forcibly separated for years it seemed, and now we were together, the bad apples who had been thrown off the cart, with the added beauty of the two little girls and Nigel's wife Leonice.

When we arrived on the 23rd of December, Nigel and Leonice had decorated a huge Christmas tree that stretched to the ceiling. Leonice had many wonderful Christmas goodies already baked and cooked and the house smelled wonderful. As it was the height of summer, Nigel set about making drinks for us, and he produced them whilst we sat around the dining room table chatting. The drink was called caipirinha, and it tasted so very good and thirst-quenching with its crushed ice and limes. I drank down one glass and started on the next and before I knew it I was swaying around in my head as if I was a feather drifting on the warm night air of Brazil. My naughty brother Nigel laughed and only then enlightened me on the content and strength of alcohol, now that he had safely seen my reaction. A little while later with some great food inside me I was fine, and able to enjoy another drink!

Christmas Eve was one enormous celebration with lots of wonderfully diverse food, fun and laughter. Whilst we were still eating and enjoying ourselves the house began to fill with friends and neighbours. Some hours later in the wee hours of the morning Nigel began to groan under his breath, and whispered to me that he detested this Brazilian habit of swarming into each other's houses on Christmas Eve. This gave me leave to be honest and tell him how much I agreed with him. I was thoroughly exhausted and almost claustrophobic with all these people filling every inch of space. Gradually they began to disappear, and we were just family again. By now it was early Christmas morning and we all toppled into bed for a few hours of much-desired sleep.

Leonice did us proud on Christmas Day with the most delicious fare anyone could imagine, and we sat under the Christmas tree and shared presents. It was absolutely delightful, especially watching the two little girls faces light up in delight, Jeanne over the wrapping paper and Sheila over the contents of the parcel being unwrapped. I was home, at long last!

After Christmas we stayed in a beach house for three weeks. This was Nigel's summer leave and Christmas holiday all rolled into one. Many people took this as a long holiday in Brazil, it being the height of summer and Christmas time, with schools closed.

It was the longest, laziest time I had ever experienced. It filled me with peace and I was in a blissful state the whole time. Little did I realise that this was to be the start of a long and wonderfully deep connection with this beloved land.

We spent much time on the beach, but we also took drives up into mountainous areas and to one special place up on top of what seemed to me a very high cliff. This place was one of Nigel's special places where he would go and watch the night sky whenever he was in that region. We lay down on the grass and with the southern night sky above us and the little town across the bay far below, I saw my first UFO or flying saucer. It was different from what I had seen years before in Paraguay, but was certainly a lovely and peace-giving sight. As we watched we saw more brightly-glowing objects that certainly were not stars, nor were they aeroplanes. They seemed further away than the first, but so lovely to watch. At other times, as we sat on the beach in the heat of the night, we could enjoy the constellations and planets of the southern hemisphere, and UFOs were not that unusual, as well as shooting stars. My heart's horizons were widening, and I could imagine that we were not the only forms of life in this great cosmos. All was pure wonder for me. My heart and mind were broadening, and this gave me much peace, joy and love within.

One night when my little nieces had gone to bed with their mother, Nigel, Michael and I sat on the beach in the moonlight. The moon seemed enormous and so very bright. It felt at once powerful yet peaceful as it shone on Mother Earth. We sat saying nothing, just sponging up the beauty. After a while Nigel said in a quiet voice that tonight there would be an earthquake. I asked what made him say this, as all was so clear and calm. The waves were gentle and low, and peace seemed to reign supreme under the light of the full moon. He explained something about the moon, indicating what power it had, which I didn't understand. I was somewhat awed.

As we slept that night, maybe because I was exhausted having stayed up so late, I never heard the wind or waves. Next morning as we rose we heard from a neighbour that there had been a quake out at sea and that several fishermen had been lost. Nigel tuned his radio in and listened. It was all too true. The family in the house a few yards from our holiday home, whom we had got to know fairly well, had lost their father and two sons in the night, as they made a living fishing. The boys were only around ten and twelve years old, and the father was the parent of ten other children; this left them and his wife, with no income whatsoever, to say nothing of the agony they endured going through such a heartbreaking loss. I seem to remember that Leonice shared food with this family and I remember feeling so very helpless, wanting to relieve their pain but absolutely unable to do so.

Not long after this we were on our way back to the Rimes' house near Blumenau. Michael had had to leave for England due to his shorter holiday, but I still had a few days of very happy, blessed times with my family in Brazil. What a blissful month this had been.

Back in England I turned the lock to enter my very cold flat in London and under my feet was a pile of post. I bent, picked up the post and ran upstairs to put some heating and the kettle on. Shuffling through the post I saw one in the familiar handwriting I had known so well from schooldays in Paraguay so long before – it must be from Jörg! And yes – it said so on the back! Cold and coffee forgotten, I opened the letter and started to read, savouring every word. He was so happy that I had found him, and now he knew where I was and we could meet. He wondered if I could take a vacation and travel to the States so we could meet up and talk. Of course that was not possible, having just used up my annual leave in Brazil. He had written about his circumstances. He had only left the Bruderhof a year or two before and was renting a house in a small town in Pennsylvania. He had a job as a mechanic. I was so very happy that we were now in touch, without a Brotherhood to censor anything we said, did or wrote. As I wondered about the possibility of a future together I suddenly started to get cold feet, wondering if he would feel anything for me, as I had more than likely changed enormously in the intervening years, twenty in all. Way back then I had been so attracted to Jörg. It hadn't been the passing crush that we get in our young years, but a secure feeling of love for him. I had never been told by a Servant of the Word that he loved me, but I could tell that he had some feeling for me, at least in a corner of his heart. Now after all this time might he be disappointed? Looking back, I realise that it never crossed my mind that I might no longer be attracted to him.

I wrote back, almost apologising, amongst my news, for the possibility that I could be very different from the girl he had known. From his reply he didn't seem to mind, or maybe he took change in me for granted. I had after all been twenty, and now I was forty!

A very short while after finding one another I received a phone call from Jörg suggesting that he should take time to come over to London to visit me, and asking if this would be all right. I was absolutely delighted. I realised through what he had said on the phone that he was what we would have to call 'poverty stricken'. The Bruderhof had put him out without a penny to his name, with no winter clothes, even though it was approaching the winter season when he was sent away, and he only was given enough money to tax and insure a beat-up little VW they had sent him off in. To do a mechanic's job in the USA in those days you had to buy all your own tools. So when he had finally found a job, he had to work at a loss until he had paid for the tools. He had to find some good winter clothing and of course with bills piling up and no bank account, he was in a very bad way. In addition, the man he was working went bust owing him six weeks' wages. So for months after leaving the Bruderhof, Jörg had eaten only chilli beans and had coffee to drink. He had gone to do the drilling job in Nigeria for a Swiss firm and had received my letter just as he returned from Nigeria, but the firm had put the money into his brother's account in Switzerland for safe keeping until Jörg could open an account in the USA. Prior to this he had lived from hand to mouth. Andy, his brother, working for the same firm, and wanting a good mechanic, had got Jörg on board to get him well away from the Bruderhof, so he had paid Jörg's fare to Nigeria.

Interestingly, it was only by slim chance that he had got my letter at all. A colleague of his had picked it up from the old abode they had shared together prior to Jörg's Nigeria venture and meant to give it to Jörg but kept forgetting it in his pick-up-truck. It took this guy three weeks to remember it and give it to Jörg. Now Jörg was suggesting he should visit me, saying that his boss had said that since he owed him money, he would at least pay the ticket to England and back.

Jörg had to phone me from a pay phone; not a great convenience! As I spoke to him I could hear coins clanking into the box every few seconds. We quickly arranged that he would arrive in a week's time. I was so excited and happy as I shared the whole story with my friend Leslie. She was wonderful, taking the place of a good friend and family all wrapped into one.

On the appointed day I scheduled myself off duty. I waited until the time arranged, but no Jörg arrived. Maybe his plane was late and he had missed his train connection. Leslie came to see how I was doing and she did well in keeping me from pacing up and down incessantly. We drank coffee, which is extremely silly when you're in a nerve-racking situation. The day came and the day went, and still Jörg didn't turn up. Leslie was back on duty, so I told myself that he would come when he could, although I wasn't really convinced.

The following morning I had scheduled myself an

early shift, so I was down in the children's home by six. I was able to go up to my flat after noon, and was pacing up and down getting really very up tight with no news from Jörg, when the front door bell rang. I ran downstairs, and when I looked through the fortified glass panel in the door, there was Jörg with the biggest, warmest smile wreathing his face that ever has been seen!

Realising that I had left my Yale key upstairs, I dashed up to get it, ran down again and within seconds the door was open and the old and real flame was right there within both of us. Immediately we were in each other's arms kissing and hugging. It was a supremely precious moment and meant very much more than anyone could possibly imagine. It was a love kiss, a victory kiss, a purely joyous kiss and a healing kiss, all of which reunited us without a word being spoken.

Later Jörg told me that when he saw my face and it vanished immediately, his heart did a somersault – he wondered for those seconds if I had taken a look at him and fled! But deep down I think he knew that wasn't so, because he was still smiling when I reappeared.

It had been twenty years since Jörg had asked me to marry him. He had, of course, not asked me, but had done the correct thing by the Brotherhood, and gone to the Servant of the Word saying he loved me, and could the Servant ask me if I felt the same. This man told him that he should wait for half a year and see how he felt then; 'test it' were his words. I felt at this time so much for Jörg. I felt very drawn to him in my heart and was hoping that one day we would get together. I didn't know that Jörg felt the same. Half a year went by and the Servant had said nothing to Jörg, so he approached this man again with the same question. This time the answer was that he had forgotten to ask me, but he said it was not all honey that shone from me, and Jörg should let go of the hope and idea of me being with him. This last conversation happened just as the American Brothers were about to arrive in Primavera from the USA and all was chaos in every sense of the word. It also happened just before I got left in the ghost village of the abandoned Ibate. A couple of months later I was to be sent to America myself, with Jörg following six months later.

Over the years Jörg and I had seen each other whenever I had been allowed onto a Bruderhof to see my family, as he was, as often as not, in the same Bruderhof village as they. I had even dared to tell those in authority how I felt about him, and the end result had been that I had been given a verbal dressing down and was shouted at so fiercely that I felt guilty for even thinking of Jörg. This time I was told that I was never going to be allowed to get married, that I should stay and be 'faithful' to the Bruderhof and be happy to work for the Kingdom, and accept that I was never to be part of the Brotherhood or get married. 'We will just carry you' – that's what is said many, many times over to someone who doesn't suit the Bruderhof.

Even though it had been twenty years since Jörg had first asked the Servant of the Word if he could marry me, even though we both were so much older and had had many experiences in very different worlds, we were still the same in our hearts. Jörg had stayed on the Bruderhof until just two years before our meeting up, and I had lived 'in the world' since I was 23; now I was 40. I think we were soulmates, and soulmates click and connect despite other people and what they think and do. Soulmates are soulmates before, through, and beyond Time.

So here we were back again with each other and absolutely shimmering with joy and love. I think that if anyone had seen the room we stood in they would have seen that it was lit up by our love. I was blissfully happy.

That day was the 13th of February. On the 14th we made our way into Peckham Rye and bought an engagement ring, with its promise to each other that come rain or shine we would walk life's walk together. We didn't actually know that the 14th was Valentine's Day. Nor did we have any idea how our life would pan out practically. At that moment we were blissfully happy and genuinely didn't care what happened to us in life and where our paths would lead.

It was lovely sharing our joy with the children I cared for. They really were infected by our happiness and celebrated by play-acting our wedding, with Andrew, aged twelve, performing the wedding ceremony and saying, 'I now proclaim you man and wife'.

I also lost all the anxiety that always preceded any contact with anyone on the Bruderhof. I phoned one of my brothers, who lived at the time on an English Bruderhof. When I told him Jörg and I were engaged, he said, 'How wonderful!' But then his tone changed and he became very flat and wary – he knew he wasn't being a good member of the Brotherhood by rejoicing over a traitor's happiness. He became the other kind of Brother.

Someone who had been with my parents at the time of our engagement told me that my mother's response was, 'Ah Chris, she's still doing her own thing. Why couldn't she and Jörg have done this with the Brotherhood and become engaged here?' This only went to show that even though my parents were part of the Brotherhood, they had no knowledge of what had happened to me through the years whilst still on a Bruderhof, which confirms that those who take authority over the rest are deceiving us all by saying 'We all sit on the same bench', 'We have all things in common' and 'We do everything in unity'.

Those cousins, aunts and uncles who had never been part of a cult or religious community were all so happy for us, and for me in particular. Jörg's relatives in Switzerland, Sweden and Paraguay were all very happy for us too, although Chris, Jörg's oldest brother, was worried that we had perhaps been a bit too hasty in becoming engaged, which was very understandable, but he became joyous when he later visited us.

Jörg and I enjoyed the following week together. There was much to talk regarding past, present and future. Trying to arrange our future was on the one hand so simple and easy, yet on the other, as we talked it through, it might be rather complicated. At first we almost took it for granted that I would move to the States. However once Jörg had seen me with the children I cared for, he said he felt uneasy and sad about me leaving these children, as they clearly saw me as a mother figure, and they would need time to get used to the idea of my going. I was glad for this insight. We decided that Jörg would go back to the States and close up anything that needed seeing to, then come back to England.

Looking back and knowing what a big deal most people make about moving to be with a loved one, even dropping one another 'because we live too far apart', I am amazed to be able to say that neither of us had the slightest worry or anxiety over what might or might not happen. Nor did we worry about losing our jobs, or what we would do in the future. We both had an incredible trust and, for me at least, a kind of knowing that all would be well.

A week after his arrival, Jörg returned to the USA. By now I had totally forgotten what the psychic had read for me; her insights had started, however, to become true. Life continued as ever in the children's home and I was quite happy, putting heart and soul into my work. On Jörg's departure I did have a slight niggle, and was vaguely worried that he could be tempted back to the Bruderhof once back in the USA. I knew how deep the Bruderhof brainwashing was for all of us, but for some it had even greater power in its confusion of the senses and sensibilities, of the emotions and heart-mind. Since Jörg had not been shown respect by others, let alone reverence as a person, he more than likely hadn't met himself yet. So would he come back to me? This was only a fleeting discomfort, because on a deeper level I knew he would.

We made arrangements over the ocean through the phone lines regarding our immediate future. Jörg would come back to England as soon as he could and move in with me into my flat. We would get married, and when he returned we would see to putting a wedding in motion.

Within a few weeks Jörg was to arrive back; he had given me the date over the phone. The day arrived and I was so happy, feeling strong and new, full of anticipation for the future. Then I received a phone call from a strange voice. He said he was calling from Heathrow airport and was I Christine Rimes? When I said I was, he told me he was an immigration officer, and had a Jörg Mathis with him; did I know this Mr. Mathis? I said that indeed I did, telling him the story of our engagement and that we were soon going to get married. We were both entirely ignorant of the proper procedures of immigration in our situation, and hadn't even thought of the implications of just 'turning up'. We had no roots —the whole world was ours!

Thankfully the officer was delighted to tell me that Jörg had told him almost in the same words what I had just said, so he was going to let Jörg go with one condition – that he did not start to work until we were married. He would have to go to the Home Office and get the correct paperwork for him to start work.

I was glad that he was now safely on his way to me. Jörg arrived well and happy and with his return we had another celebration.

I had previously become very well acquainted with the pastor in my friend Sina's church. In trying to deal with the very strong antipathy I now felt towards anything remotely religious, I had challenged this pastor on various ideas and practices of the Christian Church. He was such a lovely, kind and open man; indeed he seemed to agree with all I said in my chats with him. He hadn't 'excluded' me for daring to disagree with his Church!

We had become friendly with a bunch of others who also attended. They were all praising the Pastor to such a high degree that he could not do wrong in their eyes. It was always 'The pastor says this, he is wonderful, and we should all do the same.' Although I had come to love this pastor as a person, it was quite repulsive to hear how he was put on a pedestal and revered in such an over-the-top way. I saw the dangers. People were losing themselves to him, yet he was the innocent one in this. They were learning not to think and take note of their own intuitions, as if they had no minds of their own. They were becoming like sheep, and unknown to the pastor, they were putting a heavier and heavier burden on him. It seemed that they were relying on the pastor for their very path in life and not taking responsibility, but leaving it to him. It could get to the point where, if the pastor ever said something disagreeable to them, they could blame him for everything, and as I have witnessed before, getting rid of him with nowhere for him to go. If a person doesn't take responsibility for themselves but puts all onto another, then it can turn upon that person.

I shared with the pastor my unhappiness that a large part of the congregation was putting him, his wife and children into this lofty position in their minds and I found this tribal attitude quite uncomfortable. He was very disquieted with the notion that he could be seen as perfect while others would not have their own opinions and thus put themselves below him. The following Sunday he addressed this issue and made it clear that this was not what his vision of God's Kingdom was.

Since we belonged to no church but had it in our heads to be married in one, we went to the pastor to ask his advice and see if he would marry us. To our amazement he joyfully agreed. We talked and shared quite freely, as Jörg felt as free as I had done with this man, who seemed not there to judge us, but to help with such love and kindness that we couldn't help but feel relaxed. We shared some of our background with him. I remember saying to him that the Bruderhof church leaders had refused to let us marry, and although we didn't know their reasons I would understand if he didn't want to marry us. I saw a shadow come over his face, and briefly hoped it wasn't anger towards us. At this point in my life I still imagined I was in the wrong in any disputes, and soon I might find out what it was that was wrong about me, when I came to the crash.

The pastor looked angry, but then the sun came out and shone brightly from his face and he said that he would be very happy to marry us. Looking back, I believe he felt angry that we had been manipulated and controlled in such a big and personal way by other pastors and their church, so that we had spent twenty years on hold, and in a kind of desert. We had had some fierce decisions to make; either we could have gone back to the Bruderhof, confessed our 'sins' and then 'if God gave it' get married, or we had had the option of following our hearts, not going back, getting married and then be separated from our families, our parents and siblings. Since I had been separated for so long anyway, I guess it was easier for me to grasp this fact than for Jörg. Whatever our unconscious minds knew over this matter, our consciousness had not caught up, for now we were both so happy; life was wonderful and we would get married with no worries about the Bruderhof or our families.

Six weeks and a day after we had become engaged, we were married. We had no idea what needed to be done in preparation for a wedding. We had ordered no flowers and no photographer, and but for the love and wonderful kindness of my uncle and aunt, Basil and Stella, we would not have had a reception either. As it happened, a kind man from the Church took photos of our wedding day, and one of the Church members had decked the place out with a mass of yellow and golden daffodils. It was absolutely glorious.

During the ceremony there were only a few seconds when I did hold my breath. This was when the Pastor said that if anyone had a reason for us not to get married they should say so – now! I was shrivelling up inside, in case Jörg came up with a reason for not getting married, knowing how incredibly brainwashed folks on the Bruderhof were, and that he had known no other way of life until a couple of years previously, when he had been turfed out. Was he going to get sudden false guilty-conscience pangs, and remember that we were not worthy of being married, as several

Servants of the Word had reminded us on a number of assorted occasions throughout our Bruderhof lives? Indeed, Jörg had been told this on more occasions than me. But all was well and he didn't murmur a word, and nor did anyone else.

The reception we were given in our aunt and uncle's house was absolutely wonderful. Such happiness and love flowed throughout; it was tangible, you could not mistake the love-filled energy that flowed. My cousin Isabel and Aunt Stella had done all the cooking themselves, including the wedding cake. Their home was also decked out with glorious daffodils, giving happiness to the soul with their scent and brightness. Not all who had attended the wedding ceremony could be there at the reception as we could only fit 45 people into the house, but all those who came seemed to glow with happiness. It had been a day of blissful joy.

Even though we had told our Bruderhof families about our wedding we didn't receive a single card, letter, or loving congratulations from them for the day, and certainly no phone call. Looking back it seems inconceivable that the Bruderhof Church can afford such coldness, such unforgiving judge-mentality, such arrogance regarding their belief in 'clear love', saying that they act in this way out of their desire to follow

Jesus ('we want to put Jesus first'), therefore it would be 'emotional love' to put family into the equation. Being 'emotional' is quite some sin to them!

To this day it remains the same. Recently I heard that two of my sisters had been quite ill. I managed to get a message and a gift to the one of them and she responded in a real and genuine way. When I tried to phone the other, I was told by the telephonist that she was away in town and would call me when she got back. I didn't hear from her. I phoned again and again and again, each time being told the same thing; she was always in town and would call me back. I still don't know whether this sister is all right, better, or whether she has an incurable disease. Her husband has been one of the worst at keeping me from my family. Often whilst my mother was still alive he would prevent us from speaking to her when we tried to phone. One time, with our three children on the line as well as Jörg and me, whilst on a trip in the USA, he cut us off when we had managed to get through to Mummy. Our three children, aged eleven and the two younger ones eight, wept bitterly. This brother-in-law of mine said that Mummy didn't want to speak to us. Some years later his own daughter, who had left the Bruderhof by then and had been caring for Mummy in her old age whilst still on the Bruderhof, told me that my mother kept saying to her 'I don't know why the Brothers don't want me to contact Jörg and Chris and their family.' Other such remarks from my mother showed that she was being prevented by those in authority; it was not true at all that she didn't want to be in contact, hear us or see us.

We could not have a honeymoon straight away as I had already used up too much holiday time. Back at work we made our home in my flat and I continued in my job whilst Jörg sought employment. Very soon he was taken on as a mechanic for a company with a fleet of vans. We settled in for an indefinite time to our jobs and our little home in London. We became the proud owners of a new bed and a pinewood table and two benches to go with it. Other furniture was second-hand from the children's home.

Time crept on, and in June we could afford to take time out for our honeymoon. We headed for Switzerland as we were keen to visit all of Jörg's cousins, uncles and aunts, and his youngest brother Andy, to all of whom we had free and normal access as they were not part of a Bruderhof, and more importantly, they were 'normal' in their kindness and love towards us, their relatives. Jörg's parents hailed from the Romansch part of Switzerland, so we headed for the mountains and his uncle's home in a village near San Moritz called Celerina.

Whilst still in the valley we went to a Migros superstore to buy some provisions. Along with other foods, we bought some Swiss cheeses from the 'sale' basket. When eventually we arrived at Uncle Giovanni's House (he was at the time in hospital) we had started to unpack when a horrendous stench greeted us. We quickly found out that it was the aroma of a certain cheese we had bought. That was no doubt why we had found it in the 'sale' basket! So vile was the smell that Jörg put the cheese out on the veranda for the night in the fresh air. I couldn't stomach the smell next day, so Jörg ate it, nibble by nibble, whenever he vanished onto the veranda for a look at the view, and a cosy moment with a cigarette!

I had been so looking forward to this holiday and had enjoyed every moment until, on the last lap of the journey as we had ascended a mountain in a little train, I had the sad experience of losing the hoped-for little life that had started growing within me. We were both so hoping for a baby and despite my age I had conceived. It was all so amazing and wonderful, although I had told no friends or family as yet, and now my joy was dashed in a moment. The depth of sadness is so great in such an event, that I have no words to describe my feelings. I just sobbed. Jörg was so loving and supportive, but at the moment I still felt bereft. However, the following day as I took in the beauty and peace of mother earth I began to heal very quickly. There was still a chance for us to have children, and now I would enjoy this time with Jörg in Switzerland with his relations. It turned out to be a very blessed time as we enjoyed the majesty of the mountains, in fact the beauty of Planet Earth from this different perspective. I also learned to enjoy Swiss cheese and to this day I love it! It is second to none – on second thoughts I should say, apart from good old English mature cheddar!

Every day was special. We were taken by a friend, Migg Fischli, to the top of a mountain, which was a wonderful experience in itself. Migg was a 'reject' of the Bruderhof, and had known Jörg's parents for years before even joining. As a Brother on the Bruderhof, Migg had been quite severe, even nasty at times towards us children. He did let his true kindness through occasionally, which was then very sunny and free; more often he had been harsh though. He and wife Hilde had a big family, all around the same ages as me and my brothers and sisters.

Migg had known my father in Paraguay, as he had Jörg's, and all three had been good friends, as far as friendship can go on the Bruderhof (one can never afford to get too happy in friendships there, as it always gets pounced on by those in authority – friendship is not 'clear love' so it is looked upon with suspicion). So I had known Migg as a child, and now he had become a free and very happy and friendly man. Here we were years later on our way up to the greatest height. We were very hot, as it was summer. There were such beautiful blossoms to be enjoyed, crystal-clear blue skies and the cow bells ringing from down in the valleys and dells, also herds of goats to be seen. Gradually as we ascended it became brighter and brighter until we had reached the snow level, which was amazing to me. The sun shone purely and brightly.

Eventually we found ourselves in a restaurant, very high up and surrounded by snow with people sunbathing, some even in bikinis, on the verandas of a hotel restaurant. I stood there in amazement and felt as if I had truly left my prison of yore and was flying free. To find people and the rest of nature so relaxed and at peace, as one, was a very precious experience for me. The freedom of the folks wearing bikinis was no small part of this freshly-found joy. Back on the Bruderhof Migg would have swept us rapidly away on encountering people dressed in an 'unseemly' way by showing too much flesh. Maybe this is why it hit me so at this point, but it was a great sensation of freedom and love that swept over me. It was all the total opposite to the life Jörg and I had known when last we had been in each other's company prior to the wonder of finding one another again. And here we were with Migg, a freed man too. His freedom enabled him to be true to himself, the genuine soul he was meant to be, with a compassion he had barely displayed whilst a Brother on the Bruderhof

We stayed a while with Migg and Hilda before getting on a boat and travelling over to the other side of Lake Zurich to visit Andy and Erika, Jörg's brother and sister-in-law. Andy was a free spirit and fun to spend time with. It was a great release for us to be able to speak with our own truth about the Bruderhof and not feel any guilt. (Andy had been pitched out from the Bruderhof as a very young teenager.) Andy shared with us the 'naughty' things he had got into when first pitched out from the Bruderhof – he gave us much to laugh about. Once he had hitched up walkie-talkies in the women's toilets that were placed in a park. One gadget was placed under the seat of a toilet, while he took the other away behind a tree. When he saw a woman enter he gave her time to sit down, then said through the walkie talkie, 'Please move over a little, I am trying to paint down here' From his hiding place he saw the woman dash out still dressing herself! He hadn't used this trick on only one innocent soul either! This is how his mental, spiritual, moral oppression on the Bruderhof had left him. We enjoyed Freedom in sharing together.

This we had also managed with Migg and Hilda, and it helped us much on our journey towards healing, a new kind of healing, where we allowed ourselves to express negative feeling towards the Bruderhof experience, instead of denying those feelings to ourselves. In retrospect it was only the beginning of a long journey we were to make in coming face to face with our own gremlins and owning our own truths, thus being able to accept and love ourselves sincerely. It was a very happy time though, as we were living in the moment for much of our holiday.

We met all Jörg's cousins, which was a great treat. Rudi, Gianni, Emerita and Evelina Mathis all became very dear to me. They and all their spouses and children were so perfectly welcoming, loving, and accepting of us. I was simply amazed by that. One day with Gianni we went from mountain peak to mountain peak in what seemed like a glass box travelling on a string! Even at those heights there was a stop-off place for refreshments; amazing; but more amazing was that thanks to Gianni's love and kindness, I was able to enjoy, without panic, every moment of that trip. In my experience total love casts out fear, and his love, together with Jörg's, made it impossible for panic to get in as we flew across valleys at such a height. The majesty of those mountains and the fact that we were soaring above them really took my breath away.

Before returning to England we met Jörg's Uncle Giovannes, his father's younger brother, who went out with us for the day in his wheelchair. He became very dear to my heart, and the closest I would ever get to Jörg's father Peter, who had died long before we found each other again. Peter was a lovely gentle man in his spirit and actions, and genuinely humble. He was extremely elegant in looks and spirit too, almost regal. He had very black hair and beard, swarthy skin and a distinctive Roman nose. There were not too many grown-ups I could feel at ease with as a child, but he had been one.

Back in London we were both in work and beginning to build our lives together. Being a country child I never did take kindly to living in London, and as I sit here writing I am more than grateful that life took us away from that great disharmonious city. By now I had become second in command of the children's home I worked in. This was not difficult in any way where the children were concerned. Although they all came from disadvantaged backgrounds and had landed in this particular home because no other had 'managed' them, in fact they were all close to my heart. I got on well with the staff, and life was happy, generally speaking.

Despite our love for each other, our first year of marriage had its difficult moments. This was largely due to the trauma Jörg had experienced on the Bruderhof; he would get very angry telling me about it, and would sit and simmer, brooding in his mind over many different and deeply disturbing situations and the treatment he had experienced from others on the Bruderhof over many years. He had been grossly abused, physically, mentally and spiritually. As he related various stories to me regarding the abuse, it would trigger off the panic I had often suffered there. Sometimes this became useful to both of us, as we were able to discover answers to things we had never understood before. For instance, Jörg was relating an incident where a Servant of the Word had concluded a diatribe at Jörg (it was supposed to be a dialogue) by screaming at Jörg in an accusatory manner, 'All you see is naked women!' Jörg had no idea what this person was referring to, or why he had been so angry. Worst of all, Jörg had thought that he alone must be an 'evil' person and that since he couldn't understand what this man was saying, it meant that he must be brain impaired on top of it!

I was really surprised at what Jörg told me, because this same man had shouted the very same words to me when I was young. At the time I had not the faintest idea why someone should talk like this to me. I just accepted that although this Servant seemed really sick with anger, I must be a very bad person. When you get a lot of this kind of treatment under the canopy of religion, you tend to become brainwashed with the thought that you are to blame for everything that goes wrong. As for the 'naked women', it would have been impossible. Young women were kept well out of the way of young men where accommodation was concerned. In fact we all had rooms on the third floor of a building and the young men were mostly housed in a cabin in the wood, or in a house up on a hill on the edge of the community. It helped us both to know that we had not been alone in this mad kind of treatment. We concluded that it could be this particular Minister's issue, and given the Brotherhood's take on 'purity' versus 'sex', well maybe he in his fear could have been needing to blame someone else for his own perceived 'sin'.

Jörg had also had to account for every deed, thought and reaction to everything in life, with the result that if I asked him any question his immediate reaction was that I was criticizing him. Or he would give long explanations for whatever he said or did as if he needed to defend himself. In years gone by I had caught myself doing the same thing, and noticed that others never acted this way, so I had trained myself to become aware of this need to be highly defended, and free myself from it.

The Bruderhof religion taught that we should confess every evil thought to rid ourselves of them. This would then be followed with some smaller or greater degree of church discipline. This still affected Jörg's nerves in a powerfully raw way. He had been the underdog for a large part of his life, and it was hard to know how to handle freedom and find self-respect. Because I had been through the same emotional and psychological pain, I could absolutely grasp where he was at, but I didn't know how to help him. Mostly it is a slow and long process to reach one's own truth, to allow that truth, and to find self-respect and self-love, and I still had a way to go. I now know this as I look back.

Our joy and happiness outweighed our downs though. We had a wonderful time going to musicals, enjoying hours in the cinema and finding the green areas of London to satisfy our need of nature and the land, whenever we had a day off together. When I was not working weekends we would travel to see various friends and relatives, a joy that had been denied us on the Bruderhof. Many of my relatives and one of Jörg's uncles and aunts lived in Gloucestershire with their many children, so we enjoyed immensely getting to know this area and learned to love the Cotswolds in particular. Jörg's uncle and aunt were very welcoming and afforded us the time to unburden ourselves over our many issues and what had happened to us whilst living on the Bruderhof. Lini and Wilhelm had been members of the Bruderhof and had been sent away in 'church discipline' with all their children some twenty years prior to us visiting for the first time as a couple. They had never wanted to go back, in particular as Wilhelm was very disturbed by the attitude of *'Verbrechen an Jugendlichen'* (criminal actions against young people). He felt very clear about this, also knowing that he had been part of the system before he left. They were fun to be with, but it was also very cathartic for us to speak freely with them without condemnation being thrown our way.

Jörg was now very happy and in a solid job that was beginning to be much more lucrative than he had imagined. However I was now feeling the need to get out of London for various reasons. It wasn't just a need to leave the city life, but something I had had my suspicions over for some while within the children's home. Then evidence was pushed under my nose that I could not ignore. I had sensed that a couple of the male staff members were abusing some of the children. Prior to this we had had to let another male staff member go because he was abusing the younger boys. Apparently the law had not been involved.

One day when I was on late evening duty I found a ten-year-old girl crying in bed and her room-mate white with fear and close to tears. Susanna told me in a rush of frantic tears what had happened this evening, and said it had been going on for ages. She said she hated this particular staff member, and was sick with worry whenever he was on duty. Now the other child joined in and as she was new in the home I could see that she was feeling very insecure indeed. Each evening, just before going off duty we were to write down a brief report of anything of import that had transpired on our shift. There was nothing for it but to be honest. I didn't doubt the children one bit, and it tallied with remarks other children had been overheard saying. I wrote my report, put it in the Cardex and went in search of the member of staff who had been accused by this child of sexual abuse. I was absolutely honest with him and told him I understood what this would mean. He was very angry, but I couldn't pretend I hadn't been advised by these two children of what was going on.

Next day when the borough headquarters opened I phoned the two people responsible for children's homes in the area. By now the children had found the courage to speak up about the other member of staff to me. As I phoned I found I had my heart in my mouth, but I realised the absolute need for those in authority over me to take responsible action. They came to speak to me and tried to get me to say that I was mistaken. I was utterly shocked when I realised over a longer discussion that they were going to do their level best to cover this all up. This made me feel very angry, yet I was able to keep calm as I told them calmly that it couldn't be covered up.

A few days later they came to speak to me again. They tried again to talk me down and out. By now they were saying that if I didn't recant, they would sack me. However, now I knew that abuse had been going on from three members of staff, with two of them at least for years, within positions they had held in other homes.

I went home and told Jörg about it. He was quite disgusted and not a little angry. From now on we were in a very difficult position, as the people from headquarters were making my life very difficult indeed. I was the Deputy Head and as the Head was rarely there I needed to keep the home running smoothly. The other member of staff implicated in the abusive behaviour was in fact really gifted in many ways, which made it harder still to stick to the truth, but I couldn't betray the children just to keep my job.

Jörg and I decided to move away before I could be sacked. We looked around for jobs and Jörg found something we hoped would last for a long time, which was going into business with a friend in the car repair industry in North Wales. Up there the houses were also more affordable, so we moved to our first house on the edge of the village of Cefn Mawr, taking Susana with us, with the permission of course, of the Foster Care Society. I found a job in a nursery school in Wrexham.

Many years after our move, I received a call from the police. Three of the children, now grown adults in their thirties, had arrived at three different police stations complaining about their experience in the children's home I had worked at in London. The officer wanted me to give evidence at the Crown Court in London, adding in a kindly voice that if I didn't want to, I would be subpoenaed. I answered all the questions they put to me, giving the names of all the staff who had been working at the time. The police told me that they had contacted them all, and each had said they knew nothing about what had been going on or any abuse. This was a huge shock to me, as some of them had been very uneasy regarding these three staff members, and had indeed spoken in quiet voices about them. I was shocked at the length perfectly normal and balanced human beings would go to keep their own lives safe and unruffled. I felt betrayed, and deeply hurt on behalf of the children.

After a very long time, after the police had put their case together, I found myself in London giving evidence on behalf of the children. They were found to be telling the truth and what's more, some of them received compensation money so that they could start to build their lives back.

Where I was concerned, this was a very helpful and cathartic exercise for me to be going through. I was terrified at the thought of standing in the witness box in court an ordeal which turned out to last 1 hour and 15 minutes, to speak the truth on behalf of other human beings and against three people that I had worked with and trusted. But instead of being cowed and bent before those people, one of whom had been my boss, I had to do the opposite and stand no matter what. I couldn't allow myself to be manipulated and crushed. The barrister who worked on behalf of the three men said some things to me that were outrageous, childishly untrue and as I saw, unconscionable. He was clearly bending the truth big time. I didn't know the rules of the court requiring one to say just 'yes' or 'no' to questions, and at one point I burst out to the barrister for the accused, 'you are just lying and you know you are!' Although this was out of order, no one said a word – you could have heard a feather drop. I had learned a big lesson; that it's OK to stand up for yourself and what you see as the truth.

Money can't heal on its own, so I hope that these precious beings, for that they are, have found the healing they needed to become rounded and secure citizens – who knows? The three men were found guilty and the children's faces, now young men and women, showed visibly that they were freed up.

CHAPTER 13

A gift from God

After two years Susanna was called back to London to live with her natural mother, and we started on the route towards adoption. Whilst still in London I had visited a doctor in Harley Street, because the NHS were very unfriendly and unhelpful to couples who were forty or over wanting children and finding it hard to conceive. In fact one doctor had very rudely and hurtfully taken me by the shoulders and literally pushed me back out of his door! But Doctor Jack, working at his Harley Street office, had been wonderful to us and had talked things through with kindness and honour. As I was about to leave one day he slipped a newspaper cutting into my hand, and when I got home I shared it with Jörg. It was about couples who went to third world countries to adopt. It suggested that this had come about due to the difficulties our own country made over adopting children. We applied and eventually received permission to adopt in the UK, but before this could be fully approved the adoption board had to give all the relevant documents they had gathered to the county doctor for his approval.

Eventually our social worker came back and almost shamefacedly told us we had not been approved by this doctor, although we had been told just prior to visiting him that we had been approved. Some instinct told me immediately that this had to do with the Bruderhof doctor, who was a member of the Bruderhof. Jörg was furious and I remember he thumped the table with his fist, making her jump, along with all the cups on the table. He told her that we were done with the British Social Services and would go back to South America on our quest.

I was seething inside too, and straight afterwards we visited our solicitor. We asked him if he could get all the papers from our doctor's surgery, telling him what had happened. We guessed that with our British system the Bruderhof doctor's papers had followed us from one country to another – very useful in most situations, but not in our case. The Bruderhof doctor often visited the Bruderhof in England and buddied up with the doctor the English Bruderhof used from the NHS.

A week later our solicitor called us to his office and gave us all our notes. Sure enough there was a lengthy letter written about myself to the English medical contacts. In short it said that I was a hypochondriac, and that nothing I might complain about could be taken as truth. I had been away from the Bruderhof for years, yet this had followed me! I had been scorned years before by these Bruderhof medical staff, and had not been taken seriously. Now for years I had simply not visited a doctor for anything apart from the issue of trying for a baby. In fact I had had no need to visit for any other reason because all my physical troubles had subsided and then vanished with my leaving the Bruderhof. Whilst still living there, I had had constant back pain, and often felt very nauseated, with frequent headaches; I constantly needed to push myself to keep going throughout the day, no matter what. This was all very much related to my struggle and difficulty of living on the Bruderhof and constantly being told that I was nothing, a nobody, and that I should be seen but not heard. I would sometimes not attend communal meetings or meals due to fear which brought on panic attacks. These attacks had made me feel very afraid of being in the public eye, so to speak. It was this that the Bruderhof doctor was talking about. I would be confronted and asked why I had missed this and that communal event and my answer invariably had been that I didn't feel well. In fact I now know that it was fear; I would be tensed up and anxious much of the time, which of course had a physical impact on my body and made me feel very unwell.

Now years later this letter had brought the same Bruderhof attitude in to my life again over our wish to adopt a baby. We had known our solicitor for some time, and he had become a friend over similar interests in life. He now consented to take the infamous letter out of the file and rip it up. My medical forms were sent back to our surgery minus this letter.

It was now the right moment to take out the newspaper cutting given to me by Dr. Jack in London. We felt really keen to follow the route of going to South America to adopt a little baby. It would be either Paraguay or Brazil, but which? We kept very tight lips over what we were about to do; we couldn't afford anyone throwing a spanner in the works. We needed all our resolve, love and single-mindedness, without anyone putting spokes in the wheels.

We chose Brazil. We both had family and friends

out there, and felt confident and safe in our choice. We also knew that the Brazilian judges do not ask for adoptive parents to pay them, whereas in Paraguay it could turn into thousands of pounds.

It took us nine months to prepare. We needed to get medical documents, three references, one from a social worker, which could prove tricky. Most social workers wouldn't contemplate helping us in our quest. We also had to get evidence of our financial state and have a home study done. A police report was also on the list. For the social worker's report we asked a friend who had all the credentials, and although not working at the time, she could put all the correct stamps on what she wrote. After collecting the paperwork together we had to get it legally translated into Portuguese.

It is hard to find the words for how we both felt. It was so wonderful to do something on our own, without Big Brother looking on or indeed having anything to do with it. We were both highly sensitive to social services being involved as they came with the same flavour as the Brotherhood on the Bruderhof. Our freedom was very precious to us, so being controlled in any way was difficult to stomach, be the control physical, mental, psychological or spiritual. We had learned that because the Brazilian adoption law didn't tally with British law at the time, there was nothing

Britain could do to stop us bringing a baby back from Brazil. This suited us very well and gave the whole venture a sense of happiness and freedom. Sadly for those coming after us, things have tightened up since then.

We were asked to take photos of house and garden along with us. We were not very solvent and lived in a little three-bedroom semi. To help the Brazilian authorities feel more positive towards us we borrowed a decent car, a better make than ours, from a friend as ours looked rather dilapidated, and we parked both cars out front, thereby giving the impression of a two-car family, should they really take much notice of the photos! I think that is the closest either of us have ever got to swindling anyone!

The preparations for our baby strengthened my capabilities, desire, love and happiness so much that when I was at last ready to book my ticket to Brazil I was riding high and felt safe. I felt as if I was cocooned in a bubble of love. I had absolutely no doubts, even though I was sailing into completely unknown territory. I had to go alone as we couldn't afford for Jörg to lose his wage. This would not just be a week's holiday, or even two – it might take longer.

The one sure thing about my journey was that a couple by the names of Roger and Nora Allaine, who lived in Brazil, had invited me to stay in their house for the duration. They had taken all their children and left Primavera during the 'clearing' and 'cleansing' and upheaval that we all had experienced. In their case, unusually, I understand they had gone of their own volition, because they were so unhappy with the Brotherhood life. From Paraguay they had eventually gone to Brazil to make a new life for themselves. My brother Nigel was great friends with them, but he lived in the wrong area for adoption proceedings. We had been in contact with Roger and Nora for some years and had shared with them our resolve to adopt a baby. They had asked their children for help where accommodation was concerned.

Finally the day was upon us for my departure and Jörg took me to Manchester Airport. I said goodbye to him for an unknown period of time, but I held him very close in my heart as I needed him there to give me the courage, love and the strength I needed for my journey. It was October 8th. We left home at five in the morning and having given each other a final hug and kiss goodbye, the KLM flight took off at 9 am on its way to Holland first; from there I would board another plane to South America.

On landing in Amsterdam I was met by Bette, a friend of ours whom we had not seen for years; she too had been turfed out of the Bruderhof long before. She was now married and lived in Holland. She was such fun to spend time with, and took me to visit her parents-in-law, then on to see the sights and have a meal together. Towards evening we went back to the airport, said goodbye to each other and I took off to continue the journey to Brazil at 10:30 at night. Finally, after a journey of almost twenty-four hours, we landed in Sao Paulo. Once through customs I was met by Roger and Nora – what a relief. From here on I wouldn't be alone.

On our way to their house, 'Innisfree' near Vinhedo, we talked non-stop. We had known each other and lived next to each other way back in Ibate, Paraguay. They were my parents' age and Roger, a Frenchman, had been one of our teachers back then. As a child I had been afraid of them, but they were much nicer, freer and happier now that they were no longer tied to the Bruderhof.

It was simply remarkable that we could meet again in such wonderful freedom and find that we could be totally relaxed in each other's company, and indeed really treasure each other. I had been at school with several of Roger and Nora's children and they had said they would try to help me with my search for a baby. Francisco, one son, lived in Vinhedo, and Jacques, another, in Sao Paulo. I met them, as well as Betty and Jeanne Pierre, more of the family I had been at school with. For about four days I stayed at Allaine's house while Roger did some investigation with a social worker friend of his regarding adoption. He came up with nothing helpful, and he and the social worker said I needed to be in Sao Paulo to be able to fulfil my desire. We went to see Ebo, another of their sons, in his summer house at the seaside in Ubatuba, and Roger told me that he intended to ask Jacques if I could stay with him and his wife and two little boys as they lived in Sao Paulo.

It seemed like the whole family had gathered in Ubatuba, and we had a great time in and out of the ocean, eating and drinking and laughing fit to cure all our ills. One of the family owned a boat, and we took some trips out on it and spent much time jumping from it into the warm ocean. All this was not getting me anywhere in my search, but I was the guest and couldn't be pushing the family for what I wanted.

After this wonderful weekend I went with Jacques and his wife Monika back to their Home in Sao Paulo. The house was enormous and had a huge courtyard in the centre with all the rooms around it in a big square. Jacques and Monika lived there with their two little boys and a live-in maid who had a baby boy. Monika was a wonderful help to me in more ways than one. By profession she was a psychotherapist and working privately. She took time out to visit various mother and baby units/places/houses with me. Sadly they were all government owned, and although there were so many tiny babies who needed the love of a mother and father, they would not easily give the babies up as they were being paid per capita and the money meant more to those in charge than finding security and love for these tiny little new souls. What's more, they were guarded by police with guns all around the perimeter of these large buildings, so you could never just go and find the director but were blocked at every step. Once permission was granted to enter the building and have a talk with the Director, we were put under guard until she arrived. At that time in Brazil, children from children's homes would be sent away from the guardianship of a home at the age of ten. These little ones would end up taking care of themselves on the streets when they turned ten, so it was even more shocking that the directors would make it so impossible to adopt a baby.

Whilst we sat in a second-floor room, waiting under lock and key for the Director to arrive, I looked out of the window and down into the courtyard below. On a long, raised stone wall lay a row of babies, all swaddled up and being fed two at a time by a nurse. Some she would prop the bottle up for, then walk away and leave them. It was nearing summer and very hot indeed. These babies just lay in the scalding hot sun with no protection. I was appalled. It made me sick at heart to see this.

When the Director arrived, Monika translated for me as I explained what I was in Brazil for. From Monika's body language and tone I could tell that she was adding to what I had said. I could also understand that this woman was answering in the negative.

When we left we passed a large group of little ones who were just about walking. They were just toddling along with absolutely nothing to do or look forward to. I could see no adult caring for them. There would be no loving arms around them at the end of the day – there were just too many of them, even for a warm-hearted worker, to find time for. That picture haunted me for a very long time.

Time went on and we were getting nowhere, and one day I sat alone in my bedroom in meditation. Even Rosangela, the maid, was out with her little boy. I had spent much time with her and I had helped her in the house, and she had helped me with sewing for my baby. I had brought no clothes from England for a baby! As I sat quietly I sort of spaced out and suddenly

I seemed to hear the words *'go to the Salvation Army, they will help you find your baby'*. I could actually hear a voice and feel a presence. I felt that I was in a bubble of love; I felt very secure and all my worries about what to do had vanished. It was deeply peaceful being in this space, and I hung around in it for some while.

Then I heard the door go in the outside courtyard, and jumped up to see Monika. I was at her side before I could blink and I heard myself say 'Monika, we have to go to the Salvation Army!'

She looked somewhat shocked, but she was willing to drive me to the nearest Salvation Army House. I found a number and phoned and to my delight a man answered who spoke English. His name was Don Hennessey and he was a New Zealander. I asked him if I could visit him, only briefly mentioning my mission. When I arrived by taxi he was waiting with his wife, Lorna. That meeting was one of pure delight and love. He and his wife were the Commanding Officers of the area of the State of Sao Paulo, a vast area. They had a children's home, and a mother and baby home amongst other places, such as homes for elderly, places of further education for older children, soup kitchens, places of worship – so much under their care and supervision. I was glad and humbled that they would take time out for me. They listened to my story with honest and open hearts; you could actually feel the love oozing from them. I found myself telling them my life story with great ease, not trying to hide anything as I had done before with other people, out of shame.

Don said that they could not promise anything but that they would definitely help if they could. We had coffee and cake, and as I said goodbye my heart told me that I was on the right road at last. My happiness just overflowed!

It wasn't that long before Lorna phoned me saying that a baby was to be been born, but that it was an unusual situation for them. She explained that they normally were there for the poor people and that mothers came to their mother and baby home very early in their pregnancy so that they could eat good food, have proper shelter and medical care when needed. In return the mothers would run the home and do the cleaning, cooking and care for the little children that sometimes lived there. This was all supervised by a Salvation Army officer. Now a young mother had come to them from a wealthy home and said she couldn't keep her baby when it was born because she was a university student and would not be allowed to continue to study if she had a baby. In addition her mother was seriously ill, and she couldn't let her know of her pregnancy. This girl had refused to move into the mother and baby home, but the Salvation Army had thought to help her anyway. The baby had been born, like all the others, at the charity hospital nearby, and if there was no one to care for her she would be brought straight back to the Salvation Army home until someone was found for her.

Lorna phoned me and asked me if I would like to go straight to the Charity Hospital, because a baby girl had been born and the mother would like me to adopt her. I went and a Sister (the place was Catholic) handed me this newborn baby just outside the front door. I looked at this tiny bundle of humanity and saw that she was very perfect, a beautiful baby. I was overjoyed, yet felt a pang of pain in my heart. I cradled her for a long time beneath the beautiful, majestic trees that grew around the front of the hospital, and then took a cab back to Jacques and Monika's house.

But somehow I did not feel as joyous as I had expected. I had a distinct feeling that this was not my baby. I gave her all my love, but there was no bonding. This disturbed me silently. I felt as if this little girl was telling me she didn't belong to me.

When she was about four days old, there was another phone call from Lorna. This time it was a sad voice I heard at the other end. She explained that the mother's father had been home when she had gone to visit her parents for the first time after the birth and he had taken one look at her and said 'you've just had a baby, what have you done?' The mother had kept it all secret from her parents and was shocked at her father's questions. She told him what had happened and he said she was to get the baby back at once, and he and his wife would care for it. We had yet to legally adopt the baby, so I felt a sense of peace and relief when I gave her back into the Salvation Army's care until her grandfather could collect her. It is strange how tears, relief and happiness can be all mixed up in one emotion. That was how I was! I knew that this little girl was meant to stay in the family she had first come to.

But what would I do now? Lorna said she felt terrible for me because she didn't know of any other young mothers they were caring for who could not keep their babies. They seemed to all have places to go to after the event, even if they were very poor places. The Salvation Army, quite rightly, encouraged young mothers to keep their babies and would indeed help them after birth for as long as money held out.

I was alone again in the Allaine house when the phone rang once more. It was Lorna again, and she said to me in a very peaceful voice that a mother had come to them saying that she couldn't keep her baby when it was born as she had absolutely nowhere to go; no one would take her in. Her mother had died and she was the oldest of a large family and couldn't ask her father to support her and a baby as well. Lorna told her that the Salvation Army would help her for the first two years if she would keep the baby. The mother had thought, and then said, 'What will I do then? I may still have no place and no job. What will happen to my baby?' She said she wanted her baby to have a mother and a father, and wished someone could adopt her. So Lorna had showed her photos of us and she laughed with joy and said 'Oh, my baby is going to have a daddy who is thin on top!' Jörg had lovely black hair, but it was indeed thinning on top!

Lorna told me that the baby was expected in two weeks' time and could I wait that long? I said yes at once, because just as I had known the other little child didn't want us, I knew that this one yet to come would. We get messages in this life in two ways. One is by listening with your physical ears and your brain, and the other is listening to your heart-mind. Hearing your heart-mind is a wonderful experience and very warming. It gives one a very secure and lovely feeling. This is our intuition, our instinct.

A week later Monika put on a fashion party in her

dwelling and of course I was invited. I had never been to such a party and felt very alien. I had nothing wonderful and fashionable to dress in. Before long the house was buzzing with loud raucous women, mincing about and all glammed up, wearing what I thought to be very loud lipstick, eyeliner and anything else we women can stick on our faces. There was very good food and plenty of it, and lots of luscious drink too.

I sat there just looking on and gradually felt a bit of a thick head coming on. Just as I stood up to go and find a quieter spot, the phone rang. I took no notice, never dreaming it could be for me. I then heard Monika's voice shouting for me – it was for me. I took the call down the other end of the building, as I could hardly hear the voice. It was Lorna. It couldn't be the baby come, as it was too early.

'Hello Christine, do you believe in miracles?' she said, 'because you have just become a mother!' She said the baby had been born the previous day but she had wanted to give the mother time to change her mind about the adoption. The mother had just asked Lorna to fetch me and could I get a cab? My heart was bursting with happiness and joy.

When I arrived at the mother and baby home I was awestruck at the thought of holding the most precious gift of my life in my arms. I met Lorna at the door.

Both mother and baby were very well, although the baby weighed only five pounds and a few ounces. I followed Lorna up the staircase of this beautiful colonial villa with its gleaming wooden floors, stairs, stair railings, and doors, and she quietly knocked on one door and went in. There, sitting on a bed covered in a white bedspread, sat a young girl looking at the baby girl she had not long given birth to. The mother looked very beautiful with particularly expressive black eyes and auburn hair. The baby looked perfect, tiny but round with very dark thick hair, and all dressed in white. The curtains were of fine white material and the walls were also white, trimmed with the dark brown wood that was everywhere in the house. It looked very fresh, clean and cool in this very hot climate.

We sat down beside the mother and Lorna chatted with her, sometimes translating for me. The mother wanted me to promise that I wouldn't let her baby suck her thumb! I promised, but at the same time I was thinking that if the baby insisted on sucking her thumb there would be little I could do. From somewhere deep inside I had the knowledge that everything would be all right.

We named this little one Giovanna, gift from God, and wrapped in Christ love, and she never did manage to suck her thumb. She tried, but soon gave up. Have you ever felt love and pain hugging and holding hands? I have. Have you ever felt so unworthy, yet so worthy of something? I have. Have you ever stood in a holy place on this Earth? I have. There was something at that moment in that room that felt as if guardian angels were there, guarding, guiding, loving.

The mother stood up, picked her precious little one up and held her out to me. Her pain would be my joy. She didn't show any pain, but I knew better. This dear mother was doing this out of pure love for her little one. Later Lorna said that the day her baby was born the mother was overcome and wanted to keep her, but then in the morning she had come downstairs and resolutely said she wanted her baby to be given the kind of care she couldn't give.

I held her baby, absolutely speechless. She was perfectly serene; to me she looked like an angel, and she had a light shining from within at that moment. 'Thank you' is so weak an expression at such a moment and I couldn't bring myself to utter it; I didn't want to cheapen what was happening. I heard my voice saying that we would love and care for her child for always and do our very best for her. I also said that we would be glad if she wanted to keep in touch and that she was welcome to have our address from Lorna if she so desired. I put my arm around this twenty-year-old girl and then we silently left, Lorna saying something in a motherly voice as we were about to close the door. I felt glad for Lorna's motherly, secure kindness and love towards this young girl.

We climbed into Lorna's little VW and bumped along through part of the city until we reached the Hennesseys' house. Only when we got there and I sat holding my baby could I afford to express the absolute bliss and joy I felt in receiving this little bundle of five and a bit pounds of humanity into my heart; our little two-day-old baby; our little Giovanna Krista. I knew that she had chosen us to be her parents, though how I knew I could not tell you. One thing I do know is that adoptive parents don't really choose their baby as our society likes to impress upon people. It is more like they choose you! Even from a logical, practical point of view it is not true that you go out anywhere and 'choose' your baby. Your baby comes to you. There is no place on Earth where there are shelves of babies to choose from, they don't grow in supermarkets. Those who help with adoptions in the various agencies often like to say to you, 'You are lucky as you can always say to your child that you chose them'. Not so. You chose to want a baby, but you didn't choose the one that came to you. Just as physical parents choose to want a baby and get pregnant, but don't have a chance to choose who their baby is, the soul they give birth to after nine months of waiting is an absolute surprise to them. That little body they have given birth to is the beautiful vessel that holds the Spirit, the person, whom they do not yet know.

It was such a precious experience; deep down love overflowing, sitting there, holding this dear little soul and looking forward to getting to know her, I realised that I had an immediate bond in my heart with Giovanna. The Hennesseys were all home and sharing my utter bliss and happiness. Don and Lorna, I noticed, had put a wonderful spread on the table and were putting the final touches to it when Lorna announced the meal. We opened their bedroom door, which was next to the living room, and laid my baby on their bed where we could watch her as we ate. Giovanna was peace itself. She slept all the while and every so often one of the Hennessey girls would get up and sit on their parents' bed just looking down at this lovely little baby, and then rejoin us at the table.

At the end of the meal I was presented with a present, all carefully wrapped up. I opened it to find some beautiful baby clothes, one being the loveliest little embroidered cream yellow dress. Another gift this family gave me was to allow me to phone Jörg to tell him that our baby was there so that he could book a flight to come out, as he needed to be there for the formal adoption. In those days overseas calls were extremely expensive. It was great to hear Jörg's very happy voice and his reaction to my news.

That evening, back with Jacques and Monika and family, I had the joy of sharing their happiness over our baby. Their two little boys looked on in quiet awe. The following day Monika and I shopped for some more baby clothes while Rosangela cared for Giovanna.

A couple of days later, Jörg arrived. I took Giovanna in the taxi to the airport to meet Jörg, much to Jacques' annoyance as he said she was far too young to be travelling around. I guess he was right, but no harm was done. Jörg was overjoyed to be with us and looked at Giovanna with happiness in his eyes, but he didn't reach out to hold her. I could see his hesitation, so I just placed her in his arms and he had no choice but to care for her as well as look at her. He said he was afraid he would drop her! So I promised him that babies are tough and don't 'drop' and 'break' very easily. He grinned and felt in command of the situation after a few minutes.

The next days are a bit of a haze. I remember going to the Judge of Minors courtroom where we met the birth mother. The Judge had studied our documents and request before we arrived. We and the mother had questions shot at us almost aggressively. We answered, all three of us, in our own ways, and then there was signing of several documents and we were dismissed.

We also had to go to get a passport for our little baby from the federal police. They were very friendly and helpful. At the adoption Giovanna was not present but for the passport she had to be, and I remember queuing in the hot sun for what seemed ages. Photos were taken of Giovanna and the passport was handed to us very quickly after this.

We were now ready to book flights back to the UK. Jörg had to travel a day ahead of me because his brother worked for Scandinavian Air and he was travelling for next to nothing with them, and needed to get back to work the following day. I needed to pay full price on a different airline, which I booked for the following day.

Congonias Airport was lined with flamboyant trees, which were in full bloom at that time of year. They were so beautiful with the brilliant red blossoms hanging downwards and the vibrant bright green leaves lifting up towards the sun. They looked like umbrellas of the most exquisite kind. Because of this lovely farewell to Brazil I have always associated Giovanna with the beauty of flamboyant trees. Interestingly she has always loved and suited red.

I was made very comfortable by the staff of the plane, and Giovanna was well cared for by them. They gave her a little hanging bed, like a hanging basket, which was hung at just the right level for me to reach in and take her out as I needed. She was such an easy baby to care for on a long flight as she was so peaceful.

When we took off I sat back feeling that I was very near the end of a long journey, in fact, exactly nine months from start to completion of our quest. We had been blessed with our lovely little angel and here we were a night's journey away from home.

A shadow stood blocking the light from my book and I looked up to see the producer of the BBC programme we had been a part of quite by chance; it had been called 'Other Lives' if I remember rightly. Whilst on our search in Sao Paulo I had somehow come by chance into the acquaintance of Louise and the BBC company who were following a couple on their search for a baby from Brazil. This couple had so far been unsuccessful and here we had received our little one, and Louise wanted us in the film with Giovanna. So we had given permission, and in our delight of having our baby, we found it quite easy to play our small part in making this documentary. Now Louise was on the same flight back to the UK. She proved to be a great companion and support for some of the long trip back. She also took some lovely photos of Giovanna on the plane and a couple more just before we parted at Heathrow.

However, at Heathrow something had gone wrong with the flight bookings and the one I was to take up to Manchester didn't seem to exist any longer. So there I was, tired and stumped at the very last hurdle. Here again the Salvation Army came to our rescue in the form of a young girl named Julie, who had become a very good friend, and was an officer in the SA. She had booked us a new flight and also came to pick us up at Manchester, driving us all the way home to Cefn Mawr in North Wales, as Jörg couldn't take any more time from work.

My friend Sina, one of the few we had trusted with my reason for going to Brazil, had made our home ready for our little baby to be welcomed into. What a delightful homecoming it was. Sina had three children of her own, all very young, and she had used her own baby cot and bath for our little girl. We were welcomed with such joy by Sina's whole family, and those who lived on our little village street too.

Such happy days followed and on Christmas Eve

we celebrated with our own little baby angel in her rocker under the Christmas tree, which was lit with real live red candles. My heart was full and running over. Now, for the first time in my life, I took time away from work to just be an at home mother. I so loved it. Life was extremely happy and fulfilled for me and for Jörg too. He would be the one to put our baby to bed each night when he had been on a morning shift. Sitting in the armchair, he would hold Giovanna in his arms and sing her all the German, Swiss, Austrian, Spanish and English lullabies we had known as children. It was his special time, and Giovanna came to love it so much that it became part of her happy little life.

I remember one day needing to go to the village pharmacy, which meant a very steep uphill trudge pushing Giovanna in her pram. When I arrived, there was quite a long queue of people waiting to be served. I was right at the back and the lady just ahead of me turned with recognition in her face because we had often crossed paths; then, seeing I had a baby, she said in a very loud voice that seemed to echo off the walls to the entire waiting queue, 'I didn't know YOU were pregnant!' To which I replied, 'I shouldn't think you did – I didn't know either!' I couldn't contain my laughter and just burst forth with uncontrolled mirth.

She looked so shocked that I hadn't 'known myself' so I felt that my laughter could be hurting, so I explained my story. Although I tried to keep my voice low, the whole queue were entertained. Those at the front forgot that it was their turn to be served and turned back to listen. The pharmacist stopped, hand in the air with her customers' wares, and smiled at my story before going back to serving.

By early February when the BBC programme aired, we had settled into our family routine with much happiness. The morning after we had watched the programme on television, I was on my way down the road with Giovanna; Jörg was at work, and I was walking along in my own little world, Giovanna all wrapped up and as 'snug as a bug in a rug' against the cold, when I was brought to a standstill by a very loud screech from across the road. Looking across I saw that a woman was trying to get my attention. She was standing at her garden gate and there was another person silhouetted in her doorway. Connecting my brain to what she was saying, she shouted, 'Weren't you on the television last evening?' I said I was. She then turned to the silhouette in the doorway and shouted, 'See, I told you so!' She then proceeded to run across the road in her slippers, housecoat held around her against the cold, and landed at my side, excitedly pulling back Giovanna's covers to take a good look at her. I felt quite indignant at this intrusive behaviour, and gently but firmly pushed the covers back so that Giovanna would not get cold on this freezing day. For a few seconds there was a tug of war going on, but I wasn't going to lose this one, and eventually she got the message and left my baby alone. This woman was acting as if she had met up with a film star. She was still going on about how they had seen us on telly and her husband had not believed it was their neighbours from around the corner, so she had set out to prove herself right. Now she was like the cat that had got the cream and she went back across the road, shouting to her husband, 'It's her all right, I told you so!'

I enjoyed many happy times with Sina and her family as they lived on the same little village street as we did. Two fields and a steep hill away was the River Dee, where we spent many a happy hour together with our children. The days were long and hazy happy times for me, with very few worries to distract me. Our car was small but Klaus, Sina's husband, had a Land Rover, the kind with wooden seats round the interior. Sometimes when the men were home from work we would all pile into it and go on wonderful trips around Snowdonia. The Horseshoe Pass and the hairpin bend took us to lovely walking places high up, where we became the kings and queens of the mountain.

We had wonderful neighbours on our little street. One couple, Trish and Jim, lived a few doors down. They had a young son, Jamie, and then a younger daughter and son later on who eventually became really good friends and close to our hearts. In years to follow we spent many a wonderful hour with this family. When I think of them, pure love and joy fill my heart. Maybe the reason this is so important to me is simply that we had been brought up on the Bruderhof to understand that you could only experience true love and joy 'when you are in full unity with others'. We had no idea what Jim and Trish thought, believed or understood about life. Their actions said it all; they were love and kindness personified. Why would we need to 'be in unity' of thought and 'sharing all things'?

Winter turned to spring and one day Jörg and I went for a walk with Giovanna in our arms instead of in a push chair. We passed under a huge beech tree with its leaves just opened. Our baby lay in my arms and I knew she could see something in that tree that we couldn't. She started talking with baby soft cooing noises, and her eyes seemed to be seeing fairies and elves at play up in those branches. As she gurgled and cooed to herself her little arms and legs would scrunch up in delight at what she saw and heard. Such a deep concentration was in her eyes and such warm love. Maybe it was angels, who knows, but she saw and communicated with beings that had long been veiled from us adults. We stood there for a long while in awe of her connection. I thought of the phrase 'become like little children', which of course does not mean to become childish, but childlike, and then we will know full life.

As time passed we started to feel the desire for another baby; we were beginning to feel a build-up of the courage we would need to start again on the next part of our journey on Planet Earth. It was the law at the time that we had to adopt our baby again in the UK a year after her first adoption. She would then get what they called the 'long birth certificate'. We had been assigned a social worker for this purpose. The day of her official British adoption dawned and the social worker said she was glad for us but then added, 'but you won't do this again will you?' The British social services considered us too old. We didn't want her to know that yes, we would 'do this again' so I said, 'Did anyone ask you before your second child if you were going to conceive and have another, then decide whether to give you permission?' The poor lady was floored. She stuttered 'I should think not!' I went on, 'Nor would we seek permission if we wanted another child.'

The day of Giovanna's second adoption went happily. She was a year old, and with this there was a cessation of any social service connections or interference.

As time passed, Jörg and I discussed what we would do to extend our family. In the end we decided to make a phone call to the Salvation Army in Brazil and again approach them for help. I made the call only to find that the Hennesseys had been sent to another country, but their replacement was a couple who came from Atlanta in the USA. Evelyn Deuel came to the phone so there was no language difficulty there, a good start! She and her husband Jim had taken the position the Hennesseys had held, so I plunged in and told them what we were hoping for and asked if they would feel able to help us out again. Evelyn was a joy to chat with and was so very positive, ending by saying she would look out for a baby who needed parents and promising to keep us in the loop.

I was excited and couldn't wait to tell Jörg the news. For now it would be our secret. We knew it could be a long wait.

It wasn't too long afterwards that we got news that my father was ill and had had an operation. No one from the Bruderhof had notified us; we heard through a third person, who gave us the impression that he was seriously ill. My father, my mother and seven of my siblings all lived in one or another of the Bruderhof communities still. Most of them were married and had children. Sadly they failed to involve me in any news of their families; on very rare occasions I would hear from my mother that there was a new baby with occasionally, a photo included in the letter. They certainly did not seem concerned to tell me, his daughter, what was going on with my father. I didn't know which community my parents lived in; nor did I know where my siblings all lived – except that they were in the USA, or so we were given to believe.

I can't recall how it came about, but amazingly Jörg and I were invited to go and visit my parents, because my father was now ill with cancer. We had been married for six years, but most of my family had not even sent congratulations—they had no happiness for us, no love towards us. It had been painful indeed on this account. Jörg's family on the Bruderhof had also been very silent and distant, and if ever they contacted us it was to give us a dig in the ribs to try to persuade us that we should go and 'join' them, 'as you belong to us'. All contact only happened for one purpose, either to make us feel guilt by 'love bombing' us, or by writing moralistic letters to challenge us to go back and join them.

Thankfully Jörg had three brothers who had been rejected from the Bruderhof when they were very young and now they lived 'normal' lives, one in Sweden, one in Switzerland and one in the USA. These brothers had all visited us on various occasions and this was a delight to us, making us feel we belonged. At this time, besides Nigel in Brazil, one of my sisters had just very recently left the Bruderhof, but we were not informed and didn't know where she was; I also had one brother who had left the community long since, and we were able to have normal, open contact and great times together. Sadly, since that time, he has picked up the Bruderhof bug, the Bruderhof sickness, and been tainted by the same attitude, and will have no contact with us or our children.

It is deeply sad what this form of Christianity has done to the millions on Planet Earth. Jesus certainly never meant such cold-hearted meanness in people. He must weep when he hears people say that they will have nothing to do with their own because they want to be loyal to Jesus and put Him first, turning a blind eye and a cold heart to their own families. They quote something Jesus is supposed to have said that goes something like this: 'Leave father and mother for my sake, and follow me' and 'If anyone comes to me and does not hate his father and mother, his wife and children, his brothers and sisters, he cannot be my disciple' (Luke 14: 26). In my heart I know Jesus never said this and was grossly (and probably purposely) misquoted. The unparalleled enormity of the Bruderhof member's ridiculous mindset beggars belief and leaves one speechless. We were, and we are, treated like the lepers of the Old Testament, especially in this matter of relationships with family.

But now back to our invitation to the Oaklake Bruderhof, now renamed 'New Meadow Run'. At this time Jörg and I could hardly stomach being on a Bruderhof for too long, yet we wanted to spend time with my parents. By now we had knowledge of where many of those who had been 'sent away' lived. One of these was a woman who had been in school with me in my Wheathill years. Gwen lived in Uniontown, near the New Meadow Run Community. I got in touch with her and asked if we could visit her while we were with the Brothers if things got too much for us on the Bruderhof. Three weeks was an awfully long time to be stuck on a Bruderhof when it brought such fear back to mind and heart.

I remember arriving at the community and being welcomed by some of my siblings and in-laws. We were led to a house that was big enough to house something like three or four big families. Our little Giovanna, just eighteen months old, tagged along happily. She spoke very well and clearly at that age. We were led to an apartment of just two rooms. In one lay my father in bed, and in the other was my mother, preparing for him and us a cup of tea. Mummy came out and straight away gave me such a hug of love and happiness and understanding that it will stay with me for always. Daddy was very loving towards us, but clearly quite weak. His voice was deep and soft. Two of my brothers-in-law seemed to hang about like shadows in the corners. They were quite welcoming, one in a shy sort of way, the other very clinical. They hadn't the tact to understand that as it had been years since I had seen my parents, it might behove them to leave us and get back to work!

I soon noticed that if one of them slipped away the other would quickly reappear. It was obvious they were acting as guards and minders, and we were clearly not going to be allowed any private time with my parents in case we said something that might not blend with the 'Bruderhof spirit'. It was obviously awkward for my parents, and for me it was extremely hurtful.

We were given a room upstairs in this house, which shared a bathroom and kitchenette with another family, so during our time there we would take

Giovanna down to the bathroom that my parents shared with yet another family. Mummy enjoyed these times, as she could spend a little family time without the Brothers breathing down our necks.

One evening I was giving Giovanna a bath and Mummy came in. Giovanna stood up in the water and poked her finger into the little recess in the middle of her tummy, saying 'Look Mummy, my belly button!' My mother looked amazed and said in a rather disgusted voice, 'whoever taught her that?' I said, 'I guess I did'. With her Bruderhof hat on she was embarrassed, and she hadn't been able to adjust by putting her motherly hat on fast enough. It was 'impure' to talk of body parts!

We managed to have some lovely breakfasts with my parents, but they were short and sweet because very soon one of the in-laws appeared to become our minders again. My father was in bed much of the time. One day we stood in his bedroom doorway trying to chat, but it was awkward as this brother-in-law was so close all the time that I could easily have stepped on his toes accidentally on purpose. I controlled my desire to harm this rude, bombastic human being, as my father could do without any conflict at that time.

All of a sudden this guy was called away on some urgent task, and we were left alone with my father. We stepped into the room and Daddy began to talk to us. He shared his heart for a brief time, telling us that he felt that the Brotherhood had been wrong in the way they – he included himself – had acted in the past. He said 'One day the Brotherhood will have to see how wrong it was the way they had closed Primavera down'. They had not been closed down by a united decision of the people who lived there but by the American members from the USA. Being 'united and having all things in common' means that the rich American Brothers and Sisters would need to help out the poorer South American ones, which they did not want to do. Just a little bit more 'Animal Farm'!

My father was a very sensitive person, and I felt a real glow in my heart that he had said this because he had addressed it to Jörg, knowing what pain he had gone through; he had felt deceived and hurt that his home in Paraguay had been taken from him in such a deceitful way and right under his very nose, landing him, and many of us, feeling like displaced persons.

But now the conversation abruptly ended as the brother-in-law appeared again. He looked questioningly at all three of us, but we did not enlighten him.

Many years later, when I had managed to get one of my brothers on the phone and brought up the question of what they call 'unity', I told him what our father had said to us about giving up our homes in Paraguay. By now my father had died, so I was safe to speak without him being hurt in any way. On hearing what Daddy had said, this brother of mine completely lost it and screamed almost hysterically over the phone, with great fear in his voice, that Daddy had never said this. It would have meant to my brother that our father had died in 'disunity', which is the most dreaded and fearful thing to my Bruderhof siblings. I would say that at that moment he was in terror, which made him totally irrational in the way he talked thereafter before hanging up on me; he sounded as if he was in abject, piteous fear. That was sad indeed.

There did come a day when we felt suffocated and gave Gwen a call to ask if she could pick us up and take us for a breather to her house in Uniontown. On the Bruderhof everything was done as a big bunch. You could never see the beauty and wonderful delicacy of a single flower so to say, it was always a bunch, and put together at that by the same people, on any Bruderhof. All the communal meals and meetings were stifling us, though we said nothing to anyone. When the day came we told my parents that we were going to a friend for a couple of days, then we just walked to the entrance of the Bruderhof and were picked up by Gwen, unseen by anyone. We wanted to avoid the Bruderhof's way of 'unity', and their incessant need for reasons for our actions, thoughts and intentions. Also, we didn't want to give them the chance to cut our time short with my parents and send us back to the UK before we were ready to say goodbye. We had already been challenged about returning 'to the life' and attempts had been made to make us go back by the pathway of guilt; 'because your father has cancer and would enjoy having you nurse him', was one woman's way of expressing it.

We spent a fun time with Gwen and were able to go back to the Bruderhof for the rest of the visit with a brighter, lighter feeling inside us. It was very hard to say goodbye to my parents when the time came. We had been left alone with them for precious little of our visit. Even in the evening we had to leave them by 9.45 as my mother said that if we didn't have the lights out by ten, the Night Watchman would tell the 'responsible Brothers' and we would hear about it next day. I told my mother that I didn't care what the Brothers said to me, and that I definitely would be reading much later than ten o'clock with the light on, but that we would leave them to go to bed so they would feel comfortable. This is one example of the masses of rules of control that beset the cult. Of course the rules keep changing.

Saying goodbye to my dear and precious parents was so very painful. It left a heavy darkness in my chest. Yet again, it wasn't a private farewell, because so many others invited themselves into those last moments. I sensed that I would never hear or see my father again, and I never did see him again, in the ordinary sense of our human being.

CHAPTER 14

A family complete

Back in the UK I went about my life in a happy kind of anticipation as to when we might see and hold our new baby – not that we had heard anything as yet. I just knew that we would be blessed with another new little soul some time. Giovanna was such a joy and love to both Jörg and me, so life was really quite beautiful. Howard and Judy, a couple who had become great friends of ours, were the Salvation Army Officers in the village where we lived. This connection had proved to be very helpful with us connecting with the Salvation Army in Brazil and finding our first little baby. Now the link was firmer, as we were also spending time with Army people and going to some of their meetings, which at the time we enjoyed very much. We found a great freedom in spirit that seemed to emanate through Howard and Judy and was quite catching. Their love and happiness, despite the burden of pain they carried with their ten-year-old son having cancer, just radiated out to all from them.

One night at one in the morning the phone rang and it was Evelyn, from the Salvation Army in Brazil. She informed me that a baby girl had been born whose mother was unable, due to poverty, to take care of her little one and would we like to be her parents? What a question – of course we would! She asked if we would be able to travel out as soon as possible to go through the adoption processes. I was joyous and my heart was full to bursting. I glowed so much inside that it is a wonder I didn't light up the pathway in the dark for others. But we said nothing to our friends apart from a very few, like Sina.

A week later we were on our way to Brazil with Giovanna, now nearly three. All our documents had long since been completed. When we had arrived Evelyn and Jim picked us up from the airport. They were in uniform, so we couldn't miss them. They were immediate friends to us and were so kind and loving to Giovanna too. We were to stay with them in the quarters provided by the Salvation Army. It was a big house, all on ground level, with a nice outside garden cum patio area, the same one I had been in on my first night with baby Giovanna when we had been befriended by Don and Lorna nearly three years earlier.

We enjoyed a couple of days with Jim and Evelyn, and while they were at work they trusted us to use their house – it was very touching to the soul. On about day three Evelyn said she was going to ask the Salvation Army Officer who was responsible for the mother and baby home what was happening with our baby and if we could see her. That evening Evelyn came home looking quite troubled, saying she hadn't been able to get anything out of Mrs De Avila. The following day the same thing happened. Our baby seemed to have vanished; Evelyn couldn't even get an answer as to where she was, in the mother and baby home, or the Charity Hospital. We were a little troubled, but we had a deep conviction that all would turn out right in the end.

While Evelyn promised to look into things, we took a trip out to our friends in Innisfree near Vinhedo. I enjoyed this time greatly. It was a lovely small holding where Roger and Nora lived, and we enjoyed their farm produce for meals and the freedom of long walks. Giovanna played happily with their donkey, giving it lots of hugs, which the donkey thoroughly enjoyed.

After a few days we said goodbye to our friends and travelled back to Sao Paulo. Time on our return tickets back to the UK was running out and still we could not squeeze a word out of anyone as to what was going on with our new baby. We were even being told that we could adopt another baby, as there were many little souls without parents all over Sao Paulo. I just couldn't feel happy about this idea. I already felt a strange bond of love in my heart for the baby we had come for. We had even given her a name – Marcella. For some strange reason the suggestion of adopting a different baby left me grieving for *my* baby; the very thought was too difficult. If we listen to our heart-minds, we will see in the end that we come to our own truth. Then to follow that truth becomes completely fulfilling. Somewhere in my heart-mind I had promised our little Marcella that we would love and care for her during her sojourn on Planet Earth – I could simply not break from her!

We had only a few days left on our air tickets. So desperate did the situation become that Jörg went to the Pan-Am offices to try to extend them. Meanwhile I took Giovanna for a walk around some quiet streets nearby. My heart was very heavy and I was close to tears. At last we came upon a lump of concrete that had come from a fallen telephone post and I sat down on this ugly lump and with my head in my hands I burst into tears. It was grief at what seemed impossible. My small girl, not even quite three, put her little arms around me and said, 'Mummy, don't cwy, God will give you your baby'. I turned and hugged her. I hadn't even realised that she was so in tune with what was going on. Surely she was right but I had reached the end of my strength at that moment and it took an innocent child to bring me back into life.

I stood up and holding her hand I went back to the house, where I sat motionless while Giovanna played quite happily. I came out of my curled-up state when Jörg walked in. His face registered defeat, but I willed myself to ask whether he had good news from the Pan-Am office. No, he said they wouldn't extend the tickets. Now what? When Evelyn came in and then Jim and I had to tell them we could not extend the tickets, the dam silently burst again. Evelyn was angry that her colleagues had not been able to tell us what was going on.

Suddenly, in the still silence, I heard in my mind the name 'Rosina' and 'Amparo Maternal Hospital'. I heard myself shout out, 'Rosina!' Everyone looked up in unison, maybe wondering if I had become a bit touched! I explained, knowing this was important.

Some years earlier a woman who had adopted from Brazil, and knew how tough things could get, had told me that if things were not working out I should get in touch with Rosina of the Amparo Maternal Hospital. Almost falling over my words, I related this to the others. It had been so long ago and I had totally forgotten it – until this second. Opening my diary, there were the names scribbled on the first page. Amazing! It was as though the Angel Gabriel had whispered into my ear; the whisper rang loud and clear in my heart-mind.

At the mention of the Amparo Hospital, Evelyn said in amazement that it was just at the end of their street. Jörg and I stood up and asked Jim and Evelyn if they could care for Giovanna. We gave our little one a kiss and were out of the door. With my breath caught in my chest but a knowing in my heart, we sped down the street. At the hospital we went to the front desk and Jörg asked in a mixture of Spanish flavoured with his limited smattering of Portuguese if we could see Rosina, trying to convey that it was about a baby we were hoping to be given.

The faces behind the desk looked puzzled, but after giving each other a few questioning looks, one of them told us to wait and vanished. In a minute she was back and told us to follow her, leading us to a small very bare room with a desk in it, behind which sat a very calm looking lady. She was introduced as Sister Rosina. She indicated two chairs for us to sit down.

Now we were given all the time in the world to try and explain our situation regarding what had gone on with this huge wall of silence and our time constraint with our tickets, and we watched her expression with bated breath. Her face registered understanding and peaceful kindness. However when we asked whether the baby was in this hospital, being the Charity Hospital the Salvation Army used, and could she help us, she shook her head. She opened a drawer in her desk, took out a bit of paper and drew a street map which would lead us to the Judge of Minors. It is amazing how people can understand one another when they really have to, despite having no language in common. Rosina made it clear that we needed to visit the Judge of Minors.

We both felt that we were on the right track now, so we thanked Rosina gratefully and found ourselves almost running as we followed our little map. As it was all uphill, and the anxiety had started to come upon me again, I found that breathing was difficult and we stopped a moment. I said to Jörg that I desperately hoped my intuition was right and that this would be the last leg of our quest. He said he absolutely knew it was! This calmed me. Next we were standing in front of this rather forbidding building, then walking up the steps to the door. Inside was a great long counter top; some people stood behind it, others tapped away on typewriters back in the room behind them, a huge open space office. Someone came up asking us what we wanted. Again Jörg tried to relate our story in his Spanish and pigeon Portuguese. As we talked a woman at the back of the room lifted her glasses onto her forehead and gave us a long look, then came over, and we repeated ourselves. As we explained, a warm smile spread over her face, it was a knowing smile, as if she had been waiting for us and at last we had appeared. She asked us to return the following day and said she would have two psychologists ready to interview us; the Brazilian way of adoption at the time. It was now closing time.

The following day at the crack of dawn we arrived at the Judge of Minors again, along with our friend Monica, who had consented to accompany us for translation purposes.

Monica made all the introductions and explanations go like greased lightning, and soon we found ourselves sitting with the two psychologists – we didn't need Monica, as one woman had excellent English and the other could understand us. They chatted with us in an easy way, asking about us and our lives. After some very friendly, warm chat they said they needed to speak to the Judge and would be back very soon.

The two returned very quickly and told us that the Judge awaited us. We sat in front of this very Brazilian-looking Judge, wondering how we were going to communicate with him. and he started to speak in perfect English. This felt like a good beginning to a good ending! On his right sat a little mini-judge typing down all that was said, mostly by the Judge. He picked up the papers that we had sent ahead and flicked through them, then made his order for us to have our baby. He then told us to go back to the Amparo Hospital and Sister Rosina would give our treasure to us. We were handed five official documents that sealed our parenthood. We were SO happy, filled to bursting, and my cup was truly running over.

The lady who had first looked at us for so long across the room, and had got the ball rolling, told us that she had seen such sincerity in our eyes that she couldn't help but push us forward in our search. She chatted with us for a minute before leaving, and gave us a huge hug.

Now we sat in a visitor's office in the Amparo Maternal Hospital. The faces of workers coming in and out were wreathed in smiles as they went about their business; they seemed to know well why we were there and what was about to happen. It was a room filled with light, with a huge tree-like plant in one corner, the sun shining through the green leaves.

After a short wait we saw Sister Rosina coming down a hall toward us with her arms holding a bundle that could only be a small baby. We had not seen Rosina smiling fully in joy before but now her face radiated happiness, with a smile that seemed to light her whole face. She said to us, 'This is your baby. Which one shall I give her to?' I held out my arms to receive our little Marcella and as I gazed at her she gazed back with that innocence and wisdom that only comes from a little one who is still free of the veil between us and love-creation-life, the veil that starts to block us from seeing as we grow in ego and as we get older. Marci's life was still pure love. This beautiful little angel, four weeks old, looked deep into my eyes, holding my gaze. She seemed to say 'you'll do, I'm all right with you.' I am able to relive that wonderful day whenever I choose; there are no words to describe that true and complete love. When we have ascended completely, we will know such feelings of unconditional love wherever we are, but for now it was a moment of ascension for me.

We had only about 36 hours to get ourselves together and get on a plane bound for home. Giovanna's little face lit up with pure joy when she was invited to sit down and hold her baby sister. Jim and Evelyn loved our little Marcella and Giovanna. They were so helpful and happy to have been there for us.

Great was the day when we walked into our home back in the UK with our two little girls. We had decided that we would not start procedures with the British adoption agency until we had enjoyed our little family together for six weeks or so. We would involve them later; we didn't want to spoil this very heavenly joy by involving the authorities.

One morning when we had been back home for approximately a week I received a phone call and the person on the end of the line said, 'I hear you have another baby'. I asked how she knew, but she didn't respond. Next she asked if she could come round and visit today; she was the same social worker who had been there for our Giovanna. I said no, and explained why. She pressured some more, but I stuck to my answer, so she put the phone down.

An hour later there was a knock at the door, which I innocently answered, and there, right in my face, stood the social worker. I shook my finger in her face and said 'YOU—are naughty!' It just popped out that way. Inside of me I knew I had the choice of being awkward and sending her away or of being kind and letting her in. She meant well in a slightly patronising way, 'just doing her job'. In my young life I had lived so much under the control of the 'authorities' so I felt very rebellious towards anyone trying to tell me what to do and when to do it. Yet here she was, the professional expert trying to push her righteous self into my life! It did rankle, but I let her in.

This lady took a look at our little Marcella and an unwilling smile crept over her face. She said she would register us for a date of adoption with the Judge in Wrexham and then before leaving she said 'You won't do this again, will you!' She had of course told us we were too old to be adopting babies. I reminded her that she had not asked the authorities' permission to have a second baby before she conceived her own child, and that folks like us needed the freedom to follow our hearts in the same way she had. When she said again 'But you won't do it again?' I said we had not planned to, but if a baby came into our lives we would not say no, we would be glad.

I stayed home with the children, so Jörg was the sole earner. I just loved every day that rolled around. Life was sweet, beautiful, glorious and loving. It was also full of small child adventure. Sina and Klaus, our friends down the road, by now had a clutch of four little children and she and I spent many a happy hour wandering over the fields and down to the River Dee, sometimes with a picnic, sometimes without – but it was always a joy for us and our little brood.

One night the phone rang. I woke and dashed down stairs to pick up –it was our friend Monica in Brazil. She told me that there was a little baby boy in the Amparo Maternal Hospital, and said the Judge of Minors had asked her to get in touch with us to ask if we would become his parents. I was so quite overwhelmed with joy! Surely if the Brazilian legal team trusted us for a third baby, then why would we not take this little fellow with open arms and hearts? I told Monica that I would talk to Jörg and ring her back tomorrow.

Back up the stairs as on the wings of a dove, I eagerly woke Jörg to tell him of the phone call and asked what he thought. He rolled over sleepily and said 'of course, if the little fellow has no parents then we won't say no'. He added that we would be given the financial means if it was what our path intended, and if our God was in it. I sailed back downstairs and phoning Monica I said yes, we would like the baby boy.

Monica said that this little one had been born a few days after Marcella and in the same hospital. After his birth he had been taken home but then brought back because his family did not have enough food and shelter to keep him. The waiting for our little boy got longer, as Monica informed us that they were doing health checks because he didn't seem quite well. By now I had fallen in love with this little boy and didn't want to lose him, either through illness or through the authorities changing their minds. We hadn't told many people of our intentions, because we didn't want the British Social Services poking their noses in and more than likely managing to put a stop on our little one coming to us. Monica kept us informed of what was going on as to blood tests and so forth.

Meanwhile we were preparing. We had no money, so we just put that problem to the front of our hearts and minds, feeling sure it would come from somewhere. Help came in different ways. Firstly a Morris Minor that Jörg had refurbished, which he had been trying to sell for a couple years, suddenly sold, giving Jörg his return ticket to Brazil. Now we needed the money for the baby's ticket. In a very short time we received the exact amount. It happened in an unforeseen way. An envelope came through the door from Jörg's eldest brother in Sweden, containing the exact amount needed for the baby's one-way ticket! Chris, Jörg's brother, said he had received this money from his parents long before when they had been 'out in the world' and excluded from the Bruderhof, and now he wanted us to have it. It was totally unexpected – Chris knew nothing of our desire for a third child.

Now we had to find the money for myself and the two little girls. We were both expected to attend the Brazilian Court for the adoption. We had no one we could leave the girls with. Most of our extended families were on the Bruderhof and since they wouldn't communicate with us we couldn't involve them. So it was all of us or nothing.

The answer came to us in the form of a letter from the Judge in Brazil. He said that since he knew us well, and as he still had all our documents with him from Marcella's adoption, I could give Jörg Power of Attorney, which meant the adoption could go ahead without me being there in person. Now we just had the hospital to wait for. I was a little sad that I would not be there to receive our little boy but relieved that the Judge had made it possible after all.

After what seemed a long time we received the call to tell us to go over to pick up our little lad. Time had passed, and he was now nearly 18 months old. Jörg went off alone, and within a week he was back with an absolutely beautiful little boy, whom we called Jonathan. Jörg was the very last to emerge from passport control with the most lovely little one sitting upright on his arm and putting his little arms tightly round his daddy's neck. We burst forth to embrace them both. To me, Jonathan looked for all the world like a little angel sitting on his daddy's arm so upright, and viewing everything around him. Right from the start Jonathan had formed a very strong bond with Jörg and was almost indignant when he saw me giving him a hug. His little face seemed to say 'and who are you?'

Jörg passed him to me so as to give his little girls a hug, and as he did so I could feel Jonathan easing up and almost beginning to enjoy us all. He truly was the most beautiful little one-year-old and I felt very emotional as I thought how I had been given a third precious soul to care for and love. The love had been waiting for a year, and now it burst forth from my heart like a flower bud blossoming in the sunshine.

The hospital had found nothing seriously wrong with Jonathan. He seemed a strong and healthy little lad; he had dark brown eyes like deep, still pools that were very wise, and seemed to see everything, taking it all in with interest. He had lovely black ringlets and was exactly the same size as Marcella; they were just nine days apart in age.

It was sweet to see that after some silent weighing

up of each other, our two little one-year-olds completely accepted each other and even began to share little unvoiced jokes ending in chuckles – shy chuckles at first, but then carefree laughter. Giovanna was a wonderful 'big' sister to them both, looking after them as if she was made for it.

In my brother and sister-in-law's house both Jörg and Jonathan took a bath as the flight had made Jonathan sick, so they needed freshening up! We were kindly fed and watered and then we left for home, saying goodbye to Mike and his family.

Within the shortest time the three children were almost welded together. Jörg and I fell in step with the love, needs and care of our three little folks and my utter delight was complete. Each day was so very lovely and fulfilling. At this time it was hard for me to grasp how so many parents around me seemed to complain about their children, even wishing they had never had any. I guess we had waited so long for our family that when they were there it seemed a constant wonder to see our little daughters and son developing, loving, showing disapproval when they didn't like something, defending each other, going off in peals of laughter as they began to grow and understand their own humour; all of their lives were gifts of precious wholeness and the pinnacle of creation's love and loving.

We had the same worries as any parents do, the same hurdles to get over, the same demands on us. Looking back, the difficulties that life can present were far outweighed by the beguiling, bewitching heavenliness of small children. There is magnificence in people, even more so in little children. These were halcyon days. Life and love are very precious when both are in full bloom. Life became love and love became life.

As our children began to reach an age where they were all three in school, it was time for me to go back to work. It was also a time when we found ourselves facing the influences of other people in our children's lives. Some of these influences were lovely, and some, we thought, were not so good. Now I realise that everything they experienced was part of their journey on Planet Earth, and it would teach them much and bring them eventually to a mature and loving knowing.

We had lived in our little house in North Wales for ten years, the longest time either of us had ever been in one place, and now were moving to the Wirral. Jörg and I had found ourselves drawn to the Salvation Army, and receiving employment with them. This was what necessitated our move. Renting our house out, we moved to the Salvation Army quarters in Morton.

We were both excited about our work with them and saw only the positives in our minds' eyes. We had first met the Army Officers in Cefn Mawr and they had been such a wonderful example of true love and compassion in their work towards others; this had given us the happiness to have the chance to work in this way too. We were both drawn to the work the Army did for the homeless, the very poor and lonely and sick who seemed to be, very often, passed by in this world of ours.

We both got the idea of working for the Salvation Army in an amazing way. We had never discussed it, or even thought of it. All we realised was that to keep five of us, we both needed to work. One night Jörg went off to his night shift with a woodwork company that worked continental shifts. At around ten in the evening I was cleaning up in the kitchen, with Jörg working on a huge saw, when each of us got the idea that we would like to apply to work for the Salvation Army. I felt almost as if a presence stood at my left shoulder, talking to me. It was comforting. I had no idea what this would entail, but was much excited at the idea, and not at all worried.

The following morning Jörg went to bed at seven as I got up with the children. Around 2 pm he woke up and came downstairs for his breakfast. I went into the kitchen just as Jörg stood at the sink and on half turning he said in a shy kind of way that last night he had had a kind of visitation, and heard that he should be working for the Salvation Army soon. I was dumbstruck for a couple seconds; then impulsively giving him a hug, I told him what had come to me the night before, the same thing. Neither of us stopped to pick it to bits – it was what it was. We were both happy.

After several interviews, some of the strangest kind, we were in Morton and at work. During one interview we were told that we had to give up smoking and drinking if we wanted to work within the ranks of the Salvation Army. I remember thinking that such stipulations were quite childish, but well, if Jörg could give it up, it sure didn't bother me. We never had the money in those days for much drink and I wasn't a smoker, only Jörg. He thought he could manage it. We were also told we would have to commit to a correspondence course in philosophy, or was it theology? Interesting, but that could be shelved until it happened.

So there we were in a very cold bleak quarters, ready for work. One lady in Morton who belonged to the Salvation Army, had prepared a little tea for us. It was hard to enjoy it as it was freezing cold in the quarters. However it was nice that she was there to welcome us, even if her welcome was very reserved.

We had found a school very close by for our children and we also set about making a home of the Army quarters, a three-bedroom house with a long unkempt garden, but very promising for three little children to grow up in. They had rabbits and two guinea pigs which were dearly loved. It wasn't long before they all began to feel at home. I think the little animals helped.

We put in many happy hours, if very busy and hard-working. Jörg would work more than 40 hours a week and I would work around the children's school hours, as they now all had to be taken to and from school. I did enjoy life so much in spite of my full-time work and family. I would be with the children from 3 pm when I picked them up from school, until they were safely tucked up in bed, having had stories and a goodnight winding down time; these hours were only for the family. Jörg would try to arrive for around five o'clock and so it would turn into proper quality time. It was simply lovely and we both felt quite privileged. Then we'd clean up and start on more Army work or on the infamous correspondence course which it had quickly become. It might have been great if that was all we had had to do as university students, but we were working and running a home and family. The course began to feel rather a ridiculous requirement. However, we did complete it.

But cracks began to appear in our work for the Army. The religious side would come to haunt us at times. My time on the Bruderhof had taught me that I was not a religious person, but there I was, being reminded of religion and how hideous it was to my heart. Jörg was feeling the same way. Yet the work was so fulfilling, and gave us much joy. We realised that yet again we were up against religion versus spirit. For most of the time we were free to follow our hearts, intuition, and spirit. Our boss was across the River Mersey in Liverpool and very seldom seemed to bother with us.

I set up a Kids' Club, as there were many poor in the area and folks were squeezed into tiny living spaces with children having no space to play, let alone gardens. Of course I had to take our children with me during these Monday evenings. The Hall would be full to bursting at times, but generally speaking a good time was had by all. I also spent much time counselling, as so many seemed to come to me for help. I didn't always feel well-equipped over some issues that would unfold, so at my request, the Army sent me on a year's evening classes in psychology and counselling. This proved very helpful; however it was a real stretch on my time as a full-time mother and full time worker.

Our children were always the main source of happiness and joy. Of course we had our moments of frustration, sometimes feeling tired and ill-equipped. The overlying memory is of the wonder and preciousness of childhood, the fun and rascally tricks that the children would get up too.

One day from the kitchen I could hear squeals of laughter coming from the garden, and on stepping out into the summer sunshine I discovered that Marci and Jonni were racing their guinea pigs across the children's paddling pool. The pool was very full with slippery straight sides. As I approached I noted that both animals had reached the opposite side but couldn't climb out, with Jonathan's guinea scrabbling on top of Marcella's to get out, forcing hers to go under. The children were squealing with delight, but I only saw disaster happening with at least one drowned guinea pig. So, running round to the other side, I rescued the two creatures, to the huge disappointment of the children. I guess I was shouting at the children as I rounded the pool too. I then felt so sorry for the sad little faces which moments before had registered such glee and happiness. The disappointment didn't last long as we agreed that they could race the animals as long as they picked them out of the water at the other side, thus safeguarding them from drowning. Their guineas lived on to a ripe old age!

The Scouse accent was very pronounced in the area. One day I was walking home from school with our children and one of Giovanna's little friends joined us. Victoria asked Giovanna if she could come to our house. Although I had heard her, as she was only a foot from me, Giovanna asked 'Mummy, Victoria says can she come to our house' and I answered, 'not today'. I had enough to do without more children and was not keen to add to my work. So Giovanna turned to Victoria and translated by saying, 'Me Mam says yer can't cum,' in the perfect sing-song Liverpool accent! I guess Giovanna thought in her little seven-year-old mind, that the children here spoke a different language which her mummy couldn't understand!

Jörg and I were required to lead the Sunday meetings for those who came to the Army Corps. Morton was not very blossoming or gifted where music and singing was concerned. We were both used to singing a capella, but most of these dear souls couldn't hold a tune in a bucket, or at very least their buckets would sound as if they were leaking and gradually the music would drop and drop, half note by half note until by the end of a song everyone was in a different key.!

It could be hilarious, but at times hugely distracting and annoying. I had to use my lungs to full capacity to try and hold the people up and on key.

There was a piano in the hall, but no pianist. Eventually we pinched a willing pianist from the Church of England, and he stuck with us for a long time. He was great in some ways, but always ended every song on a third chord, which amused our children greatly, and then began to bore them.

When the pianist went on holiday disaster could strike, as it did one day. A couple appeared from Chester to join in the meeting, and when they found we were without a pianist the wife offered her husband in great gushing pride, saying he was an excellent pianist, and he agreed with a broad smile. I was taken in, and agreed to his accompanying us all. The first song was started with a wonderfully full chord, but then it all went to bits. This gentleman was so incapable that he caused havoc. We crawled through a song that should have been full of reverence and heart, but it failed completely because our children, Jörg and a friend of ours, as well as myself, were all in stitches and bursting with laughter, but having to hold it all in. I had never heard such a dreadful racket in all my life!

We managed to keep going with the meeting,

avoiding any singing for a while. I then suggested we sing another song minus piano accompaniment. Oh no – our gentleman friend from Chester had to add his mustard to the song and managed to get the children and friend Pete into such peals of laughter that it was impossible to get to the end of the song, especially as I was leading, while laughing so much that tears were pouring down my cheeks. At last the 'pianist' noticed that he was out of sorts with everyone else and crawled to a silent end. I was in hysterics by now, but not wanting to hurt his feelings, I tried to calm my tears of laughter by standing there with bowed head and talking to my self very seriously to get a grip! Maybe the people thought I was being very pious and praying!

At the end of the meeting there was another song lined up, so I suggested this time, and in the most commanding voice I could muster, that we would sing it without accompaniment. Mr 'Chester's' face fell like a little boy whose balloon has been pricked, but we managed to stay in rhythm and in tune for our final song. That meeting, the message, and medicine of the day, were pure laughter.

One year all the churches got together to celebrate Easter. We gathered with the rest outside in the sunshine next to a Baptist church. Amongst the many stood a sandalled monk, all dressed in a long brown gown with a rope around his middle that hung down with tassels gracing the ends and a hood hanging rather languidly, it must be said, down his back. Our small son looked around, no doubt seeking something of interest to keep his mind busy, because after all, a churchload of people can be somewhat drear, and spotted the monk. Jonathan's eyes lit up, and before I could stop him he was at the monk's side, tugging at his tassels to get attention, and asking quite loudly, 'Are you Santa's brother?' This particular monk was sadly of the humourless persuasion, and he answered in a tight voice, 'No, I am not'. The many standing around were happy to have something to laugh at; the laughter rippled out through the crowd, as when a pebble is thrown into a lake. The day had been made brighter!

Every weekend we were happy to be able to take the children out into the 'wilds', into nature. We also went swimming a lot and later on, biking, and Jörg would take them to a park where they could ride the little cars around – at a cost!

One place greatly loved was Thurstaston Common, where there were huge rocks to be climbed. The children spent many a happy hour up and down those rocks with me standing at the bottom with my heart in my mouth trying not to infect them with my anxiety, in case of them falling. We often went to a beech wood, where Jörg had discovered a very long rope hanging from an extremely tall tree. After testing its strength, he attached a crossbar, a small branch from a tree, and helped the children to sit on it, giving them some huge swings back and forth over a steep drop. Again my heart was quaking, but their joy outweighed my worry, and after all Jörg obviously thought it was all safe. I guess he never thought that a child could or would let go of the rope by mistake. He was an excellent balance to me for our children. Looking back I realise how much richer their lives were, having the father they had.

As time passed on I was faced with triggers to my past that started to touch my deeper emotions. There were regulations that seemed to have nothing to do with spirit, with love. It began to grind in some ways. I noticed that Salvationists would become very opinionated when talking about Army matters, such as uniform, the Mercy Seat, hats or bonnets, the Salvation Army flag, who could or couldn't play in the band. All Army culture stuff, but which meant nothing much to me, or indeed to those many who had come to join our band of seekers for love and spirit. Back in the day of William Booth no doubt there had been reason for all this outward expression of the Army. Because Jörg and I along with our children, were 'footloose and fancy free' in spirit and understanding, our Salvation Army Corps of six when we first arrived could swell to a room full with up to a hundred people. This was only on special occasions, but even ordinary times would bring fifty to sixty odd souls together. Our boss and Major across the Mersey didn't much like this free and happy spirit because we were 'not making soldiers', thus not adding to official numbers. We would let folks know that they could become Salvation Army Soldiers, members, if they wanted, but very few were interested.

There was a vast variety of people coming to our gatherings; we found it all great fun and derived much joy from them all. There were professional people, would-be musicians, people living on the street; those emotionally hurting, a world-renowned boxing champion who joined us with his wife, and several young folks. Once in a long while there would be a Divisional Officer's meeting during which officers would announce how many had become Soldiers during the last year. We could never open our mouths to declare such amazing additions because there weren't any.

This must have been noted. At one point we were called over to the office in Liverpool for a chat with the Major. Bless him, and let me say he meant well; however he told us, with a face growing bright red as he spoke, that he wanted us to resign. We were stunned! What had we done wrong? We were not traditional Salvation Army people and there was a lot missing from our work within the Army.

I asked him to tell us what we were doing wrong, saying maybe we could rectify things. We were not bred and born Army people, and didn't really know what we were supposed to be like. As he was speaking I remember thinking, 'no, not Army bred and born, bred and born in a briar patch. I still had a tendency towards an inferiority complex, and I often felt as if I belonged nowhere. At the time I wore my hair long, never cutting it as I thought it looked all right, and it saved us money, which was necessary for us on the very skimpy salary we were receiving.

For a second there was silence, then with face the colour of puce, this man who had been in the Salvation Army all his life said,' Why don't you give your husband the correct colour socks to go with his uniform? And can you not put your hair up like my wife does or cut it short as do most Salvationists?' I was dumbfounded, to say the least, but only for a moment. I was also indignant that he should blame me for the way Jörg dressed. I wasn't in the habit of dressing him, and he could put on what he wanted. It took me back to those long-ago Bruderhof days and being taken to task over my hair then. However I was a much stronger, more whole person now, and I had some love and respect for myself, even if it floundered sometimes. This time, instead of being cowed, I blurted out the truth. 'What have colour of socks and length of hair got to do with God's kingdom?'

It must be said in the Major's defence, that the uniform was navy blue and Jörg had white socks on, both of us being totally ignorant of such matters as proper dress. For me, every time they spoke of God's kingdom I had visualized the Planet Earth back to normal, filled with love and wholeness of mind, body, and spirit, everything in harmony, with much fun, laughter and joy freely scattered around for man and beast, for all flora and fauna. And here we were back to the right and wrong, long hair versus short, white socks versus navy. It was just beyond grasping at the time.

I don't remember if this man gave me an answer. He pushed a paper towards Jörg and asked him to sign his resignation. Jörg had been tipped off by another Officer that this might happen, so he refused to sign the document. I was asked to do the same and refused too.

The reason this is significant for me is because years before, during our Bruderhof time, neither of us would have had the wherewithal to speak up for ourselves, being totally brainwashed and fearful of the fists of church discipline raining down on us. Now we had come a long way on our journey to peace and freedom and finding love and respect of self. I could speak up for myself and say my truth. It was a wonderful feeling. It added strength to my person as I walked my path through life.

Later that day back at home, the situation gave us a laugh, thinking how years before that Bruderhof woman had caught up with me, also to berate me about my hair and its unholy state yet again.

Life unfolded much like that of any other family, only for me it was all new. For instance I hadn't known an education system that gave you certificates and diplomas, helped and guided you to pass exams, helping you to pass on to the next step in life, at least not during my childhood. So I learned, only one step ahead of our children, what was expected of them from the school system. As they grew older they were able to guide me, unknown to them, by explaining what teachers said, wanted, and did for their education. Most teachers were just wonderful and I enjoyed the way they worked with our children enormously. One or two however seemed unjust and out of order in their ways. In such cases I was like a lion. Nothing could keep me quiet if I felt a teacher was being unjust. Looking back

I believe that now I had found freedom, I was reacting somewhat more strongly than most would. However, it was refreshing for me to be honest, even with those who I deemed 'better and more gifted' than me, such as teachers. I still had a tendency to an inferiority complex, so it was such a relief to tell a headmaster that I felt he was being unjust towards my child.

There came a time when we started to think about where we would like to eventually move to, in anticipation of retirement, and where we would like to stop for always instead of the constant moving around that had characterised both our lives. So in weighing our feelings and reasons, we decided on Gloucestershire. The move was smooth and although it was a great upheaval, it turned out in the end to be the best thing we could have done.

We both thought that we had truly got over any pain and trauma regarding losing our parents and siblings to the Bruderhof (or should I say, their unwillingness to accept us as part of our birth families) and by now, in my estimation, it had become a full-on cult. They still refused to let us have contact with our parents, still kept us apart from our siblings, and would only allow contact with people who lived in the Bruderhof, under their control.

We were very happy with our own family, our three

very dear children, and really believed we had mastered our pains of abandonment and rejection. We had been able to forgive. I thought it had all been put to rest with the joy of living, and the acceptance that I could change nothing where the Bruderhof and my birth family were concerned. All I could change was my attitude to the pain; this I thought I had done.

One day I got a phone call from someone who did not live on the Bruderhof to say my Mother had died there and was being buried that day or was already buried. It was a shock that threw me back into a freeze. I stood there with absolutely no feelings, except an extreme choking from my stomach to my throat. I couldn't feel my emotions. I had never had any indication that my mother was even ill.

I seem to have a very acute instinct and intuition. Sometimes this is great, and helpful, but at other times it is extremely painful and difficult. For some time before this message of Mummy's passing over, I had had the distinct feeling that she was at the end of her tether with her Bruderhof existence. She had put up with huge hurts and injustices, she was a 'named' person, as far as the birth of my oldest brother was concerned, and although she had risen above these horrible hurts, I know that after my father's death 'The Life' became more and more dead to her, more and more unbearable. I had vaguely sensed this, but it hadn't occupied me unduly. She hadn't lost her real self completely. Now I was gleaning much about her from various people who had themselves been ejected from the Bruderhof, mostly much as I had been, only far more recently. Excluding people has been a constant over the several decades of the Bruderhof's existence. Many stories and incidents had been related to me over the years about my mother, from various people who had been rejected, and now we had met along life's way. I am told, for instance, that at the wedding breakfast of one of my nephews, my mother was asked to tell the gathered guests, many of whom were her grandchildren, the story of my brother Nigel's conception and birth. The lady who related this to me had been present when my mother had burst into tears as she told the story. This at a wedding breakfast for her grandson! She hadn't offered the story, but the Elder and Servant had made her relate it.

Another instance was that on several occasions when we had tried to phone my mother over the years, we had been told that my mother didn't want to talk to me. Then we had been cut off, not by my mother, but by a Brother listening in. This was mostly a brother-in-law who caused this pain, he being in a position of authority. Some years later we met someone who had been looking after my mother at the time, and was now expelled from the Bruderhof. She said my mother used to show her photos of me, my husband and children and say in a sad, injured tone, 'I don't know why the Brothers never want me to talk to Christine and her family'. There was also the precious and unique occasion when my mother had been granted a visit to us, the first and last in my entire life. She had one amazing week with my little family. The children were all pre-school age at the time, and she absolutely loved every moment. The night before she was to be picked up by a Bruderhof Brother and taken back to them, she said to me in the most haunted voice 'Oh Chris, I don't want to go back'. I said, 'Then don't go Mummy,' and she replied, 'but where will I stay?' I told her that we would be delighted to have her stay with us. She thought for a long moment, during which her hopeful face turned to black agony, and suddenly she said, 'I'll have to go back'. When I asked why, she said very quietly and quite lamely, with no life in her voice; 'Because they have bought my return ticket'. It was a heart-wrenching moment. Of course the ticket was just an excuse for her fear of disloyalty to the Church that lurked in her heart and mind. Fear the Bruderhof's existence.

The next day she was taken away back to the Bruderhof. I was never to see her again. This treatment of family relationship I owe to those self-righteous Brothers, living in 'clear love' and within a 'united brotherhood' and having 'all things in common'.

Someone I know who had left the Bruderhof many years after me, and knew my mother intimately, confirmed my intuitions about my mother's wanting to leave the suffocating Bruderhof confines. This person told me that Mummy had no wish or zest for life any longer; her soul was dying.

So now my mother was dead, gone, for ever, never to be heard or seen again, at least not in this physical world. I realised that I had always nurtured the faint hope that the Bruderhof pendulum would swing to the free and positive direction, unconditional love as the guiding force, and we would be able to have and treasure the normal and precious child-parent relationship that should be everyone's; something which in my view they preach but don't practise. Now all hope had been blown out with a puff, with a single phone call.

My immediate emotions when my frozen heart began to melt were deep sadness that I had been denied my mother and now all was lost forever, and on the other hand a gladness that she had gone and that this negative force, the Bruderhof, could no longer control our relationship.

My children remarked that I didn't cry, and asked why. It was because I had been excluded from the true run of life, and now death; excluded from creation's love and pain. It was because my hurt and pain was so deep that the tears were still unable to flow; the pain was so deep that at times I couldn't even feel it. It was as if a doctor had anaesthetized me so that I wouldn't feel the incision in my heart, but I was still awake. In addition, when you're separated from a parent for most of your life, it is difficult to grasp when it becomes real and final. My mother had remained at a distance to me and me at a distance to her in my emotions, at first.

I made efforts to contact my brothers and or sisters on the Bruderhof, which proved very difficult. Eventually I managed to get one of my brothers to respond. I asked him all about our mother, what had ailed her, had she had an illness that I should know about, had she lived in pain – I had questions like this aplenty. However, I had only got one or two out before he took command, gushing falsely about the fact that Mummy had not been ill, but had been 'sick' (vomited?) only the day before, and died the following day; with all her family around her. All her family? What about me? And Nigel, Michael and Olwen, the four who were not part of 'the life'?

A friend of mine who lived in Germany and whose mother had lived on the Bruderhof had just died too; this friend was given almost word for word the same account about her mother's death. Then a second person, who had also grown up as a child on the Bruderhof and who we had both known, was given the same story. Now it was me. I felt a huge unease while this brother of mine was talking. As far as he was concerned, there was no cause of death. But how could three people, all living on one of the Bruderhofs, be sick one day and die the next without being ill beforehand?

There was something in his rather eager speech that seemed not quite to fit. For instance, since some of my siblings lived on a Bruderhof about 300 miles away from where my mother had lived, and apparently didn't know she was ill, how could they all have been at her bedside as she was dying? It didn't hang together.

In my experience of the Bruderhof, it is all right for the members to deceive and mislead you if it is from the 'united brotherhood', a 'united front'. I think of that line by Sir Walter Scott: 'O what a tangled web we weave when first we practise to deceive'. Deceit will always be revealed to the deceived; the deceiver is blind to the fact that others see it. I guess we have all been there.

Some years later, I met someone who had been with my mother and nursed her at the time, and had since been put out of the Bruderhof. Her factual account made far more sense. She had no points to score and nothing to hide, so I could accept what she said. But even she did not know the cause of death. This person told me my mother had been slowly ailing and going downhill since the wedding of her grandson. She thought my mother had been almost traumatised by the forced telling of her private life, in public, during the wedding breakfast. The wedding had taken place on New Year's Day. By spring it had been decided that my mother was too frail to walk and had to be taken around in a wheel chair. By summer she had fallen and had broken her wrist. From then on she had gone downhill rapidly and ended up being fed her meals. In September she died. No reason given. Over all these months the Bruderhof Brothers didn't feel it 'right' and acting in their 'clear love' to inform me, her eldest daughter, of her situation, allowing me the chance to spend time with her before she died. I can only conclude that my brother's cover-up story to me had been to keep me quiet and unquestioning.

The Bruderhof have the very warped idea that if we 'outsiders' are close to them during such times as a death, we will pollute their atmosphere. They believe that if they are in unity, they will go, eventually, to the 'Upper Church'. That is, if they remain in unity with each other in their Brotherhood! What a very sad state of affairs to live under such an illusion. This is what religion can do to many who follow its rules.

As time passed I found I was battling with depression. Even so I was able to keep going and present a fairly even picture to the world. In fact, I hadn't really accepted that I was depressed.

Nigel, my eldest brother, who still lived in Brazil, had been ill for quite some time, so I journeyed over to help my two nieces and sister-in-law to care for Nigel, as there was little he could do for himself. He was very ill and both he and I knew he was slowly losing his grip on this physical life, losing the body we are clothed in, or inhabit, during our earthly visit. All his organs were very slowly but surely closing down.

This time with Nigel was very precious to me, and we were able to talk, during the moments when he was feeling a little better, about everything that mattered to us. How precious were those days! It was such a delight, in spite of what I knew was to come, to be able to love and live with my oldest brother; this was real life. There was pain, for his children who were still quite young, for his wife, and for me, but it was almost a privilege to be allowed to feel that pain. Nigel was losing his physical body, but life was real.

I had to return the UK after 16 days. We could say our goodbyes, we could touch and feel each other's embrace, we could feel each other's emotions, we could look at each other knowing we would not see one another in this form again, and Nigel had given me a greater and more secure understanding of life. My dear brother!

When I had been back in England with my family for a little while, I received the news from Nigel's family back in Brazil that he had passed away. He had died; he had left this Earth life. It was almost good to be overwhelmed with grief and sadness. It was almost a privilege to feel the pain of loss and to be able, in time, to accept it. It is a wonderful thing to know truth. Truth, whether painful or joyous, sets a person so very free. Here was the difference between my mother's passing and my brother's; truth. My heart was not frozen into anaesthesia as with my beloved mother; it was awake in loss and pain for my brother and his wife and children. My heart was free to love, and show love to my sister-in-law, Leonice, and my two nieces, Jeanne and Sheila. Without pain we don't know the deepest love. Without love we don't know the deepest pain. Such is our journey through life on Planet Earth.

There had been so much joy and happiness in my life since finding Jörg and having our three children that I had not paid too much attention to the hurts that had not been dealt with regarding my former Bruderhof life. Occasionally something came up to stir up sadness, or anger, or fear, but it was as if I could sweep these feelings under the carpet and not look too closely. I believe that perhaps my mother's death was a trigger that came to overwhelm me regarding all the hurt from my Bruderhof life. It seemed that their long tentacles could still reach me, and they were still doing the same thing where family relationships were concerned; they could still sting with impunity, and it hurt deeply. In any event, whilst finding it hard to lift out of my depression, I went and sought help from a counsellor. I certainly never thought at that point that it was my former life that was catching up with me. All I knew was that the clouds hung low on my heart and they didn't shift to allow the sunlight in.

My sessions with the counsellor were so very freeing, and I came to cherish them, as they became firm stepping stones on which to cross through the river of my life at that time, so as to land on the dry and sunny bank on the other side. I came to cherish those times. I was taken to look at all my many painful experiences, hold them close, and then let go of them. I had hidden from them and the emotions that they would have brought. I remember so well opening up to talking about the time when my own father was sent to pick me up after an operation in the hospital, so as to take me home to recuperate, as I thought, only to find that he was taking me in another direction. When I enquired as to where we were going, he told me he was dropping me off at a bed and breakfast in the country so I could spend ten days recuperating there, as the Brothers felt I shouldn't be allowed to be with the family on the Bruderhof. I had always felt such deep abandonment and shame over this incident, for which I felt I was somehow to blame, not being good enough for family or Bruderhof. Yet I had never looked at it, but covered it up in my own way so as not to live in shame. Now in one session with the counsellor I uncovered it and looked at it closely for what it really was. At the time no tears had stung my eyes, nor had my heart accepted hurt, as that would surely only have brought recrimination, but now tears came as the remembrance wrung my heart so deeply. How could my father have betrayed me so? How could he have loved his Brotherhood/Church community more than me?

I became so distressed that I could hardly breathe, but now I was allowing my anger at my father, my fury at the Bruderhof and all it represented, my fear of accepting that it ever happened, my anxiety at daring to admit that perhaps it wasn't my fault, my shame. Ultimately this enabled me to let go of the incident completely, finding peace and forgiveness for my father (less easily of the Bruderhof). With that, the love for my father came back in all truth and strength, and it has never left me. It also gave me a profound sense of loving my father precisely because of his weaknesses, his fallibility, and it enabled me to appreciate his strengths more wholly.

I was able to relive another incident when my father had been sent to the UK for a last goodbye to all his relatives before going back to the USA to 'his Brothers' to die, as he was terminally ill. He phoned me to say he was coming to visit in a couple of days, and I was overjoyed, sharing this wonderful news with Jörg and the children. I could hardly wait. There were no words to hold my joy. But on the night before his arrival I received another call. My father told me, 'The Brothers have asked me to phone and tell you it won't be possible to visit.' I asked why not. His response was ambiguous and obscure. He said something about the Bruderhof Community in England having a visit from some Hutterians (another Christian sect), which frequently happened at the time. Now as I allowed myself to live the emotions through, the heartache made the tears flow freely, washing out the pain and freeing me up again to Love.

So the sessions progressed, and by the end I found that I was in peace, joy, and wholeness, and my loving was free as never before. I have found that it is vital to a happy life to look at, own, and then let go of all that is not of truth and light and love. People will argue that we are not responsible for what is done to us by others. In my experience we can always take responsibility in the way we react or don't react and for what we make of those injustices —the responsibility does lie with us. When we take responsibility, we mature and in so maturing we find gladness in the hurtful episodes of life because, wonderfully, they give us a much more profound understanding of love, joy, light, kindness, compassion, and laughter, shrivelling up the injustices, pains, and sadistic actions that we have been victim to. Then there is the wondrous chance of forgiving, giving up the resentment that could linger. We are not victims; we are whole and perfectly made and able. There is a magnificence in the human being. I know that in all humans there is at least a spark of life-light and love. Maybe we have the choice of nurturing it until it becomes all-consuming and shines with glorious light or trying to put that spark out by covering it up, and choosing to let it die.

* * *

As I take my walk back through this lovely village and bathe in the sunlight of the day, the chattering sparrows have flown from the scraggly hawthorn tree, but with the exquisite birdsong all around, the celandines blossoming at my feet, the song of the river, the chatter of small children in the distance, I am glad, so glad for all my experience of life.

I have got to know a lady who lives in one of the little houses I pass. She never had someone in her life to love her, as she was an orphan, and no one was a parent to her as she grew. My heart goes out to all those who have never known the arms of love around them as they grew from baby to adulthood. However, all is not doom. I would like everyone who reads this book to know that they are loved, that there are people around the world giving you hugs from their hearts. Sit back in your favourite place and feel those arms around you, channelling love to you. As you sit back and wallow in that love it will grow and become more real, giving you security, so that you will be able to go forward and pass it on to your children, partner, parents, friends, and even to strangers. The minute we break through the barrier of reserve and show love to another we are filled with such happiness; the spirit uniting as one. How gloriously and wondrously exciting is life!

I don't understand life fully; in fact sometimes I don't understand it at all. But there will come a day when time is no more, the veil is lifted, and we will have full knowledge and, I guess, understanding. In the meantime I am perfectly happy to live in love. Planet Earth will be fully healed, and us with it. I have found that when I transform my personal sufferings I am in peace. Maybe as people around the world transform their personal sufferings we will find world peace, and Mother Earth will rejoice and heal even faster.

I am thankful to all those who have crossed my path in life, whether they were harsh, loving, cruel or kind. Without the dark we wouldn't know light. Without pain we wouldn't know the wonder of peace, the blessing of being pain free. I can welcome the velvet darkness of night, because that enables me to embrace the morning light with knowing joy. If I didn't know sadness, I don't think I would know happiness.

I think we choose to come and experience this journey on our green and blue planet. I am glad that I AM.

The closer I get to my home, the more I am aware of a deep sense of love flowing out to my three children, all of whom have flown the nest and yet live in my heart. Whenever they visit there is laughter and happiness, and I would confess that Jörg and I are learning from them, learning much that is new, yet this is a great part of our earthly journey. With them comes the enormous blessing of our precious grandchildren.

I am also remembering my many very dear friends who I grew up with on the Bruderhof, who have left and are living in far-flung places around the world. We have a family bond, through pain and love shared.

Then I think of my own siblings, eight of whom still live on the Bruderhof with their many children, of whom I know only one. This brings a shadow and sadness to my heart, as they refuse to visit and accept us as family. But this reminds me of the blessing of my one sister who lives close, with whom I can discuss and disagree quite freely, but laugh and have such fun with, and still know unity of spirit. Being free to disagree is amazing after our Bruderhof experiences.

As I walk up the little path with spring flowers on either side, so delicately and exquisitely fashioned in some mysterious way, the joy of creation is complete. As I approach the front door of my house, the loveliness of seeing and being together with my husband Jörg is with me. How blessed am I.